NEITHER HEROINE NOR FOOL

Neither Heroine nor Fool
Anna Ella Carroll of Maryland

Janet L. Coryell

THE KENT STATE UNIVERSITY PRESS
Kent, Ohio, and London, England

© 1990 by The Kent State University Press, Kent, Ohio 44242
All rights reserved
Library of Congress Catalog Card Number 89-24403
ISBN 0-87338-405-9
Manufactured in the United States of America

Portions of this book previously appeared in *Civil War History* 35, no. 2 (June 1989). Copyright © 1989 by The Kent State University Press. Reprinted by permission of The Kent State University Press.

Some of this material was originally published as "Duty with Delicacy: Anna Ella Carroll of Maryland," in *Women and American Foreign Policy*, Edward Crapol, ed. (Greenwood Press, Inc., Westport, CT, 1987). Copyright © 1987 by Edward P. Crapol. Reprinted with permission.

British Library Cataloging-in-Publication data are available.

Library of Congress Cataloging-in-Publication Data

Coryell, Janet L., 1955–
  Neither heroine nor fool : Anna Ella Carroll of Maryland / Janet
L. Coryell.
    p.   cm.
  Includes bibliographical references.
  ISBN 0-87338-405-9 (alk. paper ∞)
  1. Carroll, Anna Ella, 1815–1894. 2. United States—History—
Civil War, 1861–1865—Women. 3. American Party—Biography.
4. Pamphleteers—United States—Biography. 5. Women—United States—
History—19th century. 6. Presidents—United States—
Election—1856. 7. United States—Politics and
government—1853–1857. I. Title.
E472.9.C33C67 1990
973.7′092—dc20
[B]   89-24403
                                                                          CIP

To my grandmothers
Bonnie Coryell Hatch
and
Florence Ray Lewis
who also love education and history

We want no Joans of Arc to make America vascular and alive . . . we want faithful and true women, who neither shriek nor protest, but pray; women who neither mount nor sink; who are neither heroines nor fools; but American women, who can stand in their shoes. . . .

—Anna Ella Carroll, *The Great American Battle*

Contents

Maps

Preface and Acknowledgments

I began my research on Anna Ella Carroll in 1982, certain I had discovered a much-maligned, forgotten heroine of American history, a woman who claimed responsibility for formulating the Union military strategy that culminated in the successful invasion of Tennessee in 1862, whom I would redefine and properly place into the historiography of the Civil War period. Her claims were so extravagant that they had to be resolved and, curiously enough, had not been, despite the overwhelming number of works on the Civil War period in American history.

To try to find the truth about a woman surrounded by so much legend has been an enlightening and educational experience, not to mention a humbling one. Sorting out her story has made me aware of how complex our past is and how difficult biography as a craft is. The late Distinguished Teaching Professor of History at the State University College of New York, College at Cortland, Ralph Adams Brown, biographer of John Adams, had taught me that in my sophomore year at college. He was right. To him I render thanks, as well as to Professors Ellis Johnson and Donald Stewart, who introduced me to history and to Anna Ella Carroll as the author of the Tennessee Campaign.

Carroll was one of the few women discussed in the Civil War course Stewart and Johnson taught at Cortland State. She was a legendary figure, and like all good legends, there was at least some sense and some truth to her claims to fame. Discovering the factual basis for the legend, however, turned out to be difficult. In part, the difficulties lay with source materials. Some of Carroll's papers had been preserved, but many had been lost during her life. Others had burned in a house fire in the 1940s. The collection in the Maryland Historical Society is extensive, but consists mostly of letters received. Tracing letters written that still survive was a hit-or-miss task. Charles McCool Snyder discovered a large cache in 1970 in Millard Fillmore's papers in Oswego, New York. His work helped the most to place Carroll into context as a valid historical figure instead of a noble legend. So did the letters from Carroll to William Henry Seward and Thurlow Weed, kept at the University of Rochester. Perhaps most important was Maryland Historical Society Archivist Karen Stuart's suggestion that I look at the Carroll, Cradock, Jensen Collection for additional papers. The letters and manuscripts therein made clear Carroll's unflattering opinion of Lincoln, as well as providing additional information on her work for colonization and on her private life.

Important figures in Carroll's life remain shadowy. Lemuel Evans, John Causin, and Thomas King Carroll left behind few papers and little information. Even tracing Carroll's family history proved difficult as probate records for the period have not survived. While there have been numerous articles and books about Carroll's life, virtually all were repetitions of her own stories about her family life and claim. Given her predilection for exaggeration, even her claim of being a blood relative of Charles Carroll of Carrollton could not be accepted at face value.

In evaluating Carroll as either a heroine or a fool, as she puts it, I found neither. I approached her tale with a certain degree of healthy historical skepticism but, frankly, I had hoped for a more likable and substantial heroine. I still don't like her very much, but I do respect her as a woman who knew what she wanted and tried to achieve her goals by using the limited methods available to her. For this reason, more than any other, her story needs to be told. She was in many ways an anomaly: a well-educated Southern woman, a Unionist who hated slavery but refused to support emancipation, a citizen of a state founded on principles of religious toleration who was virulently anti-Catholic. While I think I have been able to explain these anomalies, I have been frustrated by research that seemed to raise more questions than it answered. Was she a swindler, a fraud, a cheat? Did the military maliciously destroy the records that proved she was a brilliant strategist, responsible for the creation of the invasion campaign into Tennessee that the Union forces used with such spectacular results in the spring of 1862? The answer to the first is still uncertain. The second, I hope, I have answered at last.

One of the final tasks and greatest pleasures in finishing work is thanking those people who were helpful to you. This book began as a dissertation under the direction of Ludwell Johnson at the College of William and

Mary in Virginia. To him and the members of the committee, particularly Cam Walker and George Hoemann, I extend my thanks. Some of this material was originally published as "Duty with Delicacy: Anna Ella Carroll of Maryland," in *Women and American Foreign Policy,* ed. Edward Crapol (Westport, Conn.: Greenwood Press, 1987), copyright © 1987 by Edward P. Crapol, and is reprinted with permission. Crapol's patience, tact, and superb editorial criticism are, I hope, reflected to some degree in this entire work. Parts of chapter 7 have been published as "Anna Ella Carroll and the Historians" in *Civil War History* 35 (June 1989): 120–37 and are reprinted by permission of The Kent State University Press.

Institutional aid is always invaluable, though never thoroughly appreciated until it is left behind. The library reference personnel, computer programming departments, and the departments of history at the College of William and Mary and the University of Dayton provided logistical support, research grants, microfilming costs, computer space and time, and in general made the mechanics of my work much easier. The Research Council of the University of Dayton provided a summer research grant to allow me to finish my research. Student assistants Jennifer Davis and Amy Young were invaluable as the project neared completion, as were Director John Hubbell and editors Julia Morton and Laurel Brandt at Kent State University Press.

The historians and archivists at the Maryland Historical Society and the Hall of Records in Annapolis, particularly Phebe Jacobsen, were of special help to me. As always, librarians went far beyond the call at the Library of Congress, National Archives, New York Public Library, Baltimore City Archives, SUC Oswego, and University of Rochester.

Carroll's childhood home still stands in Somerset County and is now on the National Register of Historic Places. Dick and E. B. Warbasse graciously invited me into their home and showed me the wooden shoe that was said to have been worn by a slave at Kingston Hall during the tenure of the Carrolls. They provided hospitality and interest, even in a revisionist history of their house's most famous resident. My thanks to Paul Touart of the Somerset County Historical Trust for helping me find that lovely home and its hospitable occupants.

The love and support my family has given me during the last seven years of this all-consuming work has made my life a joy. David and Pat Coryell provided loving parental encouragement every step of the way. Ken and Nora Coryell gave me not only sympathetic conversation but a home away from home during research trips. Micaela Coryell Ayers produced two splendid maps. And the occasional curious question from the rest of the clan made me feel as if everyone cared, even if no one was quite sure what I was doing with this woman.

My friends and colleagues became my family in Williamsburg and then again in Dayton. In particular, I want to thank Holly Mayer, Gail Terry, and Camille Wells, who asked me questions designed to focus my work more clearly; the Williamsburg Presbyterian Church Choir, especially Jeanne Kent and Thomas Marshall, who gave me escape and sustenance through music for four years; Ben Kellam, who drew the first maps, served as an invaluable resource to explain the peculiarities of the inhabitants of the Eastern Shore, and helped me look at my work with an English major's eye; and Pat Johnson and Jim Smither, whose interest and affection made the inevitable stress of rewriting easier. Most particularly I want to thank John and Ruth Ann Coski, and Mary and James Perry. They not only listened, but provided caring support far beyond any call of friendship for myself and for Ivan (*requiescat in pace*).

The errors that remain, when all is said and done, are mine.

Introduction

Of all the legends of the American Civil War, one of the most enduring has been that of Anna Ella Carroll. Secretary of War Edwin Stanton was supposed to have said of her, "Her whole course was the most remarkable in the war; she found herself, got no pay, and did the great work that made others famous." Her claims were amazing, if true: that she had drawn the maps and devised the strategy for invading Tennessee in the spring of 1862 that enabled the Union to win the western theater of the war, that she was so close to Lincoln she could see him on a moment's notice and he considered her part of his cabinet, and—the claim most appealing to a historian of women—that she had been denied recognition of her greatness solely because of her gender. But was she? Are her claims true? That Carroll worked for the government during the course of the war is undeniable. Her story, however, is far more complex than her legend, just as she is far more than a simple victim of injustice.

This biography seeks to understand Carroll's place in history by examining her life on three levels. It is, first, a closely documented account of Carroll's work. Although her reputation for over a century rested on the belief that she designed the Tennessee campaign, in fact, her military strategy replicated existing Union strategy. Far more important historically was her work in the 1850s as a writer for the Know-Nothing party. Carroll articulated the platform of the Know-Nothings in a best-selling work called *The Great American Battle*. Important, too, were her pamphlets supporting Lincoln's actions at the beginning of the Civil War. The administration was so impressed by her arguments that copies were distributed to every member of Congress. Her pamphlet on the president's war powers as both commander-in-chief and chief executive was the first printed on the issue, nearly a year before the more famous one by Horace Binney.

Carroll's actions provide a case study of the methods used by women when they struggle to achieve their goals within a restrictive society. Carroll had a methodology that enabled her to participate in the masculine world of politics and yet maintain her sense of femininity. She used the imagery of the republican mother; she bowed to the restrictions of the cult of domesticity; and she defined herself as a "Southern Lady." The power of these nineteenth-century images made Carroll aware that her God-given activities were limited to the separate sphere of domesticity, out of which she could step only momentarily, only in moments of dire national peril, and always at the risk of appearing unladylike. Carroll succeeded for nearly twenty years in writing on political matters before she stepped too far outside the sphere and never wholly returned.

Finally, Carroll's symbolic value for historians is considered. Carroll's attempt to gain recognition and payment for her military strategy, a monumental labor consuming the last thirty years of her life (see chapter 6), was adopted as a cause by suffragists, antifeminists, popular and professional historians of the Civil War, and writers of all kinds who had personal points to make concerning the importance of women's activities in history and the importance of the field of women's history. Carroll became a symbol for these writers, less for what she did than for what they could say about women, using her career as an example. The suffragists portrayed her as a poor, downtrodden example of man's inhumanity to women. Antifeminists used Carroll to support the antisuffragist position that Carroll was operating out of her sphere in extraordinary patriotic service and that her asking for recognition was asking for something unnecessary, just as the suffragists were asking for something beyond their proper spheres—the vote—that was equally unnecessary. Civil War historians dismissed Carroll's military claim as absurd because anyone could have thought of the plan, while popular writers argued that such a dismissal was made solely because of Carroll's gender. The pattern of using Carroll continues: William Safire includes her in his novel *Freedom,* thus recognizing the presence of active women during the war, but she is a lusty, liberated, and distinctly twentieth-century type. The portrayal of Carroll has changed over time and she has become a symbol, reflective of the popular perception of women active in society. Thus her biography serves a dual function: her life lets us understand the restrictions under which a nineteenth-century woman worked; her story takes on added value as a lesson in the development of historiography—the history of her story.

An extra headstone on Carroll's grave, erected by the Pennsylvania

Daughters of the American Revolution, reads: "Anna Ella Carroll, Maryland's Most Distinguished Lady. A great humanitarian and close friend of Abraham Lincoln. She conceived the successful Tennessee Campaign and guided the President on his Constitutional war powers." This inscription symbolizes Carroll's life—a mixture of inaccuracy and truth, of legend and legitimacy. Those who hold her claim to be inerrant deny her the respect she deserves as much as those who denigrate her work. She was not the heroine she claimed to be; neither can she be dismissed as a fool. The truth, as the playwright once pointed out, lies somewhere between the two.

Neither Heroine nor Fool

ONE

Politician's Daughter

The Eastern Shore of Maryland seems a world apart. Geographically separated from the rest of the state by the Chesapeake Bay and the Susquehanna River, the eastern counties have a hard existence: the soil is less fertile, the climate less hospitable, and those who live there work harder to survive. Natives of the Eastern Shore are distinct in Maryland's history—independent, contrary, proud of their singularity. The unconventional career of Anna Ella Carroll no doubt owes much to her birthplace. Born on 29 August 1815 in Somerset, the southernmost of the eastern counties, Carroll was the eldest child of Thomas King Carroll and Julianna Stevenson Carroll. The Carrolls of Somerset County claimed a common ancestry with two of the most distinguished families of Maryland, the Catholic Carrolls and the Protestant Kings. Charles Carroll, patriarch of the line, had been appointed receiver of Lord Baltimore's rents from the Maryland colonists by 1691. One of his grandsons was Charles Carroll, "The Signer" of the Declaration of Independence. Another was the Most Reverend John Carroll, the first Catholic archbishop in the United States.[1]

Kinsman to Charles and John was Colonel Henry James Carroll. In 1792 Colonel Carroll married Elizabeth Barnes King, daughter of Thomas King of Somerset County and a descendant of Sir Robert King, a Presbyterian dissenter whose family had left Ireland for Maryland in 1682. One of the richer planters on the Eastern Shore of Maryland, King was not pleased with his only child's choice of a Catholic husband, but he settled the young couple on an adjoining estate in Somerset County. The marriage produced three sons. In 1798, at age five, the eldest boy, Thomas King Carroll, went to live with his grandfather King on the family estate of Kingston Hall, where he became the focus of King's devoted affection and interest. The young boy was brought up in the best English gentry tradition, with coaches driven by slaves in livery and all the accoutrements of an English country life transplanted to Maryland. About 1802, Thomas King died, and Thomas King Carroll was joined at Kingston Hall by his parents and brothers. In 1808 Carroll enrolled at the University of Pennsylvania to study law, gaining a master's degree by 1815. He worked for a short time in the offices of Robert Goodloe Harper, son-in-law of Charles Carroll of Carrollton, and on 23 June 1814 he married Julianna Stevenson of Baltimore, the daughter of a prominent physician, Dr. Henry Stevenson.[2]

While he was on his honeymoon with the beautiful Julianna, Thomas King Carroll received word that his father had died and Kingston Hall was now his. He returned to the plantation and began his career as a planter. Farming did not particularly interest him, but politics did. He stood for election and won a seat in the Maryland legislature, the youngest member ever elected. His twenty-first birthday came the day before he took his seat.[3]

Carroll served in the State House of Delegates in 1816 and 1817 and worked as a judge in the Levy Court of Somerset County before being appointed Judge of the Orphans' Court in February 1826. In December 1829 Jacksonian Democrats elected the former Federalist Carroll governor of Maryland, replacing the anti-Jackson governor Daniel Martin. Carroll's term lasted just one year, however, as the Jacksonians lost power. Political reaction to President Jackson's vetoes of internal improvements and his distribution of executive patronage gave the anti-Jackson men enough ammunition to vote Martin back into office in January 1831. With only twelve months in office, Carroll could accomplish little, but his parting address to the state emphasized the need for education and prison reform, as well as accountability of elected officials. On 13 January 1831 Carroll returned to the pressing business of trying to make a success of his plantation in Somerset County.[4]

Carroll faced a number of difficulties as he returned home to Kingston Hall. The 1819–22 recession had badly damaged the economy of Baltimore and Maryland, and the state was only just beginning to recover by the early 1830s. Heavy investments in transportation projects, such as railroads, turnpikes, and canals, led to increased taxes to pay off the deficit. The farm economy had suffered even more as those taxes strained a collapsing agricultural base of the remote old farms of the Eastern Shore.[5]

Added to the problems of recession, high taxes, soil exhaustion, transportation difficulties, and the always cyclical and variable nature of farming, was the growing problem of slavery. Maryland increasingly resembled northern states in other ways, but held onto the institution of slavery. Pro-Southern sectionalism and proslavery political positions were most prevalent on the Eastern Shore, but Carroll differed from his neighbors. Although conditions for slaves in Maryland were milder than for bondsmen further south, he disliked slavery as an institution. Kingston Hall had a substantial slave population at the time of his inheritance, and Carroll spent much of his time trying to keep the plantation solvent enough to prevent their sale. He did not free them, apparently feeling, as did many Maryland slave owners, that freed slaves had no proper or safe place in a slave-owning society, but he was an advocate of the African colonization movement for free blacks.[6]

In this environment, Carroll's favorite and eldest child, Anna Ella, "Miss Anne," was raised: a lesser branch of a well-known family, a gentry background maintained by uncertain finances, a border state that vacillated between sectionalism and nationalism in its society, economy, and politics. In a large family, Carroll had five younger sisters: Sallie, Ada, and Henrietta, who all married; Julianna, who died unmarried in 1860; and Mary, who remained single. She had two younger brothers: Henry James, known as Harry, who became a land speculator, and Thomas King, who became a country doctor. Another younger brother died in infancy.[7]

Carroll's upbringing was as mixed as the world in which she lived. Her father treated her education as he would a son's. She read Coke and Blackstone on law, Shakespearean drama, and Kantian philosophy in her father's library, as he had done in his grandfather's. Her domestic education was not neglected, but she was more interested in books than in the accepted and common accomplishments of most upper-class young women of the period—drawing, music, needlework, and household tasks. Politics fascinated her. By 1830, when her father took office in Annapolis, Carroll's political education was such that letters to her "wisest and dearest of fathers" were sprinkled with precocious political comments amongst the news of home. "It is my principle, as well as that of Lycurgus," she wrote him at age fourteen, "to avoid 'mediums'—that is to say, people who are not decidedly one thing or the other. In politics they are the inveterate enemies of the state."[8]

At fifteen, during her father's brief tenure as governor, Carroll was sent, along with her sister Julianna, to Miss Margaret Mercer's boarding school in West River, Maryland, to finish her education. Although she spent less than a year under Mercer's tutelage, her teacher's views on education and slavery served to reinforce her father's opinions. Mercer also was the daughter of a governor of Maryland and also had been taught by her father. Like most girls' schools of the 1830s, Mercer's concentrated on educating female students for the so-called woman's sphere of home and family. But Mercer also believed her girls needed an education "as may prepare them for the great and good measures, the wisdom and the virtue which are requisite to the safety and prosperity" of the South. Her curriculum included science, philosophy, ethics, and religion. Still, Mercer maintained, as Carroll would in later years, that educated women must not despise "the refinements and delicacy which communicate an appropriate and attractive grace to the female character. These can never be laid aside, no matter how great the positive acquirements without a violation of the laws of nature."[9] Educated women they might be; ladies they must be.

Like many women in the 1820s and 1830s, Mercer was interested in the abolition of slavery. Her position foreshadowed the one that Carroll would take twenty years later. Aware of the economic and social upheaval for both master and slave that accompanied emancipation, Mercer preferred gradual emancipation with compensation for owners and voluntary colonization of freed slaves. She bought slaves herself and freed them, hiring some to work on her estate, and providing passage to Liberia for those who wished to go. She asked her students to contribute to the cause, and corresponded with such Northern abolitionist leaders as Gerrit Smith, searching for support for her programs. The increasing radicalism of abolitionists, however, eventually prompted Mercer to break with them. She wanted abolition, but like Carroll in later years, chose to temper her zeal by maintaining the necessity of removing free blacks from the state.[10] While Mercer's positions on education and slavery no doubt met with Thomas Carroll's approval, his finances apparently did not allow Anne to continue her education. When he returned to Kingston Hall in January 1831, his daughters came with him. His wife Julianna was ill, and the plantation needed closer attention.

As difficult as farming was, by all accounts Carroll was a poor manager of finances as well. While he no doubt viewed his refusal to sell unneeded slaves as a humanitarian gesture, he continually used those same slaves as collateral for mortgages required to pay off loans he co-signed for improvident friends. He was still a wealthy man when he returned to Somerset County. He had thirteen hundred acres of land to farm and thirty-eight slaves to help him. He had hogs, cattle, oxen, and horses. But it all began to slip from his grasp.[11]

The slaves went first, as much as he hated to sell: three in 1833 to a relative, thirteen in 1835 to strangers. Horses and carriages followed, all to satisfy judgments against him, as lawsuits from creditors were a constant threat. Finally, in 1837, as a financial panic swept the country, Thomas King Carroll lost Kingston Hall.[12]

The youngest child, Sallie, was only six; Anne was twenty-two. She rented a house and started a school to try to hold the family together. By

1840, she had twenty students, and owned twenty-five hogs, the latter enough to feed the former for quite a while.[13] Running a girls' school was a common enough solution for gentlewomen in straitened circumstances, since it was a money-making activity still within the "woman's sphere" of acceptable behavior. But this was also the beginning of Carroll's attempts to enlarge that sphere, in part from financial necessity. As her father failed at one career after another—farmer, lawyer, insurance agent—upon his eldest daughter fell the responsibility of supporting the family and of keeping her father from signing away their money through his misguided generosity.

The Carrolls lived a peripatetic existence. Somerset County was poor and not very populous, and the panic had hurt everyone. Carroll had to close the doors of her school in 1843 and moved with the rest of her family to Dorchester County. By 1845 she was living in Baltimore, apparently working as a promotional writer for railroad lobbyists and contributing letters and short articles on political matters to local newspapers, for which she earned small sums. She commuted often between Baltimore and Washington, always searching for a way to make money for herself and her family. In one letter, written in November 1848 from Washington, she complained that her latest financial plans had fallen through and that arranging a mortgage on some Maryland real estate would have to suffice to raise funds so she could return to Maryland to care for her ailing parents. Her father recovered; her mother died on 31 July 1849.[14]

Carroll's departure from the capital city had been only temporary. In April 1849 she petitioned the new Whig secretary of state, John M. Clayton, for a job for her father as naval officer of Baltimore. Clayton, no doubt eager to strengthen the Whig party in the largely Democratic state of Maryland, acceded to her request. After Mrs. Carroll's death, the entire family joined Anne in Baltimore and maintained a precarious hold on their finances. Harry, the eldest son, found work as a clerk to augment his father's salary, and Anne continued to write.[15]

Her success in obtaining an appointment for her father inspired Carroll, and she began to involve herself and her pen more deeply in national politics. At the age of thirty-five, unencumbered by husband or child, she took full advantage of her intelligence, education, and family name to participate in the political life of the nation.

As a woman, Carroll's participation was necessarily limited. She did not choose the paths of woman's rights, abolition, or reform, as did many political women of the mid-nineteenth century. But she was determined to exercise influence over leading politicians, particularly on political appointments, through her letters and meetings. She regularly suggested her father as a candidate for office after his tenure as naval officer; she would also suggest, and eventually demand, appointments for many of her friends and for other persons she thought would serve the government well, a common practice of the politically interested prior to the establishment of the Civil Service. Carroll's education and natural inclination toward politics had trained her mind and her father's financial mismanagement provided a constant spur. Her success at obtaining appointments was limited, but by 1850 she had honed her skills as writer and lobbyist and began to work her way into the circles of national power.

Carroll did not believe in wasting time or energy communicating with the lower echelons of bureaucracy. For her father's appointment as naval officer of Baltimore she had written directly to the secretary of state, even though his appointment was from the Department of the Treasury. But, she wrote the secretary, "so high is my appreciation of yourself, so perfect is my confidence in the efficiency of your power to serve me, that I must trust to your own kindness" to excuse a daughter from making the effort to find a "loved Father" a job.[16]

Carroll's flowery phrases were typical of nineteenth-century writing and served well to attract the attention of political leaders from whom she sought patronage positions. She began with flattery, appealing first to the intelligence and discernment of those to whom she wrote, then to their sentimental side. In 1852, still commuting between Baltimore and Washington while apparently continuing her work as a free-lance writer, she began a mostly one-sided correspondence with President Millard Fillmore that would last for over twenty years. Near the end of Fillmore's term, Carroll sent him a manuscript to read, which he returned "with thanks for the privilege of perusing it." Disproportionately encouraged by his polite reply, she wrote to reassure him that while the Whigs were in disastrous shape for the coming election, at least "the American people have already stamped an impress of approbation upon your administration, which posterity will cherish for ages to come." By May, Carroll, who had been only momentarily deflected by Fillmore's suggestion that she go through channels for a position for a friend, asked for an appointment with him instead. She reassured Fillmore that it would be "the only case with which I shall ever presume to invite especial interposition." Signing her letter, "your little friend, A. E. Carroll," she played upon Fillmore's vanity and her own supposed frail femininity to convince the president to do this favor for her. After all, she wrote, "no selfish aspiration, no sordid interest, no *political distinction* has actuated me." By implication, it was just the good of the country and their friendship at stake.[17]

Carroll's indeflatable ego and her conviction that she could provide invaluable service to her country kept her in action despite polite replies from politicians that would have dissuaded most people. Even silence did not stop her. Fillmore, for instance, apparently did not give her an appointment, but a few days later Carroll wrote him again. This time, she passed on the good news she had heard regarding his renomination prospects for the election of 1852. The struggle for the nomination was among Fillmore, Daniel Webster, and Mexican war hero Winfield Scott. The major issue was support for the recent Compromise of 1850, which had averted political crisis over slavery. The South supported Fillmore for enforcing the Fugitive Slave Law, an act that guaranteed his loss in the North. New Englanders supported Webster, a favorite son and a saviour of the Union during the struggle over the Compromise. But Winfield Scott was a military hero who had helped win the war that had forced the Compromise. He inspired few, but offended fewer than either Fillmore or Webster.

Carroll paid close attention to the politicking among the Whig factions, warning Fillmore that there were traitors in his own camp who were eroding his support. Anxious to have Fillmore take her seriously, yet cognizant of the handicap of her sex in political matters, Carroll made it clear to him she was aware of the limitations placed upon her by her gender. But she had a rationale for exceeding those limits in lobbying for patronage positions and discussing politics.

> Honored Sir, it may look unique for an "American lady" to be so heartily embarked in the interest of the political condition of the country, but I am sure it will be considered a pardonable offence, when I tell you that by blood and name and spirit I am identified with those who largely contributed to achieve and perpetuate our free institutions. And that by education and social position I have been ever led to an intelligent apprehension of the structure and entire organization of our political system—And a consequent appreciation of the wisdom and virtue of those, who have signally upheld them—
>
> *Then* it is no marvel that I should turn to *you,* with an increasing admiration. . . . your very truest and best little friend, A. E. Carroll.[18]

Carroll attended the Whig national convention in Baltimore in June 1852. The convention split three ways, and Webster's delegates bolted to Scott, not Fillmore. She was crushed by Fillmore's defeat, telling him when she discovered "that friends of Mr. Webster would never come over to you and that *hope* had fled, I almost sunk under it in the gallery." Sorrow over Fillmore's defeat did not blind her to the need for speed to obtain any political largesse, however. Carroll wrote five days after Fillmore's loss, renewing pressure on him to appoint a friend of hers to a patronage position in the brief time he had left. Because they were friends, she told him, he owed her this favor: "I do entreat you by all that is *true,* by all that is *faithful,* by all that will contribute to my *happiness.* . . ." She would see

7

him that evening and no doubt expected the good word then. When "unfriendly sources" told her no appointment would be made, she refused to believe Fillmore would betray her friendship, and asked him to make the appointment anyway, just "to show that the wisdom of a certain person is not altogether impregnable."[19]

But Fillmore made no appointments, and by the end of his term, Carroll regarded his failure to meet her demands for patronage as a personal affront. "If the President had any disposition to serve me which he professes," she wrote to Treasury Secretary Thomas Corwin of Ohio, whom Carroll had known for some time, "I am satisfied such a post might be had. . . ." If Fillmore failed her, Corwin, she thought, should act on her request instead, before the Whigs left office. She was certain he would not "neglect any thing which you can do to reward the meritorious and deserving. . . . And apart from all selfish considerations, I know you will not forget your most faithful, your most devoted and eternal friend." Friendship was a recurring theme in Carroll's demands for patronage, and she maintained contact with political leaders in case their political power did not wane. Even after Fillmore and Corwin were out of office and could do no more for her, she continued to write them as if to reassure herself both of their continued friendship and the legitimacy of her continued demands for jobs. "I could not but feel," she wrote Fillmore, three days after the inauguration of Franklin Pierce, his successor, "that the *position* I occupy justified me in making it [the patronage request]—because I am yr true & *faithful* and *eternal* friend. . . ."[20]

Carroll was always aware of and responsive to the shifting sands of politics and continued to couch her requests in acceptable language and imagery. At the same time she wrote to the departing Fillmore and Corwin with protestations of faithfulness, for example, she wrote to the new Democratic secretary of state, William Marcy, on behalf of her father who would lose his position in Baltimore with the incoming Democratic administration. An interview with Marcy had failed, in spite of tears and pleadings, but she followed it up with a letter. "As a Parent, as a gentleman, I appeal to you," she begged, "to sustain the efforts of a daughter, on behalf of a pure and exemplary Father."[21] She failed to convince Marcy of her father's bipartisan appeal, so concentrated instead on working her way into the camps of the up-and-coming among the Whigs.

Even before the election, Carroll had begun corresponding with William Henry Seward, one of the major powers in the Whig party and leader of the anti-Fillmore faction in New York. She praised his political acumen and his role in the nomination of presidential candidate Scott, for "where would have been our prospects for success with any other name than Winfield Scott?" Seward's support of Scott over Daniel Webster had been in part responsible for Fillmore's inability to make any political deal that might have resulted in his renomination, but no matter. Carroll was a politician and a pragmatist. After commenting upon the stupidity of the Southern Whigs who had split from the party over Scott's failure to make clear his support for the Compromise of 1850, and praising Seward's leadership of the Whig Party, she closed her letter by asking Seward to send his opinion of the party's chances in New York to her at the Whig Committee Rooms in Washington, a location indicative of Carroll's ability to give the appearance of legitimacy even when her connections were in fact tenuous.[22]

As she had done when corresponding with Fillmore, Carroll carefully expressed to Seward her awareness of the limitations placed upon her by her gender as she wrote. "I am a *lady,* but by *blood & name* and *spirit identified,* with those, who contributed greatly to establish and perpetuate our free institutions." Carroll was very conscious of the singularity of her proclivity toward politics; but, she told him, "by education & association my interest is more than that of ladies ordinarily. I *read, think & write. . . .*" She continued to flatter Seward prior to the election and continued to apologize for her temerity, excusing it as coming "from the impulses of a frank and generous nature, without any of those considerations which the *mere* politician would cautiously inquire into."[23]

Despite the Whig loss in November 1852, Carroll remained convinced of Seward's importance in the party and was determined to continue contact. As she ceased writing to Fillmore (except for notes of condolence upon the deaths of his wife and daughter), she began to pressure Seward to use his influence to restore her father to some lucrative post. "I feel you can appreciate the exertions of a daughter for a dear and honored Parent," she wrote, "especially when that effort is impelled by sacred and imperious considerations, which may involve life itself." Once again, Carroll repeated her pattern of combining the presumed political sagacity of the appointment with an emotional appeal that placed her lobbying for political positions within the province of the woman's sphere. She was not a lobbyist; she was instead a caretaker of her father, fulfilling her domestic duty. Nevertheless, Carroll's efforts failed, and the scramble to keep her father employed resulted in "a state of mind almost partaking of dementation," under which influence she addressed a long letter to Seward that presented a detailed portrait of the degree to which her father's financial ineptitude affected her.[24]

While Carroll later apologized to Seward and asked him to forget he had ever received the letter, she was remarkably frank. Her concern for her father's difficulties required her "to relieve my dear Father . . . in freeing himself, from an entanglement, brought about by the noble generosity of his heart, which prompted him for others, to sacrifice his own." What he had really sacrificed was his family's financial security. Still, Carroll con-

9

sidered it an act of "obedience to filial devotion" to "sacrifice whatever personal comfort may now conflict with duty" to rescue her father from his creditors, "feeling the goal is dear enough to demand it." She asked for Seward's advice about buying a farm in Maryland that would provide money for her father. By this time, Carroll was well aware of the necessity of protecting her father from what she termed his generosity. The purchase price and mortgage would be in her name so her father could no longer mortgage the family's sustenance. She would maintain control of the farm, "engage myself in whatever sphere of usefulness propriety will properly permit," while "affording to my Father, all the activity of engagement his health so imperiously demands."[25]

Carroll's devotion to her improvident yet beloved father was constantly challenged. Thomas King Carroll had learned little from the loss of Kingston Hall for his debts in 1837. By 1853, shortly after Carroll detailed her woes to Seward, her father began to sell off the remaining family slaves. There were seven left, mostly young women and girls he had taken with his family to Baltimore. His daughter was dismayed by the sale of the black family with whom she had literally grown up. To prevent it, she decided upon a unique course of action.[26]

At first "impenetrably veiled," Carroll visited the offices of leading abolitionists and philanthropists in New York City to ask for contributions so she could buy her father's slaves and thus pay off the mortgages. She wrote letters to men she thought would be sympathetic to her plight, but she preferred to meet individually with them, since in a personal interview there were "many little suggestions & explanations, often important, to a correct understanding of the case." She was desperate for money, but only a bit embarassed by her actions. Slavery was a curse that had tried her fortitude, she wrote New York abolitionist Gerrit Smith as she applied for an interview. The family's woes were not her fault or her father's. Indeed, she told him, "I regard all my own misfortune—or that, in which I am involved, on acct. of my family, to that inheritance of slavery, to which for so many generations my family have been subjected." Smith sent her fifty dollars. New York journalist and editor Gerard Halleck, with whom she also met, suggested she flaunt convention by removing her veil when interviewing with people for contributions. ". . . I think it may rather operate against you," he wrote as he sent her a list of additional contacts. "In other words," he suggested, "your frank, honest face will be a passport to you where no mere name or family distinction would be availing."[27]

Carroll raised enough money to repay four thousand dollars of debt. This time, instead of having the slaves return to the family, they were freed. The loss of collateral meant more financial woes. By the fall of 1855,

Thomas Carroll had mortgaged all the household goods for a few hundred dollars to carry the family through. The crisis momentarily passed when he got a job with the Merchant Fire and Marine Insurance Company of Baltimore.[28]

As she searched for likely candidates to give her money to pay her father's debts, Carroll reestablished her correspondence with Millard Fillmore. Her father's "generosity and nobleness of nature" had "misguided his judgment & made him neglectful of the future," she wrote in March of 1855. Thus she had to assume a responsibility which, considering "the refined sensibility of my nature & my age [forty] & inexperience in life is surely without a paralel [*sic*]." Characteristically, the letter that renewed contact with Fillmore contained little more than praise for his political astuteness and assurances she would remain "with all the affection of a daughter, your faithful little friend. . . ." But slowly and surely the demands began to creep forth: first a complimentary one in the form of a request that he review the table of contents for a book she was to write, then a demand for an immediate response to that request. She wrote yet again, pleading for a personal loan to avoid eviction of her family into the streets of Baltimore, then demanded that he call to see her for "a *purpose* which you *cannot* neglect & *will not* regret!" All these letters came when Fillmore was absorbed with last-minute preparations for a tour of Europe to begin 16 May, and he did not reply.[29]

Carroll's concern that Fillmore reach her was not entirely selfish. By 1855, when she was not holding off her father's creditors, she was writing for the newly formed American party. The party, nicknamed "Know-Nothings" for the members' refusal to respond to questions about the party's inner workings, was running its first national candidate for president in 1856. Carroll wished to give Fillmore notice that the Know-Nothings were considering him for its nominee. "You may smile," she wrote Fillmore the night before he set sail, "but I believe, I can have very much to do with yr nomination by that party, which will as surely control the next election for President as that you & I live."[30]

Carroll told Fillmore that she had met with party leaders in Boston shortly after he sailed and had drafted a letter for them that requested he clarify his position regarding the American party. She revealed herself to Fillmore as the author of that letter of inquiry not for vanity's sake, she said, but rather "that you may know the movement is sincere & in good faith." Fillmore refused her request, taking the nineteenth-century candidate's traditional position of reluctance. Carroll accepted his stand, but she enclosed the opening of a book on the American party platform that she had written and asked him to review it. Once he had received it, she demanded, "write me a letter expressive of yr regard, for my efforts—I am so well assured, this will give you pleasure—I cannot feel I impose a burden."[31]

Carroll spent the summer of 1855 promoting Fillmore as the American party candidate over his nearest rival, George Law. Although she knew her gender meant most believed she had "no right to interfere in politics," she excused her actions and maintained the legitimacy of her work by arguing that "this American movement is above party and if the efforts of woman are ever to be exerted for God and Liberty, it is now. . . ." Fillmore's note wishing the party success satisfied those unsure of his loyalty, Carroll wrote, and she was convinced more than ever of his suitability over the competition. "My convictions as well as my hopes induce me to believe you will be the candidate of the American convention. Perhaps no one, vain tho it may seem, really knows more of the *true* wishes of the leading men of the Order . . . than myself."[32] Carroll exaggerated her role in the party's selection, but by championing Fillmore, who did indeed become the party's choice, Anna Ella Carroll had chosen, for one of the few times in her life, the right man upon whom to expend her inexhaustible supply of literary energy.

TWO

Carroll and the Election of 1856

The American party nominated Millard Fillmore as its presidential candidate in February 1856. Carroll was convinced that she was responsible; after all, she had been a supporter of Fillmore as far back as 1852. Now at last, her choice legitimized by the men of the party, Carroll had a national platform from which to write. While she continued to seek influence over patronage positions through personal letters to politicians, she now began to publish under her own name and to participate openly in politics. The next eight months would be the most productive of Carroll's career as she wrote and published books, pamphlets, articles, and editorials in support of the American party and its candidate.

The rise of the American party to national power in the 1850s came about as the Whig party declined, and paralleled the rise of the Republican party. The new organizations appealed to voters with moralistic stands on issues with mass appeal such as nativism, anti-Catholicism, and slavery. Many nativists were also antislavery men and vice versa, and, early on, voters supported one or the other party or both. But by the election of 1856, party loyalties were more intense. Know-Nothings were determined to win the election with a candidate who focused interest on nativism rather than slavery.

Historians have long argued the primacy of the slavery issue in the campaign of 1856, relative to such other issues as nativism, anti-Catholicism, temperance, and economics. The majority of Know-Nothings, however, were more concerned with nativist and anti-Catholic issues than with the antislavery movement, its radical leaders, or the growing sectionalism of the country. Far from being a party of displaced Whigs, former Locofocos, Free-Soilers, or assorted political cranks looking for a home, the Know-Nothings represented a legitimate attempt by a substantial group to articulate a platform and promote a party that would respond to its fears of a growing threat to the stability of the American nation caused by the huge influx of foreigners to the United States in the 1840s and 1850s. The immigrants were primarily lower class, at times badly behaved, quickly naturalized, and largely controlled by the Democratic party machine. Know-Nothings held them responsible for the growing corruption and dissoluteness discernible in the American body politic.[1] For the American party, the threat posed by immigrants was far more important to the survival of the country than the issue of slavery expansion or control.

In the border state of Maryland, as in the more northern states, corruption, nativism, and anti-Catholicism were the major concerns of the Know-Nothings, in spite of Maryland's status as a slave state. These were the issues that attracted the majority of supporters; few expressed great concern over abolition and the slavery question. Carroll, for instance, had embraced the American party for its nativist, anti-Catholic stand. Her father had been a Whig supporter, as had she, and both had been disheartened when Henry Clay lost the 1844 presidential race to Democrat James K. Polk. Many Maryland Whigs had blamed the immigrant vote in Baltimore for helping to give Polk the victory, even though Maryland had gone Whig in the election and the margin in Baltimore had given Polk a plurality of only 473 votes.[2]

An additional influence on Anne Carroll's political choice was the Reverend Dr. Robert J. Breckinridge. Breckinridge, minister of the Second Presbyterian Church of Baltimore, which Carroll had joined in 1845, was a powerful orator and ardent anti-Catholic. His tirades against foreigners and Catholics made a deep and long-lasting impression on Carroll: twenty years later she would recall his sermons as she wrote to him of her life's work on behalf of the anti-Catholic movement.[3]

Another factor in Carroll's decision to side with the Know-Nothings was the Whigs' continued decline. Although her father had benefited from a Whig patronage position in 1849, by 1853 the Whigs were out of office, and he was out of a job. The Know-Nothings, moving into the power vacuum created by the Whigs' demise, were so popular in Maryland that by 1855 they had gained control of the state legislature. National popularity was sure to follow, Carroll believed, and if she achieved power within the party, she could guarantee her father's financial security.

The economic and social disorder of Carroll's private life also may have been responsible for her political choices. Of necessity, she had been forced by her improvident father to make her way in the world. She would not blame herself for her difficulties, nor could she blame her dearly beloved father. Looking outside her family for the culprit, she found a corrupt political and religious machine to blame. In a sense, Carroll did what the rest of the anti-Catholic nativists did in blaming outsiders for her troubles.

Rivalry between Catholics and Protestants in Maryland was not new. By the 1850s difficulties were exacerbated by the disruptions to society caused by immigration, political corruption, and the ineffectiveness and dissolution of traditional parties. Nativist Protestants felt they were under siege; the world for which their ancestors had fought and worked and died was under attack by various forces. Because they would not blame themselves, they looked outside themselves and their Protestant cultural matrix to the foreigners, to incoming "tribes" such as the Irish with their clannishness, their strange languages, their different values, beliefs, and cultural systems. Immigrants became an easily identifiable enemy.[4]

If foreigners could be enemies, foreign Catholics could be doubly treacherous. Not only did they represent a threat to "Americanism" by retaining their Old-Country ways, but they were an additional threat with their allegiance to a foreign potentate, the Pope, who, "sitting and trembling upon the great shield of the Vatican at Rome," Carroll suggested, had "evinced a great desire to control the spiritual and temporal interests of this young world."[5] This reasoning allowed the Know-Nothings to leap from the undeniable (that politics were corrupt and society in disarray) to the unbelievable (that the Pope's Jesuit monks were infiltrating and subverting the American political system).

Know-Nothings felt that their access to the political process was being threatened or limited by foreigners. Considering their politically unsound demands and the growing bloc of foreign-born registered voters controlled by party bosses, their sense of powerlessness was partially justified. More important, Know-Nothings believed that their enemies' power had been achieved by conspiratorial means. Given Americans' traditional enchantment with open political systems in theory if not in practice, the Know-Nothings had created an easily despised enemy: corrupt, conspiratorial foreigners. In their advocacy of xenophobic hatred, the Know-Nothings could unite as a true political party with a viable enemy to fight. But grounded on emotional rather than rational approaches to the issues, the American party was not disposed to make any sort of compromise, a stand that in the troublesome 1850s meant death to ordinary politics.[6]

It is through the prism of fear, irrationality, and emotion that characterized the Know-Nothing party that its literature must be evaluated. Know-Nothing writers, including Carroll, were not only convinced of a Jesuitical conspiracy, but were also, like most missionaries of a cause, convinced of the righteousness of their own position. Carroll's first book, *The Great*

American Battle (1856), was "the textbook of the Cause," according to
E. B. Bartlett, the national president of the Know-Nothings, as it so accurately portrayed the party and its dictates. Like most political tracts of the
times, Carroll's works were scarcely literary masterpieces. She tended toward overly dramatic prose, hyperbole, italics, and exclamation points,
and, tellingly, found a campaign biography of Fillmore "wofully [*sic*] de-
fective in *vim* and enthusiasm."[7] Still, she clearly stated the danger and
proposed appropriate action to circumvent it.

Carroll divided *The Great American Battle* into three major sections.
The first five chapters alerted the American people and the press to the
dangerous aim of the Roman Catholic church "to unsettle the principles of
our liberties and hence to destroy them. . . ." Each member of society had
a specific duty to meet the challenge. Women should perceive the danger
and act upon it, but only as a guiding moral force, even if their actions were
political in their ramifications. Still defining political actions for women
within cultural confines, Carroll argued that women's province was the
education of children and of men. By this education women sought and
propounded "man's moral and ultimate good." Of course, to accomplish
this goal they had to be educated themselves, for it was education united
with morality that enabled women to become "an arm of strength to free
America." In her call to women, Carroll combined all the characteristics of
Victorian culture: the high status of the mother as transmitter of cultural
identity and values; a faith in the redemptive power of education over ignorance and sin; women's God-given role as moral leaders of the family
and, through families, of the nation; and the imposition of the Protestant
Christian framework upon extant institutions. Reforming those institutions to reflect more closely God's will meant that the white, Anglo-Saxon
Protestant version of His will would "govern the mind of America."[8]

The tasks of the press and the men of America were less noble by com-
parison. While the "women of American now may be said to control the
destinies of ages yet unborn!" because of their influence over children, the
press primarily was urged to take the subject seriously. Because the press
was the "judgement-seat of public opinion" its dismissal of American party
fears as "frivolous" could result in its own destruction, warned Carroll.
Men of America, on the other hand, were by the Jesuit threat afforded a
perfect opportunity to emulate patriots of old. For men, as for women,
education was the key to meeting the crisis: education was "the instrument
of liberty, property and security to America."[9]

The educational process Carroll called for had to be one that did not
involve the use of Catholic schools, popular in the United States for their
rigorous curriculum. Such schools posed a significant danger since education nourished "the very soul of America." The Catholic church, argued

Carroll, offered education only as a way to influence and eventually control souls through convents, schools, and colleges.[10]

The school issue was a particularly touchy one for Carroll as a native of Maryland. In 1852 Delegate Thomas Kerney of Baltimore had introduced to the Maryland state legislature a school reorganization bill designed to simplify the administration of state-funded, locally operated schools. The bill made provisions to give state aid to private schools, including parochial ones, if their curriculum was state-approved. In practice, the bill would have meant public funding for Catholic schools. Know-Nothings seized the issue as evidence of a "deep-dyed Popish plot" designed to destroy the traditional separation of church and state, and to gain control over the disbursement of educational funds. Catholics' next step, declared the Know-Nothings, was to seek control of all public funds, and to underhandedly unite church and state into a theocratic government answerable only to the Pope.[11]

Commuting between her father's residence in Baltimore and her freelance work in Washington, Carroll would not have been able to miss the issue. The bill was eventually buried in legislative committee, but the clamor it raised continued to be fuelled throughout the 1850s not only by such political tracts as Carroll's work, but also by arguments over the social, moral, and political implications of using the Protestant Bible in public schools, or banning the Bible entirely at the request of Catholic bishops. Censorship by the Catholic church over reading matter in schools continued the controversy with more protests by Know-Nothings like Carroll who thought that history would thus be "murdered" and literature "maimed and mutilated."[12]

The most famous of Catholic educators, of course, were the Jesuits, a special branch of the Catholic priesthood which came under Carroll's most virulent attacks in her book. Through education "the humble of our land have been made lofty, the poor have been enriched and blessed," and she herself had been able to participate actively in the political world she loved, but "Jesuitism," a term which Carroll used interchangeably with "the Romish Hierarchy" and "Popery," was "threatening . . . to swallow up America; and springing its shuttle of death across her shores it pants to be able to water its steed in her great Mississippi." Mixed metaphors aside, the American party had been formed to forestall this Jesuitical takeover.[13] Through Protestant-controlled education, anti-Catholic legislation, and deportation of immigrants, declared Carroll, the Know-Nothings were determined to defeat the foe.

In the second section of her book, Carroll developed the literary device of a garden tea party at which "America" and his mother (never named) visit with each other and friends and discuss the history of America's birth

17

and rise to manhood, as well as the enemies that will assail him once he leaves the party. Day by day, chapter by chapter, America and his mother discuss the nature and characteristics of the American party. It possessed a patriotic fervor comparable to political groups of the revolutionary period, but remained secretive because it needed time and trustworthy party members to guarantee solidity and strength of organization. On political issues, the party opposed the sale of public lands to immigrants instead of to "native American citizens for public improvements and their education!" It saw the Union's national interests and its preservation as more important than any sectional gain. The spoils system of the corrupt political party currently in power had led to the selection of foreigners over native-born citizens, and was, in reality, a "Jesuit mechanism" to take over the country. To meet those threats, the American party, a " 'purely defensive' "organization, was formed; it would retire itself from politics " 'when the aggression of foreigners ceases.' "[14]

In like manner, Carroll continued for many pages, presenting the American party stance on all the major political issues of the day and reiterating her accusations of corruption by the "timid, servile serpents" of the Pope. Carroll brought in the history of European monarchs condemned by the Pope to prove the papal interest in controlling temporal matters. She discussed the *Index of Prohibited Books* and the Inquisition to prove Catholic attempts to restrict freedom by controlling minds. Her writing exemplifies so-called paranoid scholarship: apparent "facts" marshalled in a rationalistic and scholastic manner that led to a conclusion neither rational nor scholarly.[15]

In the last section of her book, Carroll brought the troubles caused by those alleged papal conspiracies to the present day. She accused the Naval Board of Fifteen, which had reorganized the United States Navy's officer line in 1855, of being controlled by the Jesuits. The reorganization had been controversial and several officers had written Carroll complaining of their reserve status, hoping she would publicize their cases. She took up the cause and found her proof of conspiracy in the Catholic backgrounds of board members Commander Samuel F. Dupont and Commodore William Shubrick, and of Senator Stephen A. Mallory, who had introduced the original bill of reorganization. The true purpose of the reorganization, she asserted, was not to make the navy more efficient but to destroy it. Catholic officers had survived the purge, she said, because the Pope wanted his subjects in positions "to sap the foundation of our democratic liberty and our glorious Constitution," as well as to destroy the only arm of the United States government that could conceivably interfere in the Crimean War. That war, claimed Carroll, was being waged by the Pope to crush Russia and the United States somehow so there would be no rival to his European base of power.[16] Carroll's arguments and descriptions of papal activities were without foundation and at times ludicrous, but for Know-Nothings, her emotional and irrational logic was very appealing.

In the end, Carroll called for the expulsion of all Jesuits and the cancellation of all treaties with countries which did not allow the free practice of Protestantism. And, of course, she called all true patriots to join the American party. Men were exhorted to vote for Millard Fillmore; women's "holy mission" was to "plead, in Gospel sincerity and patriotic fervor," with the men of America to vote for Fillmore, thus preserving "our Sabbath, our Schools, our Bible and Liberty."[17]

Beyond a statement of American party principles of the more moderate wing of the Know-Nothings (Carroll did differentiate between foreign and native-born Catholics; the latter were still acceptable as citizens), Carroll's *The Great American Battle* is valuable for the insight it provides regarding her views of women's place and women's work, and of her consciousness of the societal strictures placed upon her. Carroll began her work by apologizing for her intrusion into the masculine world of politics, protesting her innocence of intent. "I have no affiliations with any principles which place [woman] in a sphere at variance with that refined delicacy to which she is assigned by Nature," she wrote, thus maintaining both her distance from the burgeoning woman's rights movement and the individual nature of her work. She had "no aspirations to extend her influence or position." Yet the present dangers to the survival of America meant women could not shrink from their duty. "God has given to woman to enlighten America, and to America to light the world," she wrote, and America's fate depended on the work of its daughters. While Carroll recognized the political nature of such a mission, she always reassured her readers that it was only as a moral agent that a woman should act: her sole aim was still "to develop the child for God and his country."[18]

This ideology of the woman's sphere and of the republican mother were common in the first half of the nineteenth century. Carroll also compared the moral superiority of women to the "blundering and quarrelling of men" throughout *The Great American Battle.* A woman's true vocation was to work for man's moral improvement, and to achieve that goal, Carroll continued to argue in favor of education. Only when educated could a woman secure the "respect, confidence and appreciation" necessary to become that "arm of strength to free America."[19]

Even when using analogies to compare the women of her day to the women of Sparta, Athens, Rome, and the American Revolution, Carroll was very careful to present her readers with heroic women within the accepted cultural imperative. "We want no Joans of Arc to make America vascular and alive," she wrote. As religious as Joan of Arc may have been, she was Catholic, dressed in men's clothing, and led men into battle, none of which appealed to Carroll's view of what women should do, even in times of national peril. "We want faithful and true women, who neither shriek nor protest, but pray; women who neither mount nor sink; who are neither heroines nor fools; but American women, who can stand in their shoes. . . ."[20]

Of course, the most obvious instance of Carroll using the republican mother ideology was the garden tea party device she used to present the history and platform of the American party. By employing a mother as well as a son figure as a party spokesperson, she was able to convey the respect due women as mothers and participants in the nation's life in terms of day-to-day existence, noble acts in emergencies, and as grantors of new life by their procreative abilities. The son provided a mechanism to express gratitude as a measure of women's worth within the cultural framework as it existed, and without the need for enfranchisement. " 'My mother,' he [America] said, 'you made me a man! You taught me to love God in my cradle, and to love my dear country. . . . I wish all the children had such a mother, then our dear country would have patriot sons.' " The happy result? " 'They would all belong to the American party.' "[21]

While Carroll embraced the domestic imagery of the republican mother, she occasionally used adjectives of political weight and force to describe her: "She was indeed the most original and commanding of women, an elemental force of great power, and like a solvent of such range of affinity, as to combine and reconcile heterogeneous spirits into one society." But these stronger terms were seldom used, and Carroll always returned to the less politically threatening domesticity, reestablishing the subservience of the mother to the more political animal, man: ". . . our Divine Creator saw fit to dignify woman by the name of 'Mother' when he gave her to the companionship and comfort of man. It was in this sense [as a potential mother] that she became the Eve to the American family. . . ." Even when dealing with the history of women's past patriotic deeds, for instance, noting that Washington had expressed his belief that women's sympathy toward the cause had helped win the Revolution, Carroll was careful to attribute women's success not to masculine incentives such as dreams of achievement and glory, but to " 'duty: and [they] would have fallen short, had they done less!' " To clarify her position regarding women's place in politics, Carroll finally stated, "Let no cry of *'woman's rights'* deter you [from reading *The Great American Battle*]. That charge has no significance here."[22]

The Great American Battle was a fair success. Carroll finished the book in early March 1856, and by May wrote to her father of the papers' announcement of the sale of "10,000 copies of the Battle and the whole country is alive in its praise—I wish you could see half that is said." She was startled, she wrote, to find that her publisher had employed a woman as agent for her work, but she appeared to be a good choice since there were a large number of subscribers. Her biggest concern was the number of newspaper editors who had not yet acknowledged receipt of the copies sent them. "This is *Pierce* acting through the P.O. [Post Office]," she declared, believing that President Pierce's Catholic postmaster general was taking advantage of his position to purge the mails of all anti-Catholic materials.[23]

But compliments for Carroll's work did make their way to her in New York City, where she was writing campaign tracts for Fillmore from her rooms at Holdridge's Hotel at Eighth and Broadway. One letter of praise came from North Carolina American party leader Kenneth Rayner. He looked at the book as an opportunity for the party to clarify its philosophy. A restatement of purpose, he hoped, might turn the party away from its current state, in which its principles had been "adulterated by the selfishness and sectionalism that have marked its late progress." Rayner feared the widening split in the party over the slavery issue would overshadow the more important issue of anti-Catholicism. As edifying and beneficial to the American party cause Rayner thought the book was, he did find fault with one matter: the distinction Carroll drew between native and foreign Roman Catholics. "You are wrong," he wrote Carroll. "In the main, the native papists are as intolerable as the foreigners." Both groups, he believed, gave a spiritual supremacy to the Pope which released them from the obligation of their allegiance to the Constitution, and the Know-Nothings "must make war upon the whole system. . . ."[24]

Candidate Fillmore, to whom Carroll had sent a copy of the book's opening chapters, never actually read it, but did "commend her zeal in the cause." His own zeal was a bit more suspect. As a candidate, Fillmore did not give Carroll much to work with. Not a particularly charismatic politician, he was decidedly lukewarm about most of the tenets of the Know-Nothing party, prompting Carroll to write him at one point that she "didn't feel like entering with my whole soul again into anything chilled by a want of appreciation. . . ." Fillmore was not an anti-Catholic, nor was he a nativist. But he was aware of the growing popularity of the American party and, like most retired presidents, he wanted employment which would not demean the office he had once held; a return to the White House would suit him just fine. Left politically homeless by the decline of the Whigs, Fillmore viewed the Republican party as too sectional to guarantee the country's stability. He protested that he had "no desire to mingle in political strife," but he nevertheless became a sworn Know-Nothing and accepted the nomination. He had supported Know-Nothing Daniel Ullmann in the New York gubernatorial race of 1854 and had written of his concern over the "corrupting influence" that the struggle for control over the foreign vote in the state had occasioned. But even as the American party nominee, Fillmore still spoke not of anti-Catholicism or nativism, but vaguely of adopting the party's principles, despite Carroll's urging to "proclaim . . . to the land that you go the American doctrine from alpha to omega."[25]

As the campaign progressed, Fillmore continued to refuse to take a strong stand on anti-Catholicism. Carroll hoped to ease the discomfiture felt by many American party members, particularly those from areas heavily Catholic, by drawing a clear distinction between native-born and foreign Catholics. It was the system rather than the individual against which she wrote, Carroll argued, the "foreign, ungrateful refugees" who maintained allegiance to their native faith even after naturalization. As the Gallican Catholics in France had stood for no papal interference in temporal matters, so native-born Catholics must stand against papal interference in the American political system. This distinction was crucial for Carroll to make, not only politically, but personally as well. Everyone knew the more prestigious Maryland Carrolls were Catholic. She could honor her ancestry, but "so baneful an evil" was papal control over votes that it was pardonable "in all eyes," presumably including familial ones, to work to expose the evil even if she and the American party for which she wrote appeared to some to be "bigots and blockheads."[26]

Politically, the Know-Nothings needed Carroll's distinction between native and foreign-born Catholics so states with strong Know-Nothing parties and large Catholic populations would stay with the party instead of defecting to the Democrats or, far worse, to the newly formed Republican party. Both Carroll's native Maryland and the southern state of Louisiana, for instance, had substantial Catholic populations who were Know-Nothings. Louisiana in particular presented a problem. At the American party nominating convention in Philadelphia in February 1856, the Louisiana delegation contained a number of Catholics. The convention allowed their credentials, but the feasibility of seating Catholic delegates in a strongly anti-Catholic convention depended upon accepting this distinction between native and foreign-born Catholics.[27]

Carroll could—indeed, had to—accept the distinction. She believed it, too, since her own family and state history provided familiar and familial examples of patriotic native-born Catholics. Radical Know-Nothings such as Kenneth Rayner, however, were under no such illusions as to the contradictory nature of allowing the Louisiana delegates in. "I can not tell you the deep mortification I feel at the compromise with Jesuitism made . . . by the Nominating Convention," he wrote to Carroll. The "anti-Romish element of the order has been its great element of strength with the masses," he argued. Admitting the delegates he feared "was a fatal step . . . those bodies surrendered to the enemy the citadel of our strength." But such uncompromising anti-Catholicism as Rayner's was too offensive to survive politically. If the American party wished to win the election, it had to tone down its anti-Catholicism enough not to lose voters to the other parties. Moreover, the real problem in the nominating convention had been the issue of slavery extension and control. Northerners had bolted from the convention over that issue, not anti-Catholicism. Although Rayner argued that seating the Catholic delegates had done irreparable damage to the fortunes of the American party, even he had to admit that the Know-Nothings were likely to lose the election because of their inability to resolve the slavery issue.[28]

In *The Great American Battle* Carroll had concentrated on the impending takeover by the "Romish Hierarchy." In election pamphlets she wrote throughout the spring and summer of 1856, she shifted her emphasis to concentrate on preserving the Union against the growing sectionalism in the country. The Republican nominee, John C. Frémont, belonged to a party radical enough to provide the Know-Nothings an opportunity to present Fillmore as a national candidate. The Republicans were Free-Soilers; many were abolitionists. Both ideas were anathema to many Southerners. Unlike Frémont, Fillmore was not a candidate for those who desired " 'an administration for the North as against the South, or for the South against the North. . . .' " Instead, he said, his interest was preserving " 'our beloved country, our whole country and nothing but our country.' "[29]

Carroll pressed the issue of sectionalism in her first pamphlet, *The Union of the States*. While there was still mention of the dangers of a corrupted democracy because of foreign voters, Carroll devoted most of the pamphlet to other concerns. Fanatical abolitionists had combined with Democrats to cause sectional strife in 1850, she argued, and it had been only "the Roman firmness of Mr. Fillmore," exhibited best when Fillmore signed the Compromise of 1850 after President Zachary Taylor's death, that had saved the Union. The civil war that currently raged in Kansas she blamed on the Democratic administration's incompetence, and it could have been avoided had Fillmore been renominated and reelected in 1852. Continued unrest in Kansas and continued Democratic interference with the ballot box were in store if Americans did not return Fillmore in 1856.[30]

Carroll did not directly attack the Republican party in this pamphlet, as she did the Democrats, but she did argue that Fillmore was a better candidate because he had been nominated by a national rather than sectional party. In so doing, she conveniently ignored the "Northern American" convention in New York City in June that effectively had fused with the Republicans by endorsing their candidate, Frémont. Carroll had attended the convention and been dismayed at the intransigence of the dissident Northerners. It was not only madness to nominate a sectional candidate, but "treason to the Union" as well, and since she saw both Democrats and Republicans as sectional parties, she presented Fillmore as the only national choice.[31]

Also issued prior to the election was Carroll's *Review of Pierce's Administration*. This was an exhaustive year-by-year critique of four years of Democratic blunders under the administration of Franklin Pierce. While the *Review* contained many of the same ideas as *The Great American Battle* and *Union of the States,* it is particularly informative regarding Carroll's ideas on foreign policy. Her opinions were characteristic of antebellum expansionists such as Matthew Fontaine Maury, Asa Whitney, and William Henry Seward. Not limited to the continentalism of Manifest Destiny, and not interested in the Young Americans' call for intervention in Europe, Carroll was primarily a commercial expansionist. She argued for a foreign and domestic policy that would benefit trade, a consular and diplomatic service to promote the expansion of American markets, reciprocity treaties with South America, a strong navy and forceful commander-in-chief to protect Americans abroad, and peace with Europe to avoid the disruptions of trade any war would bring. These were points upon which she could attack Pierce's administration as being ineffective.[32]

The *Review,* like *The Great American Battle,* was a coherent statement of political criticism combined with a recommended course of action for its readers. Here again, Carroll took care to reassure her readers that she knew her limits "within the province of feminine delicacy." At the same time, she knew "of no rule to exclude females from society or the discussion of any subject which has an immediate bearing on the social, moral, and political destiny" of the country. She pointed out, rather sarcastically, that "an American female is not an idle statue of a pagoda, or of a Turkish seraglio. . . ." Readers should have no fear that Carroll, or any woman expressing a political interest within these particular provinces, would "trespass either on the rights of the male sex, or wantonly expose herself to a charge of temerity." She was seeking after Truth, and all citizens should be given an opportunity to participate in such a search since the aim was to promote the welfare and good of individuals, society, and the nation. The interdependency of modern society meant "the interests and destiny of the mothers and daughters are in common with those of their fathers and brothers," and once again, it was part of woman's duty as a citizen and mother to educate the next generation. Since Carroll was not a mother, she continued to explain her own motivation in emotional terms still compatible with the woman's sphere: her love of country and her "desire to awaken the reader to the vast importance" of the subjects treated by her work drove her to political action.[33]

Carroll wrote on through the long summer of 1856. Fillmore had returned from Europe to the United States in late June and greatly angered Carroll by failing to call on her, especially considering, she wrote him, "all I did, nay permitted, in your behalf, for I have been the author of articles which were made effective by ignorance of their source. . . ." She had even had, she said, "a tender for my influence . . . decorously intimated at any amt. I named," from Frémont's people. "I replied," she continued pompously, "that I *loved* freedom so well, that I could not consent to sell my *conscience* and become a slave. I supported the American candidate of the American party from *principle* and a purely *independent* ground." Perhaps, she wrote, Fillmore feared the effect of publicly acknowledging her work printed under her own name. "For the first time in our *history* a woman has ventured openly and without disguise to espouse the cause of her Country. . . ." Fillmore should not fear but approve of Carroll's work. After all, she pointed out, it had "drawn the applause of your sex, and every distinguished member of the party . . . have [*sic*] called, while, you . . . have seen fit . . . to show so much indifference. . . ." Those men, she wrote, included Erastus Brooks, New York's Know-Nothing gubernatorial candidate hoping for a ride on Fillmore's coattails, National President Bartlett, and Thurlow Weed, a leading New York Republican and power broker. In addition to accepting their calls, Carroll kept up her correspondence with Thomas Corwin of Ohio, Kenneth Rayner, and Josiah Polk of Washington.[34]

Fillmore's continued silence may have convinced Carroll that he was uncomfortable with her actions outside the confines of her proper sphere. Carroll continued to reinforce the womanly nature of herself and her activities. "I keep myself a lady and mean to," she reassured him. Her support for him was more emotional than political in nature. "I have never known any change in my feeling for you. . . . [T]he confidence and love I have ever had for you has been next to my own Father—a better man than whom has never lived in this world."[35]

By July, Fillmore apologized for his neglect, writing Carroll from Buffalo where he spent the summer. Carroll wrote back, gratified "to know that you had not set aside from memory a true woman who is true to you." She asked for information on his previous administration to use in the *Review* and other pamphlets. He replied, promising a visit with her should she come to Niagara Falls. Her hard work on his behalf was not unappreciated, he wrote. In fact, he was pleased "that I have at least one friend on whom I can rely through good & through evil. . . ."[36]

Along with her campaign tracts, Carroll was finishing a massive tome, *The Star of the West; or, National Men and National Measures.* Her work-load began to take its toll on her health. Fillmore thought her illness arose "from overtaxing the brain with mental labor. You must desist at once and seek health and recreation," he wrote her. "In the end it will be time gained." Carroll did stop work for a while to recover her energy, but she soon picked up her pen to continue. By September 1856 *The Star of the West* was ready for the press.[37]

Perhaps reflecting the strain of overwork, *The Star of the West* was the poorest of Carroll's campaign works, the most disjointed and incoherent. Apparently it was a collection of articles written and previously published. Gathered together for the book, the essays had little in common. Carroll reexamined the Naval Board's reorganization work of 1855, concentrating particularly on the sad plight of Commodore Charles Stewart, the ranking officer of the United States Navy, who had been placed on the reserve list and to whom the book was dedicated, and on Lieutenant Washington A. Bartlett, an expert on lighthouses who was also "reserved." In "The First American Exploring Expedition," she took up the cause of Jeremiah N. Reynolds of New York. He had fought for years for congressional funding of an Antarctic expedition and then was refused permission to join the United States Exploring Expedition of 1838–42 led by Lieutenant Charles Wilkes. She wrote a promotion of a transcontinental railroad which would benefit trade by giving Americans "a hold on the wealth of China . . . and her 700 Millions of inhabitants." The railroad would have other salutary effects. The gold of California would be more accessible; it would save time, expense, and trouble in trade and commerce. A railroad would also prevent the secession of the Southwest from the United States—a worri-some possibility because of the area's isolation. Isolation in the region had already led to abuses of democracy, to "disorders . . . the villainous prac-tice of stuffing the ballot-box, the elevation of the scum of society and traitors to office. . . ." A transcontinental railway would change all that, as well as uniting the country and advancing Protestant education and civilization, which Carroll held to be more conducive to economic growth because Protestants had fewer holidays than Catholics.[38]

Incoherent as *The Star of the West* was (Carroll also included essays on her favorite topics, Jesuitism and the dangers of Jesuit education), it did have one unifying theme: Carroll's fascination with the ideology of Manif-est Destiny. Expanding ideas she had mentioned briefly in *The Great American Battle,* Carroll described the mission of Americans to "spread their Protestant Bible and their American Constitution on the wings of the American eagle," so they could throw their weight "in behalf of equality and justice over the countries of the world. . . ." Not incidentally, those actions would also mean an increase in strength and resources as well as "moral, commercial and political greatness."[39]

In a chapter on Central America, Carroll developed the subject of expansion more fully, writing in support of William Walker's popular filibustering adventures in Nicaragua. Walker's attempts to force the Nicaraguans to accept a republican government appealed to Carroll's sense of mission and duty that were so much a part of her expansionist outlook. She compared his work with what American revolutionaries such as "Lafayette, DeKalb, Pulaski, Kosciusko, had done for American liberty. . . . Who, then, can repress patriotic emotion or deep sympathy for his triumph?" The United States was right to extend to Central America the protection provided by its legal and governmental systems, according to Carroll, since the people of Nicaraugua had invited intervention on their behalf. The triumph of self-government in the American tradition for such a people tied in well not only in spiritual terms with American interest in liberty and justice, but also in economic terms. To Carroll, Walker in Nicaragua meant that "our stars and stripes will yet float over the Pacific gate of the Nicarauguan transit" on the road to the China market, and the key to the Gulf of Mexico would "never fall into the hands of savages." The Central American states, so essential to U.S. trade, must remain in friendly hands. Walker's activities provided Carroll with the perfect example of what she viewed as the nobility of the American mission in action in Central America, restoring order and peace through American systems of government, and, at the same time, ensuring the preservation and promotion of United States trade.[40]

Carroll must have been greatly pleased to receive Walker's note thanking her for the copy of *The Star of the West* that she sent him after its publication in October 1856. It was, he wrote, "a source of consolation as well as of encouragement . . . to receive such assurances" as she had manifested "in the cause of Nicaraguan regeneration." He promised to try to visit her before he returned to Nicaragua, to converse with her personally about her work. Her description of his public speaking presence ("an expression of meekness, accompanied by a nasal tone and sluggish utterance, which would arrest attention in any assembly"), was peculiar enough to suggest an encounter of some kind before his return to Central America and subsequent execution by the Hondurans in 1860.[41]

Perhaps because of the essay on the popular exploits of Walker, certainly in spite of its literary shortcomings, *The Star of the West* was Carroll's most popular book, running to three editions. Carroll had no time to rest, however. The election was fast approaching, and she cranked out two more short pamphlets. One was distributed in Boston, where she had gone to work with her publisher on *The Star of the West,* the other in New York, where, she wrote Fillmore, it had been declared "the best effort now that can be made to save" that state for the Know-Nothings.[42]

Carroll attacked Democratic nominee James Buchanan most vigorously in the first of the two pamphlets. *Which? Fillmore or Buchanan!* conjured up the spectre of war with Spain over Cuba by reviving the issue of the Ostend Manifesto, for which Buchanan had been partly responsible. The Manifesto, which had caused considerable flap when issued in 1854, was a statement of intent to purchase Cuba or, barring compliance, to "detach" it from Spain. Buchanan was secretly pledged to revive the Manifesto if elected, Carroll wrote. The result would be *"War immediately* with England, France and Spain!"[43] To prevent such a catastrophe, vote for Fillmore!

Carroll's *Who Shall Be President?* discussed more domestic concerns. Carroll dismissed Republican Frémont's election as mathematically impossible because of Southern opposition. At that, she may have at last realized that Fillmore's chances for victory were slim: "Every vote . . . cast for Frémont, is a vote really given to Buchanan." Vote for Fillmore! Buchanan would bring Kansas in as a slave state; Fillmore would send in troops to restore order. The disunion of America that was sure to result under Buchanan's administration would paralyze and eventually destroy the country. Vote for Fillmore! Carroll was becoming aware of the very real possibility of a Know-Nothing loss if the party could not attract more votes from other parties: "Republicans, Democrats and Whigs, join the American army . . . and aid us in electing Fillmore. . . . Do this now and settle minor differences at a more convenient season."[44]

Clearly Carroll did not comprehend that the Republicans would never make the necessary compromise on the slavery issue required to embrace Fillmore's candidacy. For Republicans to support the American party platform of popular sovereignty, instead of their own platform which opposed any extension of slavery, was not a "minor difference." It was political suicide. The non-extension of slavery was the raison d'être of the Republican party. Co-optation through compromise would inevitably mean its destruction.

The "more convenient season" which Carroll hoped for would never arrive. Wanting to share information "infinitely important," Carroll left Boston to meet with Fillmore one last time before the election, but was unsuccessful in her attempt to meet him at the Cataract House in Niagara Falls in late October. Fillmore, no doubt concerned with election matters, did not respond to Carroll's letters asking for an appointment. Carroll, disproportionately offended when put off, was convinced that "some malignant influence" was swaying Fillmore's mind against meeting with her, especially considering all she had done for him. Or perhaps Fillmore still did not "like

a *political* woman, but my friends say I have been more than a Jessie Frémont to the Fillmore cause," she wrote, referring to John C. Frémont's
politically ambitious spouse. Hurt at his silence, she took the train to Buffalo to await his appearance at her door. She added a postscript to a note
requesting he call on her with what might be considered a threat, and was
certainly less than gracious: "You better let me know what time it will suit
you to call here."[45] That night or the next day Fillmore must have called
and soothed Carroll's wounded feelings, for their correspondence continued after Carroll returned to New York City to await election day.

THREE

Losses

Fillmore lost. James Buchanan and the Democrats won; John Charles Frémont and the new Republican party were second. Returns came in slowly enough to New York City that Carroll hoped that the election would be thrown into the House of Representatives. On 5 November she met with "leading Republicans" to suggest a fusion between Know-Nothings and Republicans, with Fillmore as the candidate of choice should the House vote be needed. Fillmore, she argued, was the only national candidate and had successfully avoided a campaign focused on the divisive issue of slavery. "Every body now concurs with me that the campaign was conducted on a false issue." But because the Republicans had dealt with it and thus split the national vote, they had "left the D—— to sweep the stakes. If others had fought on the same principle I did, the victory would have been complete." If only men had listened to her more closely. "Had I been a man, I would have had this," she wrote, blaming Fillmore's loss in part on men's refusal to take her more seriously because of her gender. More important, though, was the lack of funds for the campaign: ". . . even as a woman, had I 20 thousand dollars to have worked with, to this end," victory would have been realized.[1]

At least, Carroll was pleased to say, Maryland had maintained its loyalty to Fillmore. She took credit for that win. After all, she wrote to him, "there my works have most circulated and my opinions been most freely consulted." The problem had been New York State. She thought it safe and sure to bring victory to Fillmore, and maintained her belief in Fillmore, despite reports of his losses, thus marking the difference between the "cold selfish calculations" of professional politicians and herself. "My heart enters into my acts and I loving the cause, *believe* in its triumph," even when political factors suggested the opposite.[2]

Carroll received a warm letter of condolence from Kenneth Rayner on 14 November which praised her for her "pure and disinterested devotion to those immortal principles of liberty" in the late election. She grew impatient to hear similar sentiments from the defeated candidate. She wrote Fillmore a letter of condolence and support, heaping praise on him, comparing him to George Washington, sure he would "be admired by yr. whole country at a future day." In spite of her earlier claim that the slavery issue was not of paramount importance to the campaign, she predicted that his recent position regarding slavery would be the path chosen by all "sensible people North & West. And the *soi disant* [so-called] Republicans and our party must fuse" on that position to win in 1860.[3]

As much as Carroll admired Fillmore and his alleged, and unappreciated, political acumen, however, he must learn to be kinder to those who worked for the cause. "My complaint is that you can't see me as I do you—I am *great* in my womanly sphere." That he still had not written her, ten days after his loss, hurt her greatly. "But no matter, I had no motive before Heaven in serving you with a sacrificing enthusiasm," she wrote. His lack of graciousness distressed her, and she would often, in the future, "recur to it with *pain, only on yr. account,* I am content to know, I have conscientiously done *more* than my duty." Her martyr's crown secure, Carroll closed her letter with a request for a letter she could use to introduce and promote her work for a book tour upon which she was about to embark. "I intend to disseminate my 3 works wherever I go and mean to be a power yet in this land, which it will be well to propitiate."[4] Showing signs of the obsession for power and recognition which would eventually dominate her life, Carroll got what she wanted this time. Fillmore sent her the letter despite her threatening tone, and thus inadvertently discovered the shady side of Carroll's life.

Carroll took Fillmore's letter, along with one from Rayner and one from Thomas H. Clay, Jr., of Kentucky, revised them to appear as if unsolicited endorsements of her work, and presented them to the press as support for a testimonial dinner to be given her to show the American party's appreciation for her labors in the late election. This practice was common in the nineteenth century, but was usually done for, rather than by, the recipient. Still in New York City in late November, Carroll was apparently having difficulties raising enough cash for her book tour. The testimonial may have been her idea, or that of her friend, William Scudder Tisdale, a writer for DeWitt Publishers, a New York publishing company that carried a number of Know-Nothing publications. Fillmore apparently discovered the unauthorized revision and use of his letter and wrote for advice to Daniel Ullmann, an attorney on Wall Street who had run unsuccessfully for New York governor as a Know-Nothing in 1854.[5]

Although Fillmore's letter to Ullmann does not survive, clearly he had not mentioned that he knew Carroll, nor did he mention the dinner. Ullmann's reply of 25 November was less than flattering regarding Carroll. "She is a regular Jeremy Diddler in petticoats," Ullmann wrote, referring to a fictional character who borrowed money and never repaid it, "and was once, some eight or ten months ago, arrested for swindling." Carroll was clearly not all she seemed to be. She had also apparently embroidered upon her family lineage, claiming a link with Alexander Hamilton, but it was "the first time" Ullmann had heard of the alleged relationship. Ullmann was not impressed by Carroll's " 'political proclivities.' I apprehend they hang very loosely upon her, and I suspect are adopted for each occasion." Ullmann had met Carroll about a year previously in a "circle of very respectable people" who had become "very much alarmed when they learned her real character." In fact, Carroll had "tried her game on two or three of my friends and upon me, but we were too old soldiers to be taken in." Fillmore's letter amused Ullmann, "as it is pretty much a repetition of enquiries that I have had addressed to me several times."[6]

Fillmore was not amused. Unaware of his perturbation, Carroll did write him on 5 December telling him she had fixed his letter to suit her purposes for the dinner, but allowed him no opportunity to approve her actions or withdraw his letter, as two days later the notice for the dinner, with the altered letters printed below it, appeared in the *New York Dispatch.* On 8 December, Fillmore heard from Tisdale, demanding money for the dinner. "The design is to make it a *national* affair," he wrote pompously. "When we remember that a lady of Louisiana was presented with a set of magnificent jewelry for merely stepping on board a steamboat on the Ohio River, as a representative of the Southern States, it is certainly right and proper that one who has performed ten thousand times . . . more than this mere physical act, should be the recipient of a testimonial ten thousand times more valuable than the one presented to the lady who stepped on board the steamboat." Tisdale closed his missive with a list of the members of the presentation committee, which included Know-Nothings Clay, Rayner, Thomas Whitney of New York, Senator-elect Anthony Kennedy of Maryland, and Jacob Broom of Pennsylvania.[7]

Not only angry, but now suspicious as well, Fillmore wrote again to Ullmann, asking his opinion as to the dinner's legitimacy. "I shall most cheerfully contribute my *mite,*" he emphasized, but only if "the money goes into safe hands." Ullmann replied the next day that he would be glad to investigate. Carroll's advertisement in the *New York Dispatch,* he continued, had announced that Fillmore was "pretty strongly committed to a high appreciation of the lady and the value of her services. I never did have a high opinion of either." Tisdale, he thought, was "a little hack writer" in publisher DeWitt's employ. As far as Ullmann could tell, he belonged "to that numerous class whose pretensions are vastly in excess of their performance." He knew of no real scandal involving Tisdale, "yet I have conceived a rather unfavorable opinion of him." In fact, Tisdale had earlier "beguiled" Ullmann into writing a favorable account of his abilities that "was made use of very improperly in an affidavit." As for the weighty individuals on the presentation committee, Ullmann suggested that they probably had been approached in the same way as Fillmore.[8]

Carroll's primary motivation for using Fillmore and the idea of the testimonial dinner was doubtless financial. Had the Know-Nothings won the election, her books would have sold well. As it was, she wrote Thurlow Weed (whom she presumed she knew well enough to have sent a flirtatious demand that he call upon her) to borrow a hundred dollars so she could "buy up 500 vols [of] Star of the West" which she could then resell for $1.25 each. She had to survive on her writing as best she could; no patronage positions would fall to her after the defeat of the Know-Nothings. But while Fillmore was willing to commend her for her work for him, he had "only glanced at her publications, never . . . read one through," and was altogether unhappy that Carroll had taken advantage of her contact with him.[9]

A letter on 15 December to Fillmore from Jacob Broom in Washington discussed party matters and made no mention of the dinner or the presentation committee of which he was supposedly a member. A second letter arrived from Tisdale, demanding an immediate reply, and a note came from Ullmann reporting that while he could not discover much about the affair, he distrusted the whole, as did those to whom he had spoken. "My own opinion is that they wish to obtain your name on which to base their operations," he warned Fillmore. The same mail also brought a letter from Carroll, replying to Fillmore's demand that she return all of his letters to her. "This is the first time in my history, amidst all my correspondence, that ever such a request as yrs was made," she wrote, and she said she was too busy to accede to his request. She was hard at work, preparing a new book of reminiscences of great Know-Nothings and other politicians, to be called *Men as they Seem and as they Are*. Besides, she had burned all but two or three of his letters. And anyway, she could not see why he was so angry. "The part published has done you more *good* than that of any letter, you ever wrote in your whole life before," she wrote indignantly. Carroll blamed Fillmore for many of her financial difficulties. "I have embalmed you so entirely in my Books that, their sale is utterly destroyed in certain sections. No one living has done so much for you." Even though she had been "repeatedly invited" to publish new editions minus Fillmore's name, she refused "to emasculate and alter my Books. . . . I will not depart from my principles to put money in my purse." It was clear Fillmore just did not comprehend how much she had done for him. "You have not *read,* you do not know, the measure of my services for you as the *public* knew them. How can you? without you read?" If Fillmore wanted to complain about the alteration of his letter, he was free to do so privately or publicly. "That man is yet to be born in this world whom I fear or am not ready to meet through the Press or elsewhere. I see clearly you mean *never* to understand me."[10]

Fillmore needed nearly ten days to recover enough of his sang froid to reply to this remarkable defense. Not even a flattering letter from a supporter, Samuel St. John, Jr., consoling him on his recent loss could help—for St. John referred to his "excellent friend, Miss Carroll." Carroll herself added fuel to the fire as she sent Fillmore a copy of the second edition of *The Star of the West* and demanded he pass it along to the editor of the *Buffalo Commercial Advertiser* so the paper could review it. John B. Floyd of Virginia and others had been to see her, she wrote; "would you believe *I* could have defended the charge of your cold *personelle* [personality]?" Seeming unaware of Fillmore's anger, she inquired innocently, "Don't you mean to answer my last letter?"[11]

Fillmore finally answered, coldly and efficiently, two days after Christmas. He had sent her book on to the editor; as for an answer, ". . . some letters are best answered by expressive silence. The unauthorized use—not to say abuse—of my former private letter should teach me caution." Weakening somewhat—after all, Carroll could be a charming woman, and, in spite of Ullmann's accusation, she had done a good job for him and his party—he "would fain believe the act" was not hers, but that of her "evil genius," Tisdale.[12]

Carroll seized upon the out graciously provided by Fillmore, but not without a few parting shots. "Of all the trying things in my life, and you know of some, your last letter was perhaps the most so," she began. She had "sacrificed & slaved" for him, had given him time and "my hard earnings beside. . . ." That she "should be the one to whom you express indignation that the world should know *you* felt proper appreciation for the same," was beyond her ken. Fillmore had given her the letter with no notice or marking of confidentiality. Besides, "Heaven knows it was not strong enough, or warm enough, to attract any particular notice," and he had "said nothing that was not *true* . . . nothing you should not have been *proud* to have the world know. . . ." She was his friend and had worked for him and the party, and both owed her thanks and recognition in spite of the fact she had neither asked for nor been given "a single farthing" for her work. As for Tisdale, well, she had little control over his activities. He had been hired to do her proofreading and correspondence, and she saw him *"very* seldom."[13]

Tiring of the matter, yet determined to maintain his position, Fillmore tried one last time to make Carroll understand the impropriety of her (or Tisdale's) actions. Unaware that he "had exhibited such a want of gratitude as to justify" her actions, he reiterated the private nature of the letter of recommendation and expressed his sorrow at her "most extraordinary lecture" and her threat to eliminate him from her works. "But you will pardon me for saying that such threats have no terrors for me." If her friends gave her a dinner, he would make a contribution, but that was all. "Standing as I do, I can not . . . single out one friend from all the rest for public honors. Your own good sense must convince you of this. . . ." Fillmore would blame it all on Tisdale rather than Carroll, "determined to believe that his *evil genius,* and not your own upright and generous heart, has induced you to suffer—rather than do—an act which has placed me in a false position and given me infinite pain."[14]

Again Fillmore provided Carroll with a graceful way out: a belief that her feminine nature would automatically preclude such trickery. Again, Carroll took it; but again, not without a few acerbic remarks about his part in the affair. If he had just told her, she would have maintained his confidence, "that I might not have been the innocent cause of inflicting a pain . . . greater than that of your defeat." She would earn her laurels from public approbation of her works in the future, though Fillmore's distaste for singling out any one friend for notice did seem to her rather curious. "Had there been other ladies—or any one lady in the land, who had also occupied a position" similar to hers, she could have understood his reluctance. But there were not. And she could scarcely believe his male friends would be so "devoid of their vaunted chivalry as to envy a poor little woman" who had received special notice from his pen. "Indeed, so far as I know every American gentleman, who worked for you, approved and admired you for it." As for Tisdale, he had taken advantage of the situation, and she had taken care of him: "I found out the man—And I have freely expressed my opinion to his own Mother, who is a true woman—He will do no more for me." She remained "your *tried* & trusting friend, and I have to live and die with an unchanged feeling for you."[15]

Like many incidents in Carroll's life, this one is frustrating in its lack of further evidence. Was she a swindler? If she had been arrested for the crime, she might not have been convicted; no record of conviction has survived, and there seems to have been a common reluctance by nineteenth-century judges to convict upper- and middle-class women of such crimes.[16] How valid was Ullmann's evaluation of her "political proclivities"? Party leaders

Kenneth Rayner and Jacob Broom certainly valued Carroll's opinions. Ullmann's opinion may have been sour grapes: after all, Ullmann had been defeated in 1854, and his party had just lost again. Anger at his party's failings might have taken the form of scorn at Carroll's claims to have done valuable work for it. If she had tried to swindle him or his acquaintances, that would necessarily have colored his judgment of her political abilities as well. Then again, it might have been a simple case of misogyny. Perhaps Ullmann just did not like or approve of "political women."

Why did Fillmore keep trying to explain his disapproval of her actions to Carroll? Why not just cut her off? Perhaps, like all politicians, Fillmore preferred to withdraw with a door left slightly open. He might have viewed Ullmann's accusations as spite; he might have been willing to give Carroll the benefit of the doubt because she was female and therefore, in his mind, not completely responsible for her actions. Certainly, she reinforced his notice of her femininity when she was in trouble. After the election she was a "power to propitiate." After their quarrel, she was a "poor little woman." Perhaps he simply preferred—vain, ambitious, and sensitive to slight as he was—to swallow Carroll's explanation whole, along with her ever-present flattery. If he chose to disbelieve part of what she said, at what point could his questioning stop—before or after her pretty remarks about his noble being?[17]

What is clear in this incident was Carroll's choice to use her sex and the ideology of the woman's sphere as defensive weapons when it suited her purpose. Clearly desiring to placate Fillmore, a powerful man still in New York and a useful contact for her, Carroll took the easy way out by blaming her indiscretions on her womanly soul. This excuse was readily accepted because of widely held beliefs about the nature of women, and, further, it served to reinforce Carroll's overall political methodology of duty, apology, and personal petition, rather than woman's rights or equality.

Ill in January "from the effect of a continued use of my brain & a crowd of matters pressing on me. . . . until the slightest agitation will put me in danger—and send my pulse to incredible speed," Carroll postponed her book tour west until late spring. She revised *The Star of the West* again, dedicating the third edition to United States Navy Commodore Charles Stewart, who wrote to thank her for her "generous espousal of the cause" of those still fighting the Naval Board of Fifteen. She was not particularly enamored of the trip, which she was to take with her brother: "To think one like me should have to push my own Books is hard," she wrote, "but if my friends will stand true, I can do it like a lady & make a competence." By April she had been to Washington and then was off to the Midwest, stopping in Chicago in June for a few weeks. She maintained contact with her New York City acquaintances, asking Thurlow Weed to give one of her friends a job in the New York City Customs House. Weed was powerful in New York, but unlikely to have control of customs positions. No matter to Carroll. She assumed power was power and it could be wielded where it was wanted. As always, she couched her demand for a patronage post in personal terms ("You have kindly promised me your aid. . . .") and appeared to have learned little from her experience with Fillmore, as she included a sentence which could be easily construed as blackmail ("The obligations I have placed [*sic*] certain parties, in *withholding* valuable information. . . .").[18] The book tour must not have been overly successful, since she continued to press politicians for patronage. Those whom she thus aided apparently paid her small sums for her letters on their behalf.

As the anti-Catholicism of 1856 gave way in national preeminence to the slavery issue in 1857, Carroll thought of writing a book on the latter. Kenneth Rayner's argument that passion had overruled reason on the matter apparently dissuaded her. "I fear that the proper, the just, the constitutional view of the question would not please either section," he wrote. "Would there not then be danger of you hazarding the *prestige* you already have in the public estimation by your failure to accomplish that which I do not regard as within the scope of human achievement[?]" She worked instead for Maryland Governor Thomas Hicks's election in 1857 and again in 1859. Also in 1859 she published another anti-Catholic text, *Pope or President?* Once again, her goal was to point out the danger facing American institutions from the Roman Catholic Church in America, since "some one should *dare* assume the responsibility of revealing the astounding mysteries of the Vatican. We have allowed *its own writers* to untangle the fearful meshes of their crafty and corrupt system." The "extreme incredulity" of Americans to believe in the Jesuitical threat had demanded she publish the work.[19]

Considering Carroll's vanity and her known reputation as an anti-Catholic, *Pope or President?* surprisingly, was published anonymously. Carroll may have chosen to hide her name and gender because of the lurid tales contained therein. She dealt with matters with which few women, and certainly no unmarried Southern lady, should dare admit acquaintance. Tales of physical torture were bad enough, but stories of incest, adultery, and mesalliances, even when couched in Victorian euphemisms, made it clear the author knew what those terms meant. While Carroll had clearly done her "research," though limiting it to unfavorable and anti-Catholic sources and citing evidence out of context, such a book presented to the public with a woman's name on the title page would cause as great an uproar as earlier anti-Catholic works such as Maria Monk's *Awful Disclosures* (1836). Carroll's intention was more scholarly than sensation-seeking. She took her Jesuitical conspiracies seriously, approaching the problem with the mind-set of the scholar and the argumentative style of a lawyer.[20] Her goal was to sway the American public, and more directly and specifically the American press, to take the threat as seriously as she did and then commit to action. Sensationalism would not do for her purposes, and a woman as author would have caused quite a stir.

A second edition of *The Great American Battle* also came out early in 1859. In March Carroll proposed a book on Dr. Robert Kane, the famous Arctic explorer who had died in 1857, writing to his brother for approval of the project. As she started the work in April, she resumed her correspondence with William Henry Seward, who was a member of the Kane Monument Association. In that same letter to Seward, she mentioned a work on Kansas that she was preparing, which would be "of immense benefit to the Republican cause."[21]

This was the first evidence that Carroll had dropped her allegiance to the American party and turned to the Republicans. While she supported the ideas of the Know-Nothing party throughout her life, particularly its Unionist stand and its fear of the Jesuit influence in American politics, she was enough of a politician to realize that the Know-Nothings were losing power. To maintain whatever influence she thought she had, and to gain more, Carroll had to extend herself beyond the limits of the American party. While the Republicans were offensive in some political matters, they were a rising force in the land, and Carroll chose to work with them. Weed, a leading Republican in New York, had written her a letter recommending her work to newspaper editor Horace Greeley. Commending Carroll to Greeley's attention, he remarked that "though for some time *Americanist,*" she had done "and is doing, much for Republicanism." But Carroll had not given up the Know-Nothings entirely. For as long as she could, she worked for both parties. Her goal was to elect a man to the White House in 1860 who could serve the ideals of both parties. By April 1858 she had made her choice: John Minor Botts of Virginia.[22]

As Fillmore had, Botts appealed to Carroll as a national candidate. "I know no North, no South, no East, no West," he wrote. "I only know my country, my whole country, and nothing but my country." "There is nothing local about him," Carroll claimed; "there is nothing sectional about him. He is emphatically, a national man. . . . He is the only man now left, who can occupy the position of such men as Clay and Webster." It might be premature to pick a candidate as early as more than two years before a nominating convention, but Carroll argued that it was going to be exceedingly difficult to find one who could "harmonize and unite the contending influences" in an increasingly divided country.[23]

By 11 May Carroll, who no doubt had met Botts through the American party, had become his campaign manager. He sent her copies of his speeches; she was to send him all her press releases. Botts was an experienced politician. A Whig, he had been in the Virginia state legislature from 1833–39 and in the House of Representatives from 1839–43 and again from 1847–49. He was an anti-abolitionist, hated the Democrats, and held both groups responsible for the agitation throughout the country over the slavery issue. He was not particularly enamored of foreigners and tended to take a conspiratorial view of Democratic party policies. Most important to Carroll, though, was his pro-Union stance. He would, he had written, "make a willing sacrifice of myself, if, by so doing, I could save the Union and rescue my country from ruin."[24]

The sectional upheaval resulting from the Kansas-Nebraska Bill had brought Botts out of retirement, and he had run unsuccessfully for Congress as a Know-Nothing in 1854. He continued to speak out publicly after his defeat, railing against abolitionist fanatics, disunionists, and the Democrats. Appealing as his opinions might be to some, however, like Fillmore, he was not the most charismatic of politicians. Carroll thought his intellectual approach to the public in his speeches and his brusque manner put off voters. He was not uncaring toward his opposition as charged, however; "on the contrary," she argued, "he was a thoroughly refined and accomplished gentleman . . . with most agreeable manners and . . . most fluent and interesting in his conversation. . . ."[25]

By 1859 Carroll was eager to determine Botts's viability as a candidate and did some checking with her political acquaintances. Thomas H. Clay, son of Henry Clay of Kentucky and a Know-Nothing in 1856, thought Botts a good choice, but only if sectional issues were disregarded in the coming election. Buchanan was out of the question for the Democrats, he wrote, having "shewn himself worse than ever his most bitter political enemies had thought him." Seward and other Black Republicans, he thought, were unacceptable candidates on the slavery issue, because they supported the non-extension of slavery into the territories. That left men like Botts, Edward Bates of Missouri or John J. Crittenden of Kentucky, behind whom all "conservative and rational men could unite" as supporters of popular sovereignty.[26]

Edward Bates indeed was being considered as a candidate. N. Ranney, a Democat from St. Louis, wrote Carroll that even he would welcome Bates in the White House, if the Democratic party split and the opposition won the election, something he thought unlikely. Carroll viewed such comments from politicians as challenges to her candidate. She wrote letters to newspapers, lauding Botts's years in politics over Bates's inexperience. Josiah Polk, her friend and occasional landlord in Washington, wrote Carroll that he too was pushing Botts's candidacy to both Know-Nothings and Republicans. Botts could serve as their fusion candidate, instead of Bates, Know-Nothing John Bell, or Republican Seward.[27]

Cautiously optimistic and properly grateful to Carroll, Botts thanked her for "the important influence you are so ready to exert in behalf of my elevation to the Presidency of the United States in 1860." He realized that her work might not be reaching as many people as he needed to win a nomination, because some of the papers to which she sent letters and articles, for instance, the Know-Nothing *New York Express,* had a limited circulation. Still, if he were denied the nomination, he thought, it would be "by the political machinery of the politicians," not public sentiment.[28]

Carroll went to St. Louis in July, presumably to measure Missouri's support for Botts's candidacy over favorite son Bates. She went on to Chicago, where she supplied newspapers with pro-Botts articles. She then returned briefly to St. Louis, where her paternal uncle Charles lived, and from there took the train across the country to New England. The trip was partly work and partly an excursion. Carroll's health was not always the best, and her friend Polk "indeed rejoiced to learn that your health is improved. This shows the benefit to you, of exercise and mental relaxation. . . . Even the *iron horses* has [sic] to stop . . . now and then."[29]

Botts began to look more and more like a winning candidate to Carroll. Jacob Broom in Philadelphia called him the "man for the times" because he was both a Southerner and a Unionist. Carroll counted Thomas Corwin of Ohio in Botts's camp, although Benjamin Wade, Judge John McLean, or Edward Bates would no doubt be considered more likely as Corwin's first choice. By November, moreover, Bates had "gone over, clean and clear to the Republican party," thought Botts, which would most likely serve to drive the Whig and Know-Nothing elements into his camp.[30]

Carroll desperately wanted Botts to win. She had supported Fillmore and failed. Botts was her way back into power. But everyone in politics knew that William Henry Seward was destined to be the Republican nominee in 1860. Carroll would have to have been completely out of touch with political realities not to have recognized that. Nevertheless, she had chosen her candidate, certain, as always, that she had made the correct choice, and she was sure Seward's abolitionism would destroy the country. So Carroll lied. She lied to herself, a necessary deception so she could continue her work for Botts. But she also lied to Botts.

Botts had begun to question Carroll's assurances of Weed's support when Weed's newspaper did not print articles supporting his candidacy. Carroll had written an article explaining Botts's views, which, if published, Botts believed would have helped his cause; however, he wrote Carroll, "I guess he is not prepared to do it—& yet, if he is seriously in favor of my nomination, why shouldn't he?" To reassure him, Carroll told Botts that Thurlow Weed, "in sacred confidence," had told her that "Governor S[eward] is as politically dead as tho' he were . . . undergoing putrefaction in his grave, that he will not now be brought forward in the Convention, *nor any other Republican.*" She told him Weed was "determined to nominate you if possible," that Botts's prospects "never were so strong as now." As the election year began in earnest, however, Botts too had heard from Weed. Weed, he wrote Carroll, had said only "that in the event of their [Republicans] having to go *South* for a candidate—he would prefer me." Was this a change in Weed's views from what he told Carroll? "Under what pretense is it they have invited others into their convention [who] . . . are entirely cut off & excluded from all possibility of a nomination no matter what their principles . . . their services or their availability?" Any fusion between Know-Nothings and Republicans was impossible under those circumstances.[31] Botts was not angry at Carroll, since he undoubtedly believed her incapable of deception. But he was furious at the Republicans for refusing to consider any fusion candidate who was not a Republican.

Perhaps because Carroll knew the degree of hatred the Know-Nothings felt toward Seward, she could interpret whatever comments Thurlow Weed made to her regarding Botts as support for his candidacy. The virulent anti-Catholicism and nativism that had characterized the election of 1856 was still very much a part of the 1860 campaign. Seward's supporters faced letters such as the one Weed received that remarked on the "widespread and deep prejudice against Seward on account of his action, as governor, on the public schools," referring to Seward's support nearly twenty years previously for public-funded education for immigrants to be taught by " 'teachers speaking the same language . . . and professing the same faith.' " Parochial schools would have thus received public funds—an idea as unpopular in 1840 as in the 1850s, and a controversy that clung to Seward throughout his attempts to become a presidential candidate. The letter-writer urged Weed to drop Seward as a candidate. "The prejudice [against him] pervades the entire Protestant church. . . . It is strongest with the clergy; but is showed more or less by the great body of the laity, even outside the council of the Know Nothings . . . while with the Americans, it is rankest—deepest—most bitter."[32]

But even a former Know-Nothing like Carroll recognized the primacy of the slavery issue over anti-Catholicism in the campaign of 1860. Sectional tension had increased greatly in the years from 1856 to 1859, thanks to the Dred Scott decision, the civil war in Kansas, Preston Brooks's attack on Charles Sumner in the Senate, the Lecompton Constitution, and John Brown's raid on Harpers Ferry. As sectional tensions rose, Know-Nothings were forced either to take a nationwide stance against slavery, thus losing Southern support to the Democrats, or to deemphasize or ignore the issue, thus losing their Northern support to the more inclusive Republicans. The Know-Nothings had achieved their victories at state and local levels because they had been able to appeal to nativist sentiments in the South and because they could combine that appeal with anti–slavery-extension stands in the North. But the Republicans had, by 1860, recognized nativism as an important political drawing card and an issue that was not going to disappear. Accordingly, Republican leaders made concessions to the Know-Nothings by incorporating a degree of nativism in their party pronouncements. The Know-Nothings' abysmal record of achieving their goals while in public office also drove Northern Know-Nothings to shift their allegiance to the Republican party.[33]

Given the decline in Know-Nothing power and the co-optation of their ideas by the Republicans, Carroll had adopted Botts, a Know-Nothing but a strong Unionist, as a logical fusion candidate for president. But Botts was too unpopular in Virginia, where Know-Nothings were weakening rapidly. More important, he could not wholeheartedly adopt the anti–slavery-extension plank of the Republican platform. Kenneth Rayner warned Carroll that unless Botts could say "no extension" and mean it, there would be no nomination. Opposition to slavery extension was now essential, and as much as Rayner had hoped for a "union of the opposition to Democracy North & South . . . on a conservative rational basis of organization. . . . I doubt if such a thing be possible." But Botts was not willing to go far enough. In an effort to compromise, he was willing to subscribe to the entire Republican party platform, except for the resolution regarding slavery extension. Where the platform called for no extension in the territories, Botts wanted to insert the words, " 'either by force, or federal legislation against the will of the people of the territories. . . .' " With these changes, which he saw as mere modifications, Botts did "not see why every Whig and American in the United States should not subscribe to the Republican platform." But his words would change the platform from the absolute of nonextension to a form of popular sovereignty, a "modification" completely unacceptable to Republicans.[34]

Carroll went home to Church Creek, Maryland for Christmas. By this time, her father had moved in with his son, Dr. Thomas King Carroll, and his family. Carroll visited only briefly, then went back to New York City to discuss Botts's future with Thurlow Weed. She returned to Washington in January 1860. A friend from New York, John B. Fry, wrote that he had heard she was "overrun by visitors—the magnates of the land" at her parlor in Polk's boarding house on Pennsylvania Avenue.[35] And Carroll feasted on the news and gossip brought to her by her visitors, including Jefferson Davis, Thomas Corwin, and Republican Representative John Sherman.

The biggest topic in town was the contest for Speaker of the House of Representatives. The Speaker's control of committee assignments was crucial to all political parties, considering the coming election year, and battle lines were drawn along sectional lines as well. The fight had begun on 5 December 1859 and lasted until William Pennington was elected on 1 February 1860. Carroll had discussed the matter with Weed in New York in early January and agreed with him that Sherman was the best choice for Speaker. By the twenty-seventh of January, though, Carroll had become "acquainted with the *Bossmen* of the Republican, Southern opposition and Anti-Lecompton parties," and wrote to Weed although he was apparently ignoring her.[36]

Sherman could not be elected, she wrote, and "I intend to tell him the whole truth as I know it and as no man . . . would ever tell him. . . ." A union between Southern Know-Nothings and Democrats was forming that would destroy the Republicans—and Thurlow Weed as well, as they perceived it was thanks to him that Sherman was still in the running and causing no end of trouble. Since Southerners flatly refused Sherman's candidacy because of his hasty and unwise endorsement of Hinton Rowan Helper's incendiary attack on slavery, *The Impending Crisis,* Carroll instructed Weed to pull back from his support for Sherman and push for Thomas Corwin of Ohio instead. Corwin's name had already been put forward in the House on 17 January by Roger A. Pryor of Virginia as a compromise candidate. Weed must come to Washington immediately and take charge of things, Carroll wrote, or he would "never survive the obloquy which will be heaped upon you if you allow a Republican organization to be defeated by the persistency of this present course." Carroll thought herself fully justified in both her plans to tell Sherman all and to force Weed to come to Washington because, she wrote, "I feel that my position before the country, my knowledge of what I am about, my principles and my sincerity in the maintainance [*sic*] of Republican sentiments, which I will cherish while I live (for better reasons than influence you politicians)" enabled her to advise Sherman to withdraw as Speaker candidate. So convinced was Carroll of the rightness of her actions, she continued, that it would "make me indifferent even should Mr. Sherman not adopt my wise and patriotic counsel. I shall have the approval of my conscience and my country hereafter—when the whole party will feel the direful calamity which will come from their own doings or those of the leaders to whom the matter is entrusted."[37]

Carroll was growing a bit desperate. She had spent more than three years trying to force a fusion of Know-Nothings and Republicans. She had spent nearly two years pushing Botts for the presidency, with no real sign of Seward losing support from major Republican leaders. Weed was not returning her letters, even if he did consent to see her occasionally when they were in the same city. Botts as a candidate seemed to be out, and Carroll wanted in. The contest for Speaker provided her a way. Thomas Corwin was an old and intimate friend; if he were elected Speaker, surely not only some of his glory, but also some patronage would fall her way.

Carroll may have seen this election year as her last chance. She was, after all, forty-five years old. Her party had almost entirely lost its place in politics; friends and acquaintances, taking her word at face value about her influence, were hounding her for jobs; she herself was chronically short of funds and, as always, concerned about her family. Her father was still poor, and Dr. Carroll had a growing family to feed. Anne Carroll was also growing deaf. For a woman whose main attractions were her intelligence, wit, and flattery, it would be disastrous not to be able to participate in the political discussions that made her parlor so lively and provided her entrée into the political world she loved.[38]

Sherman did withdraw, but Corwin lost out to the coalition candidate, William Pennington of New Jersey. The year 1860 became frantic for Carroll as she searched for the next man who would be the president to latch onto in order to ensure her own future. She even wrote for Fernando Wood, the Doughface Democratic mayor of New York, suggesting he be a candidate for president. Wood thanked her for "keeping his name before the public" and acknowledged draft attempts, but laughingly remarked that "but for the *common sense* my mother gave me I should be made dizzy" by such attention. He would be satisfied with a seat at his party's nominating convention. He complimented Carroll's political acumen, though. "You can get the confidence of us men and I know you well enough to know that no man however cool . . . and *diplomatique* can escape you. Therefore I would rather have your opinion than a dozen of the best statesmen in the country."[39]

Besides her own self-interest, though, Carroll was still vitally concerned with the preservation of the country from the agitation that seemed ready to tear it apart. She supported Wood because of his stand against the agitation promised by antislavery Republicans. In March she wrote to Weed again, telling him neither Seward nor Bates would take the nomination, and therefore Botts "is your only man." If that were impossible (Carroll's first admission of doubt), Botts would be willing to accept the vice-presidency under Judge John McLean. McLean's age, seventy-five, was a major factor in considering his candidacy. Carroll dismissed it rather callously, deciding that "if McLean did die, the North would have as good a friend" with Botts in the White House as ever Seward would be.[40]

In April 1860, just before the Democratic party split and thus guaranteed its loss in November, Carroll wrote to Weed once more. She told him that Judge McLean would be nominated at the Constitutional Union party's convention in Baltimore on 9 May. She considered him "the only man who can defeat the democracy." For the vice-president, she wanted Weed to "let it be . . . Botts. . . . You have got more power than they [the Constitutional Union party members] will have; even in their own party! For you can regulate the Republicans." Carroll doubtless wanted Weed to force the Republicans to adopt the Constitutional Union candidates as their own. But Weed, above all else, wanted William Henry Seward to be the Republican nominee. If he did have any power over the Constitutional Unionists, he chose not to exercise it for Carroll's choices, though he did later suggest Botts to Lincoln for a cabinet post. The Constitutional Union party's candidates were former Senator John Bell of Tennessee, with Edward Everett of Massachusetts as his vice-presidential running mate. McLean and Botts were both nominated in the convention, but won only 21 and 9 and one-half votes, respectively, on the first ballot; they dropped to 1 and 7, respectively, on the second ballot. Carroll, in keeping with her search for power in the winning party, quickly wrote a congratulatory note to Everett.[41]

Carroll could not have been too surprised that Botts lost in Baltimore. He himself had given up by 1 May, writing sadly that ". . . all hope, expectation and . . . *desire* has pretty well died out," as he saw "State after State, meeting in Convention and my name not mentioned with approval in any one . . . it looks to me very much like the game is up." But Thurlow Weed's inability to "regulate the Republicans" at the Chicago convention must have shocked Carroll. After the Republicans nominated Lincoln on 18 May, she must have been in despair. She had worked hard to establish a relationship with both Weed and Seward; so who was Abraham Lincoln? She went home to Church Creek, as John Wilson, another boarder at Polk's in Washington, wrote to her that things were "quiet and dull without you." But he held out hope: Bell's prospects were brightening, he thought, since Lincoln's nomination meant the alienation of votes in New York, Ohio, Pennsylvania, and Massachusetts, states that had had their favorite sons eliminated by the dark horse from Illinois.[42]

By June, Carroll had fallen ill and could follow the campaign only through letters from Polk and other friends. Botts successfully predicted Lincoln's election to her, and prophesied the immediate secession of the South upon the commission of any act of aggression by the new president. Carroll herself was soon ready to "speak of the Union as already dissolved." By September she had recovered from her illness, but her sister Julianna had died during Carroll's stay in Church Creek. She returned to Washington, needing to discover where she could fit in with the new administration, only to be met with another loss. The *National Intelligencer* announced the death of former Maryland representative John M. S. Causin.[43]

John Causin apparently had met Carroll in Chicago about 1858. She may have known him from his earlier political career as a state representative from St. Mary's County in Maryland. He had been visiting his family in Arkansas and was returning to his law practice in Chicago when he died of apoplexy. In three letters from Causin's brother-in-law to Carroll, evidence of their relationship as intimate friends and probably lovers survives.

Causin's brother-in-law, L. E. Barber, wrote gently of John's death to Carroll, and of the death of his mother as she had waited for her son's body to come home. Aware that Causin had "regarded you with affectionate esteem," Barber promised Carroll that he would return the letters she had written to Causin. Carroll requested a copy of Causin's last speech and when Barber replied, he suggested he burn her letters. There were *"many— very many* of them," he wrote, and he had accidentally read one "at a part which gave full expression to the feelings of the writer—the whole heart was bare before me." Embarrassed by the incident, he worried about sending them through the mail: "It would be mortifying if by any accident your letters should fall into other hands."[44]

Relieved at his discretion, Carroll requested Barber burn the letters. She also asked him to "suspend judgment" until he "knew the facts" regarding her relationship with Causin. Barber assured her he could not conceive that their relationship, whatever it might have been, could "depreciate you in our estimation. . . . Can it be that I would estimate less one whom he loved for returning that love!" While Barber could not "altogether acquit [Causin] of imprudence and of weakness in this respect," he hastily reassured Carroll of her innocence in his eyes. "I know nothing, believe nothing, suspect nothing . . . other than the simple fact that there existed a mutual affection." He enclosed locks of hair from both Causin and his mother, thanked her for allowing his sister to keep Carroll's daguerreotype, and sent her violets from the graves of the dead.[45]

Carroll suffered greatly during 1860 and early 1861. Ill health, the loss of Julianna and of Causin, and despair at the turn of events in her life kept her quiescent for a time. Her work would help her recover, however, as the growing threat to her beloved Union soon spurred her into action.

FOUR

"To Preserve This Union"

With the election of Abraham Lincoln, Anne Carroll feared for the very existence of the Union. "I have no doubt," she wrote in November 1860, that Lincoln's election would "lead to an attempt on the part of the Southern leaders to dissolve this Union." She had heard disquieting rumors from her home state and, convinced that the secession of Maryland would mean the destruction of the Union, she urged Governor Thomas Hicks to stand firm against secessionists. "Although you were opposed to the election of Mr. Lincoln, you are for maintaining this Union," she reminded him. Lincoln had been "constitutionally elected and . . . must be inaugurated on the 4th of next March, as the President of the whole U.S." A successful inauguration depended more upon Hicks's "individual firmness than upon all other men in the nation."[1]

Carroll may have overstated the importance of Hicks's position, but not the importance of keeping Maryland in the Union. If Maryland seceded, the capital of the United States would be cut off from the North. The loss of the capital could mean the loss of the Union as well.[2] Both sides wanted Maryland, and in the early days of the secession crisis, no one, including Governor Hicks himself, was sure how the state would go.

A slaveholder from the Eastern Shore county of Dorchester, Hicks considered himself a Southerner, as did many Eastern Shore residents. He supported slavery, saying at one point that he had "never lived, and should be sorry to be obliged to live, in a state where slavery does not exist, and I never will do so if I can avoid it." A Know-Nothing, he had been elected governor on a Unionist ticket. But the two political characteristics, slaveholder and Unionist, were fast becoming uncomfortable for politicians to enjoy simultaneously.[3]

Carroll, an old family friend, wasted no time in urging Hicks to stay with the Union. She wrote first from New York City, then from Washington, where she took up residence as Congress convened in December, hoping to continue earning her keep from her pen. Over the five months between the election and the outbreak of war, she alternated between Maryland and Washington affairs, trying to stay in touch with matters in both areas. Much of her attention focused on Maryland. There, secessionists, mostly Democrats, demanded that the governor call the legislature into special session, believing they could push through a call for a secession convention.[4]

Hicks refused. After a "fair, frank, rational examination of the subject," he told leading Maryland secessionists, he could discover no necessity to convene the legislature in special session. The expense was unnecessary, the weather inclement. Further, he argued, those called would waste time spending money instead of solving what he termed the "so-called" crisis, and Maryland was already fifty thousand dollars in debt from the previous session. Hicks counselled patience, urging secession leaders to wait to see what the other states would do, to allow Congress to convene and take action, and to let the inauguration of the president take place. He also rebuffed tentative approaches from the Southern states, turning down South Carolina's allegedly innocent invitation to join with the Palmetto State in a day of fasting and prayer. He had scheduled one already and could not change the date, Hicks replied, fearing secessionists would interpret any joint act as support for their cause. Maryland would pray alone, he wrote South Carolina Governor William Henry Gist, but "heartily with the same purpose . . . in imploring God's blessing and direction in this hour of difficulty."[5]

Carroll wrote to Hicks often during this period, passing along information and articles from Washington newspapers. It was a difficult time for the governor: "the waves of secession and rebellion are beating with great fury upon the frail bark of our State's executive," and he was "borne down at the same time by domestic afflictions almost without a parallel" (the death of his daughter).[6] Putting his personal crisis aside, by the first of the year Hicks was ready with a message to the people of his state that laid out what had been done since the election and what would be done in the future.

Hicks had consulted with the other border states, he said, but he was inclined to wait before taking any action in concert with them. South Carolina's reasons for seceding were not good enough to persuade him to join with that state. Even if the reasons had been good, the maintenance of state sovereignty would preclude using one state's actions as Maryland's rationale for such a drastic step. Despite his failure to support Lincoln and his party in the late election, Hicks assured his constituents, he believed that the Union, even under Republican rule, would guarantee the protection of slavery within Maryland. And no, he answered his critics, Lincoln had not promised him an office if the state were kept in the Union. He added one more reason for patience: considering the state's geographic location, any war within its borders would be so destructive that it behooved him to give its citizens "time to breathe" and "try every honorable plan . . . to avert the necessity of War. . . ." He saw two choices: "to allow Maryland to slide into the ranks of the seceded States," after it had been "hurriedly borne along into the turmoil of the political movements of the day," or, far better, "to wait with calmness the progress of events."[7]

Although pressure from secessionists for calling the legislature continued in January, so did support for Hicks and his conciliatory measures. Carroll was one of his most ardent proponents, writing letters to newspapers on behalf of his actions. The support was welcome, but Hicks, tired of "the harassings of calculating demagogues (and they are terrible)" expressed the "sincere wish that Congress may early do something to stave off and save a collision."

> Will not the representatives from the Border States go at once to work and effect something as a salvo and will not the Northern representatives yield more for their country's safety? They have the power, will they not display the needed magnanimity and pass conciliatory measures and put the Southern extremists at fault? This I say as a Southern man. The Southern extremists wish no offers of compromise from any quarter, but not so, the masses. And how easy a matter for Northern members to unite with conservative Border State members and the few worthies from the far South and pass a proposition of that good laboring man Crittenden or some such measure to stave off until the people can have light and the fourth of March is past.[8]

Such firmness of position and such obvious, if overly optimistic, hope for reconciliation impressed Carroll. She shared Hicks's private letter with several Republican politicians and was pleased to be able to quell rumors of Maryland's impending secession. Maryland would come out of this trial "like gold seven times purified," she told Hicks. And even if Virginia did go with the South "(which [state], in spite of the secessionists I am privately assured is true to the Union) I can see no reason why Maryland should cast her destiny with her." What would come next, she continued, she was not sure, for John J. Crittenden's proposals would never pass Congress—it would be "as easy to build a world." She was right. It was too late for

Senator Crittenden's proposals to extend the old Missouri Compromise line to California and to protect slavery in the South with a constitutional amendment.[9]

The secession of states continued: Mississippi on 9 January, Florida on 10 January, and Alabama on 11 January. "The madness of those political metaphysicians, and aristocratic Southern tyrants" so angered Northerners previously sympathetic to the South, thought Carroll, that they now viewed secession "as rank treason to the government, and believe it is the *planned* work of traitors. As do I." In spite of her love for the South and her many friends among Southern politicians, "I love my country . . . far more," and she would not support her friends in such a cause as secession. She continued to counsel patience, telling Hicks she could see "nothing for the Border States to do, but to adhere to their own conservative principles and bow to the supremacy of Constitutional law. Lincoln is the Lawful President of the Nation. . . ."[10]

Of more immediate importance to Carroll by the close of January was her own safety. Was she safe in Washington? She sought reassurance from Hicks. Rooming at the Washington House, she was "the only Southerner in the whole establishment. The ladies flock to my parlor, for news and rely far more on me, than on their husbands for information & knowledge of Southern intentions. Leading secessionists who called to make farewell visits to me, gave me the earnest assurance that it was no part of the Southern programme to attack this city. . . ." If she left prior to inauguration day, not only would it be personally inconvenient to her as it interfered with her work, but also "it would be the immediate signal of every Northern lady's leaving—supposing it be done from apprehension of danger." Hicks apparently assured her of her safety, for not only did she stay in the city, but she wrote to a New York newspaper to express her certainty the city would not be attacked, denying a report secessionists intended to seize the capital.[11]

Her state safe, her person safe, Carroll next looked to her constant concern: patronage. That Carroll thought she deserved attention and employment for her friends and family from the incoming Republicans, after she had failed to support Lincoln in the election, exemplifies her tendency to use and present her abilities, actions, and influence in whatever form would accomplish what she wanted. Obsessed with a desire for power, attention, recognition, and reward, she constantly reinterpreted her own actions and misinterpreted the actions of others until the conclusion filled her needs, however far from reality that conclusion might be.

Carroll's attempt to presume upon her acquaintance with Thurlow Weed is a prime example of this characteristic. There is no evidence that Weed was particularly close, professionally or personally, to Carroll. In her letters, though, she demanded favors of him that few people not well acquainted with the Republican leader would ever dare suggest. Weed's position as a mediator between the Seward faction of Republicans and president-elect Lincoln made him a target for Carroll's queries. She began soon after the election, pressing Weed to have John Minor Botts put in the cabinet, along with John A. Gilmer, a North Carolina Know-Nothing. Both men were Unionists, both knew Carroll well, and both undoubtedly would feel obligated to help her with patronage positions in the future. Botts and Gilmer were under serious consideration by Lincoln on Weed's advice, though there is nothing to indicate they were suggested by Weed at Carroll's instigation. In fact, her letter suggesting Gilmer for the cabinet was sent to Weed three weeks after Lincoln offered him a position. Still, Carroll would no doubt claim the credit if either man were chosen. Lincoln settled on Gilmer as the best choice among the Southern and border state Unionists, but his preliminary offer was met by Gilmer's demand that Lincoln publicly declare his intention that the new administration would back down from its opposition to slavery in the territories. Lincoln refused, and Gilmer regretfully declined.[12]

Carroll urged that Gilmer and Botts both be put in the cabinet to draw on Unionist support in North Carolina and Virginia. Failure to include either one—or any Southern man—angered her greatly. She did not know or ignored the fact that the Southerners selected had refused office on Lincoln's terms. She later wrote that Lincoln's actions constituted "an irreparable blunder" and claimed he was interested only in "constructing his Cabinet on partisan grounds. He was intent alone in harmonizing the radical and conservative elements of his party. It was a fatal error not to have taken . . . some one, or more, representing, not party, but the *Union* sentiment of the South." For Carroll, the crisis to the country was great enough that party interests should be put aside. She held the disproportionate representation of Northerners in the cabinet responsible for increasing "the power of the rebellion a hundred fold!"[13]

By March Carroll turned to more personal concerns in her correspondence with Thurlow Weed, asking him to use his influence with Lincoln for an appointment for her father to the Naval Office in Baltimore. He had held the office before, and she wanted Weed to write to Secretary of State Seward in support of her petition for her father's job as a recognition of her claims. What claim she thought she had is unclear. Weed apparently made no effort to fulfill her request, and Carroll resentfully concluded that he would not help her. She had been ill and did not want to have to go to see Lincoln herself, but, she complained, "I suppose with a hundred friends I shall have to do this myself. It is *wrong,* that I should be obliged to see him. . . . It is due to me that my Father be tendered the Naval Office."

When Weed failed her, she turned to John Minor Botts, who saluted her for being a "dutiful daughter" but pointed out that he had "established it as a rule, not to interfere with any local appointments outside my own State," a dismissal which apparently ended their relationship.[14]

Convinced that Weed possessed considerable control over patronage, Carroll continued to badger him with requests. Representative Thomas Corwin, Carroll wrote Weed, was too ill to accept his appointment as minister to Mexico. Fortunately for the president, she could provide the perfect substitute in Lemuel Dale Evans, a former representative from Texas, "eminently qualified . . . really a *great* man in intellect." Evans must have been a very close friend, because if he were awarded the post, Carroll intended to go with him. She hung tenaciously onto the idea of Evans as an ambassador; when Corwin accepted his nomination after all, she proposed Evans for a post in Constantinople, writing to Seward's son, Frederick, and then making the same proposal to Weed.[15]

In the midst of this constant and continuing struggle for patronage, in which Carroll had no reasonable hope of success, the secession crisis in Maryland came to the forefront again. The war had begun in April, and the transportation of Union troops through Maryland to protect the city of Washington sparked protests from Marylanders. A riot on 19 April in Baltimore against the 6th Massachusetts Regiment was condemned by both Lincoln and Carroll. " 'Our men are not moles, and can't dig under the earth; they are not birds and can't fly through the air. There is no way but to march across, and that they must do,' " said Lincoln.[16] Indignant at the "disgraceful and atrocious outrages in Baltimore," Carroll wrote to Governor Hicks, warning him that the federal troops must be guaranteed safe passage. "You cannot deny the right of transit to the Northern troops through the territory of Maryland, called by the President to defend their capital and your own," she wrote.

> Maryland thank God is still a state of this Union. It is the sworn duty of Mr. Lincoln to defend the seat of government—the troops can approach it only over the soil of Maryland and what power have you to prohibit their approach? That Maryland ceded to the United States a national seat of government and then withheld the right of peaceful transit over her highways essential to make it safe and suitable for the purposes for which it was ceded, or to defend it in time of war, is so glaringly absurd as to shock the common sense of any one. And such a declaration would be [scorned] by the civilized world.[17]

Carroll feared Hicks might desert his Unionist stance under the pressure from the secessionists. He did make one concession to ease tension in his state: he called for a special legislative session to meet in Annapolis on 26

April. On the twenty-fourth, however, he moved the meeting place to the more peaceable and strongly Unionist city of Frederick in western Maryland. Carroll wanted to go to Frederick to try to influence the secessionists, but safe passage to Annapolis or Frederick could not be guaranteed. "So I am flooding the *Legislators,* Heaven defend us from such, with letters. I *will* be heard there & if the miserable fools pass the ordinance [of secession], let them go & suffer the consequences." The legislature did not pass an ordinance; it voted on 27 April that it did not even have the right to consider secession, and in early May voted that it would not call a convention that could grant it that power. By 13 May, troops under command of Major General Benjamin F. Butler occupied the city of Baltimore. Control over the state by Unionists was at last realized. Hicks had held out successfully, and Carroll could breathe a sigh of relief: her state would remain loyal to the United States.[18]

In her letter to Hicks after the Baltimore riots, Carroll had begun to articulate her view of the nature of the rebellion against the federal government. By the summer of 1861, she was ready to distribute her arguments in support of the president's policies to the country at large. From July 1861 until May 1862, she wrote at least four pamphlets and countless letters to the press to disseminate her opinions on the legality of the war. In those writings, in those troublesome times, Carroll ignored the fact she was a woman in a man's world. She made no apology for her intrusion into the political arena, as she had done in her 1856 election books and pamphlets. Perhaps she had seen enough women working for the war effort to believe her apologies were no longer necessary. Her object was to save the Union; all else beside was frippery. She went straight to the point in her writing, wasting no time on decorating her arguments with the ideas of republican motherhood or the limits of the woman's sphere. If her arguments did not help win the fight, there would be no republic in which to be mother, and all spheres would continue to be sadly disturbed. After the crisis, she could return to the style of her antebellum writings, but for the present, the Union was all that mattered to Carroll. She would not weaken her arguments by making distracting references to her sex.

Carroll began delineating her constitutional theories in a published letter responding to Edward Everett's 4 July oration at the Academy of Music in New York City. Everett had argued against secession by pointing out that, in order to secede, the states had had to make war, a power expressly limited by the Constitution to the national government and one which could not be usurped by the states. As for those states, such as Virginia, that argued states could resume their sovereign powers and then secede, they were also wrong, he said. James Madison, father of the Constitution, had declared in 1830 in the midst of the Nullification Crisis that the resumption of sovereign power could be made only by the people of the whole United States, not by the individual states.[19]

Carroll agreed with Everett's analysis. She parted company, however, over his contention that secessionists were wrongly citing John C. Calhoun as the founder of the theory of secession as well as nullification. Not true, asserted Carroll. In both his essay, "Discourse on the Constitution" and his Fort Hill address, Calhoun had made clear his position on both theories of opposition to the federal government. Nullification was the arrest of one or more federal acts by a state; secession was the arrest of all federal acts by a state. Both doctrines meant states could not be coerced into following federal laws, and both were insupportable if the United States was to survive as a federal government.[20]

This idea that the federal government had the right to coerce states to follow federal laws was key to Carroll's arguments supporting the Union. Her first major publication on the subject came shortly after her letter to Everett in the form of a reply to a speech by John C. Breckinridge. Breckinridge had been senator from Kentucky, vice-president under Buchanan, and the Southern Democrats' presidential nominee. He was also the nephew of the Reverend Robert Breckinridge, Anne Carroll's old friend and minister from her days in Baltimore. With deep pain, Carroll had watched as John voted against Lincoln's policies in the early days of the war and gave speeches supporting the rebellion. Breckinridge's opposition to Lincoln stemmed from his belief that the president had taken upon himself powers he did not possess. He had established a blockade, made war on the South, called for enlistments, and suspended the writ of habeas corpus, all powers which Breckinridge thought the Constitution had granted to Congress, not the executive. The government could "exercise such powers and such only" as were spelled out in the Constitution, he declared. "If the powers be not sufficient, still none others were granted and none others can be exercised."[21]

In her pamphlet titled *Reply to Breckinridge,* Carroll met Breckinridge's criticisms by contending that the whole argument of whether or not the president had acted legally turned on the question of "whether the overt act of treason, which the Constitution defines to be levying war against the United States, had been committed? Whether the Confederate States of the South commenced the war?" Or did the president make war upon the South? The South had started the trouble, Carroll wrote. Southerners had also conspired to prevent Lincoln's inauguration, had seized federal property, acted as provisional governments, recruited soldiers to fight, "stormed Fort Sumter, and put in motion a formidable army for the capture of Washington and the overthrow of the Government." The president's response was to defend the nation against these threats in order to ensure the national existence.[22]

Granted the premise that the Confederates and not the president made the war, Carroll argued that the constitutional duties of the executive in such a position were to "faithfully execute the laws." While Lincoln was not given the power to declare war, he could, given the absence of a sitting Congress, "defend the assault on the nation's life; because his right rests on the supreme or universal law of self-defense, common to nations as to individuals." As the defender of the nation, he was expressly granted powers as commander-in-chief, Carroll argued, and that "express grant of *war-conducting power* . . . carries with it the implied power to use every belligerent right known to the law of war."[23]

Carroll interpreted the war as an insurrection (a legally nebulous term in nineteenth-century international law), which she defined as a rebellion by citizens of the United States against the United States. She thought that such an interpretation would keep the Confederacy from gaining belligerent status as an independent nation. Thus, the power of war would stay in the president's hands as a defender and executor of the national laws, rather than be put into congressional hands as the body to declare war against a foreign nation. This interpretation meant that all Lincoln's actions that followed the attack on Fort Sumter—the blockade, the call for volunteers, even the suspension of the writ of habeas corpus—were merely the means, expressly and constitutionally granted, with which Lincoln defended the Union and the Constitution.[24]

Carroll's overall interpretation of the president's war powers coincided with those of Lincoln and his attorney general, Edward Bates. She was, however, confronted with the same legal tightrope that faced all Union propagandists seeking to support Lincoln's war measures. Until the 1863 Supreme Court decision in the Prize Cases, Lincoln's actions as the chief executive could not be legally reconciled with his actions as commander-in-chief. If he were acting as an executive officer and controlling an insurrection, for instance, he had no right to institute a blockade of Southern ports. A blockade was an act of war, and war existed between two belligerents, not between the civil government and its insurrectionary citizens. But Carroll supported the president's actions by arguing that his status as commander-in-chief gave him war-making powers he could use as a law enforcer, the same distinction the Court made. Any power normally used in war was his to use in putting down the insurrection.[25]

In the long run, Carroll took the same position that Lincoln occupied when his actions were termed extralegal. "Are all the laws, *but one,* to go unexecuted," Lincoln asked of Congress on 4 July 1861, "and the government itself go to pieces, lest that one be violated?" Lincoln's answer was no, and so was Carroll's. The extraordinary danger to the survival of the Union itself outweighed the temporary suspension of specific laws.[26]

Carroll's support for Lincoln's actions was not entirely uncritical. She did not hold Lincoln responsible for starting the war; however, she did view his decision to stand firm with his party's position regarding territorial slavery as the precipitate cause of secession which had led to war. But though his decision was criticized by pacifists, Unionists (including Carroll herself), Southerners, and historians, Carroll argued that the pro-secession "conspirators" had done everything they could to ensure that no compromise on the issue of slavery would ever pass Congress. They wanted out of the Union, and they had fired the first shot. The war was their choice, she wrote, and in making war, Lincoln was merely defending the country and exercising his constitutional authority to put down the "heretical" doctrine that the government could not coerce a state to obey federal laws.[27]

The last point Carroll made in her pamphlet defended the president's suspension of the writ of habeas corpus. Attorney General Bates's own opinion on the suspension of the writ had been issued on 5 July 1861. The president's ability to suspend the writ was of crucial importance in deciding how far he could go in making military arrests of Confederate sympathizers and disloyal citizens. The question had come to the fore with the arrest of John Merryman, a prominent pro-secessionist from Maryland, who was recruiting and training Confederate volunteers in the city of Baltimore. Arrested in May 1861, Merryman was denied freedom by writ of habeas corpus. Chief Justice of the Supreme Court Roger Taney filed the writ and called a press conference to complain that Lincoln was exceeding his power by refusing to release Merryman. Taney accused Lincoln of suspending the writ itself, a power given in the Constitution only to Congress.[28]

Bates argued on behalf of the president. Lincoln could not and had not suspended the writ. He could, however, "*suspend the privilege* of persons arrested" to *use* the writ. Bates's legal hair-splitting was questionable, but still better than Carroll's on this question. First, she argued that Taney's assumption that the suspension of the writ was solely the province of Congress was invalid. True, the power of suspension was listed in article I, section 9 of the Constitution, which spelled out various congressional powers. But the next section of the article listed powers denied to states, "which Congress even cannot exercise"; thus the article might be inclusive of presidential powers as well. Carroll followed this remarkably silly argument with a more substantial one that traced the history of temporary suspensions of civil rights during wars, referring to the American Revolution and the War of 1812 as precedent for Lincoln's actions. Quoting Thomas Jefferson, she pointed out the overriding importance of self-preservation of the nation above all else, including civil rights.[29]

Here Carroll was on more solid ground, ground occupied by Bates and by Lincoln himself. It was also ground Congress would eventually occupy; by March 1863 Congress passed legislation retroactively approving Lincoln's actions of the war's early days. Such actions had included arbitrary arrests and the suppression of the press as well. This last charge gave Carroll particular pause, for, she wrote, "as an independent member of the press I will never consent to see its power trammeled or its freedom abridged by President or ruler." But the press (in this case a pro-Confederate St. Louis newspaper) had been used by Confederates to trample the very institutions it was supposed to defend by calling for their destruction through the destruction of the United States. Therefore, argued Carroll, that press should be shut down. Here again, the temporary suspension of various constitutional rights, if necessary to preserve the whole Constitution, was the proper course of action for the president as commander-in-chief to take. Martial law transcended civil law when it was imposed for the preservation of that civil law.[30]

Carroll's *Reply to Breckinridge,* one of the earliest printed pamphlets supporting Lincoln's position, was well received. Samuel T. Williams, attorney for the *Congressional Globe,* wrote that he was sure that "if spoken in the Senate, your article would have been regarded by the country as a complete and masterly refutation of Mr. B's heresies." She sent copies of it to Caleb Smith, secretary of the interior, and to Attorney General Bates, who passed along a copy she left for the president.[31] She also printed some ten thousand copies for distribution throughout the border states, primarily as a civic gesture, but also as a way to convince the War Department to recognize the value of her services and hire her as a pamphleteer. Momentarily, the tactic worked. On 2 October 1861 she would meet with Assistant Secretary of War Thomas A. Scott, who would leave her with the impression that she could bill the War Department for printing and labor costs of any pamphlets she wrote which were approved by his office.[32]

Carroll continued to write defenses of most of Lincoln's actions. In September 1861, she issued a short pamphlet supporting Attorney General Bates's defense of the president's actions; in December, she published *The War Powers of the General Government.*[33] Her primary argument therein was, once again, that the actions the president took, such as suspending the writ of habeas corpus or making arbitrary arrests, were legal as long as they were taken to fulfill his function as president, executor of the laws of the land, and commander-in-chief. But Carroll also used this pamphlet to argue against the confiscation and subsequent emancipation of slaves.

Carroll had feared Lincoln's "abolitionist tendencies" from the beginning of his administration. In August of 1861 she was sure he was bent on destroying slavery as the Confiscation Act of 1861 became law, ignoring Lincoln's opposition to the legislation. Samuel Williams had tried to assuage her fears: if Lincoln were an abolitionist, he wrote, he would, as William Lloyd Garrison and Wendell Phillips had done, rejoice "over the secession of the South, because they believe & with good reason, that separation dooms slavery by removing it from the protection of Federal law. Lincoln, therefore, if he favored abolition, would, if he acted consistently, end the war" by allowing the South to secede. Carroll may have believed this argument; after all, she had written Jefferson Davis on the occasion of his inauguration the previous February that, "Slavery will perish, for the nations of the earth, . . . cannot in this age of the world aid or abet it on this continent."[34] While Carroll hated slavery and was sure it would eventually disappear, she still insisted that the federal government could not legally interfere with the institution. If slavery were to die, it would be a natural death, not an execution.

In her rough draft of *The War Powers,* Carroll included a description of Lincoln as an abolitionist, "a renegade Southerner, narrow minded, as all ignorant men are, [who] hates the South intensely, because he did not get its votes." Carroll feared that hatred would end the possibility of restoring the Union with slavery intact, a condition which she deemed essential to preserve the Southern economy and society. Lincoln must recognize the South as part of the "great family of the Nation," in spite of its peculiar institution, she wrote, and he must respect the South's constitutional right to hold slaves. Only through the efforts of Unionist allies in the South, Carroll argued, could the North hope to restore the Union. But if Lincoln acted as an abolitionist by threatening emancipation through such acts as confiscation, "the American people may abandon at once all reasonable hope or expectation of his ending the war. It cannot be done."[35]

Carroll interpreted the government's confiscation policy as the first step toward forced emancipation. But most supporters saw the measure primarily as a way to weaken the enemy by depriving the South of money and materiel. The August 1861 act provided for the condemnation and seizure of all property used to aid the rebellion. Such property, of course, included slaves, some of whom had helped build Confederate batteries. While the confiscation of such property may have been militarily sound and a politic measure, it was legally questionable and rarely enforced.[36] Still, Carroll viewed the act as an opportunity the president had created to free slaves, and she held Lincoln personally responsible for enforcing an unconstitutional law.

At one point in her rough draft of *The War Powers,* Carroll even called for the removal of "every obstruction" that stood in the way of pursuing the war to its constitutional end (that is, preserving the Union), "even if it be a President of the United States!" But by the time she finished her pamphlet, her rhetoric had become less impassioned and more legalistic. Since the war was being waged to preserve the Constitution, she wrote, "the war power itself must not trample that instrument in the dust."[37] This was an interesting argument coming from a woman who had already declared that suspending civil rights guaranteed by the Constitution was acceptable in order to preserve the Union.

Carroll's work on *The War Powers* was prompted by congressional discussion of a second confiscation act. On 2 December 1861 Senator Lyman Trumbull promised to introduce a bill, more comprehensive than the first, that would free more slaves. Consequently, one of Carroll's primary aims in her pamphlet was to convince her readers, especially those in Congress, that the war could not and should not emancipate slaves in the South. The policy of abolition, she wrote, "can never hope to restore the Union, while it would be sheer suicide to the Constitution. Such a policy might create unity, which is a very different thing from union; but it would be the unity of a frightful despotism over both the South and North." For Carroll, the way to emancipate was not by force or decree, but by "preservation of the Union, and with that silent progress of intelligence and virtue which the Union alone can guarantee."[38]

Carroll viewed Trumbull's bill as one of many ludicrous plans being proposed and argued that all acts suggesting the government could confiscate all the property of the rebels, both private and public, were inherently unconstitutional. The United States wanted to regard the war as an insurrection rather than a war between two independent powers. It could not, therefore, abrogate the Constitution that it said was still in place within the areas in rebellion. The Constitution was still the law of the land in the South, according to the North; therefore, it should not be trampled upon in order to be preserved. Confiscation of slaves would involve taking private property for public use without just compensation, which the Constitution forbade. The government did not gain powers as it put down the rebellion; it therefore could not claim the right to confiscate private property without due process of law. If, to bypass that constitutional limitation, the government proposed to confiscate property under the laws of war, it would be admitting the Confederacy was a belligerent power—an independent nation—the very thing it wanted to avoid. Carroll was willing to jettison constitutional guarantees to such privileges as the writ of habeas corpus to preserve the Union; she was not willing to do so to free slaves. Although she had been able to maintain an argument that acknowledged Lincoln could take actions of war while acting as an executive in her earlier pamphlet, she did not maintain that duality in her interpretation of any confiscation act. Carroll saw beyond the act's stated purpose of confiscation and measured its effect of freeing slaves to form the basis of her criticism.[39]

The State Department printed *The War Powers* and distributed it to all the members of Congress, where it gained special notice by New York Republican Representative Alexander Diven in a speech on the confiscation matter.

> A specious argument in favor of what may be done under the war power, by way of confiscation, has been made. . . . Any one who desires to see it answered will find that a clever woman has done it completely. Any clever woman could answer it. . . . She signs herself in her pamphlet Anna Ella Carroll. I commend her answer on the doctrine of the war power to those who have been following that phantom and misleading the people. And I commend it to another individual, a friend of mine, who gave a most learned disquisition on the writ of *habeas corpus,* and against the power of the President to imprison men. He will find that answered. I am not surprised at this. The French Revolution discovered great political minds in some of the French women, and I am happy to see in these troublous times that there is a like development in our women.[40]

Carroll's pamphlet did not end the question of whether confiscating slaves was legal as she probably hoped it would. There can be no doubt that Carroll despised slavery. She bought her father's slaves prior to the war to keep them from being sold further South. She made sure those slaves went free. She freed her own personal slaves and supported colonization efforts. But she was well aware of the psychological, sociological, and economic upheaval that would result in the South if slaves were freed without compensation, colonization, or due process of law. Events in the spring of 1862, however, made it clear to Carroll that the push for emancipation had not been stalled by her writings or by her constitutional arguments. On 13 March 1862 Congress prohibited the military from returning fugitive slaves who had escaped to Union lines. In April Congress abolished slavery in the District of Columbia, albeit with compensation of owners.[41]

Carroll feared the impact of that legislation on the war effort. She wrote to Lincoln and urged him to use his veto power. Unopposed to abolition with colonization, she feared the bill came at the wrong time; it would alienate all the Unionists in the South, since they would see it as clear evidence that the abolitionists controlled the government. Emancipation in the District of Columbia was the first step toward the destruction of slavery that John C. Calhoun had described in 1849, she wrote. Once abolitionists obtained control of the government, "they would proceed, first to abolish slavery in the District of Columbia—secondly, in the territories—thirdly, in all the forts, magazines, arsenals, dockyards, etc.—fourthly, to prohibit the internal slave trade between the states—and finally to abolish it in all the States." The Southern Unionists Carroll knew believed Calhoun had been mistaken in his assumption that the abolitionists would one day become ascendant. The success of the Republican party had not meant "the Abolition reign had commenced," Carroll argued; any change in the raison d'être for the war now would change that perception. "Be not deceived, Mr. President, because the Union men of the South sustain you, in your efforts to suppress the rebellion and maintain the integrity of the Constitution, that they will ever submit to the abolition of slavery, by the [general] government." If the president signed the bill, she predicted, the war would be protracted "for months, it may be, for years," and the rebels would gain "a reinforcement of at least fifty thousand fighting men" from the border states, all opposed to any form of emancipation. Fifteen hundred slaves might be freed as a result of the measure, but Lincoln would "consign to a bloody grave, at least ten thousand patriot soldiers." The president must veto the bill, she wrote, for even if Congress passed the bill over his veto, at least Lincoln's hands would be clean as far as abolition was concerned. That was the important point for Carroll: the president must not be the one to change the nature of the war.[42]

Lincoln signed the bill with a note praising Congress on 16 April, never doubting "the constitutional authority of congress to abolish slavery in this District" and having "ever desired to see the national capital freed from the institution in some satisfactory way." Since the bill provided for compensated emancipation with the possibility of colonization, Lincoln's only qualm was the expediency of the matter. Unlike Carroll, he believed the time was right.[43]

Carroll must have been disappointed that she had failed to stop Lincoln from signing the bill, but she made a note on her copy of her letter to him that he had not received it prior to signing the measure, which no doubt comforted her. However, she was destined to be disappointed again over the issue of confiscation, which came up in May in final debates over the Second Confiscation Act. One version of the bill came before the Senate in the spring of 1862. On 19 May Senator Charles Sumner of Massachusetts rose to argue for its passage "to suppress the insurrection, to punish treason, and rebellion, to seize and confiscate the property of the rebels. . . ." Sumner's arguments in support of the bill led to Carroll's pamphlet, *The Relation of the National Goverment to the Revolted Citizens Defined.*[44]

Sumner argued that the peculiar nature of this civil war had placed Confederates in a sort of double jeopardy. They were criminals, guilty of treason; they were enemies because they had made war against the United States. Consequently, "we are at liberty to . . . treat the people engaged against us as criminals or as enemies, or, if we please, as both." If Confederates were criminals, Sumner said, it was the duty of the North to "pursue and punish them"; if they were enemies, it was the duty of the United States to "blast them with that summary vengeance which is among the dread agencies of war. . . ."[45]

Defining Confederates as criminals—as traitors—would make them subject to the constitutional provisions which ordered that "Congress shall have Power to declare the Punishment of Treason." Sumner argued that such punishment should be the forfeiture of property, as provided in article III, section 3 of the Constitution. Defining Confederates as enemies, on the other hand, would make them subject to the "rights of war" which provided that the "private property of an enemy on land may be taken as a penalty for the illegal acts of individuals, or of the community to which they belong." An abolitionist, Sumner extended the confiscation of property to include confiscating slaves. If slaves were considered property, he argued, they could be confiscated as the enemy's property had traditionally been confiscated during time of war. If slaves were humans, they existed in a "constant state of war" with their masters anyway, by virtue of the institution which enslaved them. Thus, in freeing them, the United States was simply taking "advantage of the actual condition of things." Freedom for slaves would "take from the rebellion its mainspring of activity and strength . . . its chief source of provisions and supplies . . . a motive and temptation to prolonged resistance," and furthermore, he argued, would "destroy forever that disturbing influence which, so long as it is allowed to exist, will keep this land a volcano ever ready to break forth anew!"[46]

Sumner's speech horrified Carroll. It encompassed all she had been fighting against: abolition, disunion, and revenge. In a letter to Lincoln, she was even willing to move away from her earlier position that the war was a rebellion. The "so called Southern Confederacy, is now to this government, as a *foreign* power and people are as much under the dominion of a foreign yoke as though the States were held by France, or Great Britain, instead of domestic foes," she wrote the president. "Davis has coerced the obedience and submission of the entire population," and recognition of the United States as the supreme power by any Southerner would be "at the peril of his life." If the rebellion had in fact succeeded in establishing a foreign government, Carroll argued, the public law applied. Under the international rules of war, confiscated property would return to its owners. But if slaves were adjudged persons, as Carroll believed they were, and set free after confiscation, they could not "under the Constitution be deprived of their liberty." Confiscation, because it would lead to emancipation, meant trouble. It also meant expense, since the owners would have to be compensated for that property not returned to them.[47]

The major problem for Carroll—and for Lincoln—regarding the Second Confiscation Act was the definition of both the status and the property of the offender, the Confederate. If Confederates were domestic criminals, due process regarding the seizure of property had to be observed; property could not be seized without an individual trial. If, on the other hand, Confederates were really traitors, the Constitution forbade punishment for treason to extend beyond the life of traitors. Since slaves were inheritable property, the government would be punishing the traitors' heirs by freeing their property, thus extending the traitors' punishment beyond their own life to their heirs. A blanket declaration that all persons in rebellion against the United States should lose their slaves posed tremendous problems. All traitors would have to be tried and convicted individually, and their property then seized. Given the size and scope of the rebellion, that was impossible. And if the government chose to proceed against Confederates *in rem* (against their property) instead of *in personam* (against the individuals), as provided for in the Second Confiscation Act, the same problem occurred. Defining slaves as property in order to confiscate them legally, *in rem,* meant they could not then be emancipated since that would still extend forfeiture beyond the life of the traitor. Simply put, the government could not legally confiscate and free slaves.[48]

Carroll saw "an express inhibition upon the power of Congress to abolish slavery or confiscate the property of rebels," she wrote. The Constitution specifically defined what treason was and "absolutely inhibit[ed] the confiscation of the estate of the traitor to the government, leaving it free to pass to his heirs." The confiscation act under consideration by Congress would adjudge the Southerners guilty without trial, decide their punishment (the loss of property), and execute that punishment (by confiscating their property). A bill more directly in conflict with the Constitution could not have been drawn, said Carroll.[49]

Where Senator Sumner had argued that the "peculiar circumstances" of the combination of public and private war enabled Congress to treat the South as either criminal or enemy or both, as it pleased, Carroll cited the same authorities and even the same passages to argue that the prohibition against confiscation "was inserted in the Constitution *only* to prevent the exercise of this arbitrary power" during such a rebellion. Sumner used the long history of confiscation to justify its recurrence. Carroll used that same history to argue that the abuse of power through confiscation had led to the inclusion of the prohibitive clause in the Constitution. The Bill of Rights further guaranteed security of property, reinforcing the Constitution's stand against confiscation. The Second Confiscation Act came not from a long-standing tradition, Carroll believed, but had originated "in the worst and most malignant passions of the human heart . . . pressed in utter *contempt"* of those constitutional guarantees. In her pamphlet, Carroll returned to her definition of the war as a domestic rebellion: only individually could those convicted of treason be punished by holding their property liable for damages.

> Before Congress can claim to exercise this power of war over any portion of the American people; it must first recognize the rebellion as a success—*their revolution accomplished, and the Union dissolved.* In short, must concede to the rebellion—what no European power has ventured to do—that they have achieved their independence, and have established a firm and stable government, against which it is no longer proper to war with the view of suppressing it.
>
> For Congress to take that position . . . is to become allies of the rebellion, and ourselves *traitors, like them, to the Constitution.*[50]

The war might be raging, Carroll argued, but the Union remained. Confederates were still citizens and had to be treated as such with all the constitutional guarantees that citizenship provided. Possession of property might pass to the government during the war, but title to that property remained, except in the case of "movable goods," with the owner or the heirs. Further, since Southerners had been subjugated by a rebel force and the federal government was unable to protect them from that subjugation, she argued, "it *cannot* hold them responsible for any act they may commit *while under the pressure* of a usurping power." It would be difficult enough to restore authority and peace constitutionally; "the Union of these States *cannot* be restored under a *mutilated Constitution,* or under a new and different one." Confiscation would continue the war "for the sake of power. For the annals of the world record no instances where the usurpers of power have ever, voluntarily, laid it down."[51]

Carroll called *The Relation of the National Government to the Revolted Citizens Defined* her "Reply to Sumner." It too was printed and distributed to Congress, probably because it argued the position Lincoln actually practiced in spite of the act's passage. In addition to writing pamphlets on the unconstitutionality of confiscation, Carroll continued to demand that the president oppose any policies she thought might lead to forced emancipation. She wrote Lincoln that all moves toward abolition, whether by confiscation act, by military orders (such as General John C. Frémont's August 1861 proclamation freeing slaves in Missouri and David Hunter's 9 May 1862 proclamation in South Carolina), or by arming freed slaves, would strengthen Southern resolve to defeat the Union until a million men would be required to defeat the South. The expense alone would ruin the country and destroy Lincoln. Carroll grew exasperated: "I cannot allow myself to speak of men so stupid, as to suppose they can change at once, the whole social ideas, which have from the origin of our institutions controlled the American people . . . [to lift] up four millions of African slaves, upon a plane of political and social equality." It was absurd, it was dangerous, and it must be stopped lest Lincoln become "the *last* President of the United States of America."[52]

Carroll suggested Lincoln find some way to antagonize the abolitionists in order to reassure the border states. The final version of the Second Confiscation Act offered such an opportunity. "This bill will inaugurate a new policy," she argued, "and change the whole morale of the war. It will no longer be regarded as a war for the maintainance [*sic*] of the American Constitution, but as one, for the subjugation of the Southern States, and the destruction of their social system. And the judgment of the civilized world will then decide that the South is in a just struggle for Constitutional liberty; against an arbitrary and revengeful government." Intervention by Europe was sure to follow if he signed the bill, Carroll warned, and Jefferson Davis and his "co-traitors" would become heroes while Lincoln and his cabinet would stand "in all the future, like George the Third and the Ministry of Lord North."[53]

Lincoln did have objections to the confiscation act, and in fact broke precedent by sending his proposed veto along with the signed bill back to Congress on 17 July. His objections were similar to those Carroll raised regarding property, and centered on the extinguishment of real estate titles, which was an unconstitutional forfeiture of property because it extended beyond the life of the guilty party, as well as on proceedings *in rem.* As provided for in the act, proceedings of property forfeiture *in rem,* rather than *in personam,* led to a forfeiture of property "without a conviction of the supposed criminal, or a personal hearing given him in any proceeding," he wrote. While *in rem* proceedings were used in admiralty cases, Lincoln thought the Second Confiscation Act should provide "a reasonable time . . . for such parties to appear and have personal hearings."[54]

But unlike Carroll, Lincoln did not object to the emancipation of slaves provided for in the Second Confiscation Act. He chose to interpret the act's provisions regarding property forfeiture as applicable to slaves, as Carroll did. This interpretation was apparently not the one Congress made, since the act provided separate sections for confiscation and emancipation, and did not mention slaves as property to be confiscated. But Lincoln reasoned that if property forfeited to the general government under the act included slaves, the government, "so far as there can be ownership," owned those slaves. He then had "no objection to Congress deciding in advance that they shall be free." As for the specific provision which declared slaves of rebels "captives of war, and . . . forever free," Lincoln suggested that Congress make clear the conditions under which that provision could be enforced.[55]

Lincoln's signing of the Second Confiscation Act, even with his reservations, made it clear to Carroll that either Lincoln or Congress was going to do something about emancipation. Lincoln's desired policy for emancipation was the same as Carroll's: gradual emancipation to avoid social disruption, federal compensation to prevent economic destruction, and voluntary colonization to ensure peaceful race relations. While Carroll's concern was for the preservation of the South, which made her hesitate to support any wartime emancipation measures, she remembered well the days when the slave traders came to buy those whom her father had had to sell. "I shudder now at the sight of such horrors as came before my own eyes," she wrote. "A daughter, clinging to her parents & in the most delicate situation—with screams that were frantic, the whole white family of females, in tears, yet powerless to interpose . . . the most tender and devoted of mothers too far bereft by the sale of her first born boy to shed a tear. . . . Scenes like this no years have ever effaced—no time can ever make me forget. . . ."[56] That tragic memory stayed with her, and in 1861 and 1862, at the same time Carroll fought against the confiscation acts because of their emancipatory effects, she worked to promote the colonization of freed slaves.

By April 1861 Carroll had begun working for Aaron Columbus Burr, a leading New York merchant, on a plan to colonize freed blacks in British Honduras in Central America. In March of that year Burr had become the agent for James Grant of Belize, British Honduras, to sell Grant's 150 square miles of land in "Stand" (Stann) Creek, to found such a colony. Aside from what he viewed as the humanitarian motive of colonization, Grant had asked sixty-five thousand dollars for the land, which included considerable stands of mahogany, rubber trees, "cocoa nut trees," and a brickworks.[57]

Burr originally had made an agreement with Grant to lease the land for a mahogany-cutting company formed in 1860. The political unrest in the area scared off investors, but Grant had received several offers for the land itelf, which Burr privately thought ought to be valued at one hundred thousand dollars. Burr kept Grant from selling by promising him that he would try to sell it to the United States government. In the spring of 1861 Burr proposed to Carroll, who was, he wrote, "known as a practical advocate of colonization," that a company be formed "for the purchase of this land for the benefit of the free persons of color in the United States." It would also benefit Burr's pocket: he offered the land at what he called a "reduced price" of seventy-five thousand dollars. Burr had never actually purchased the land from Grant, so his price reduction was scarely a civic gesture. If the parcel sold, he stood to make ten thousand dollars on the sale of the land to the government. Part of that profit undoubtedly would go to Carroll.[58]

Burr hired Carroll as a lobbyist to help him present his case to the government. The terms of their agreement are unclear, but by the fall of 1861 Carroll was corresponding regularly with Burr and apologizing that a case of cholera in August and September had kept her too ill to do much work. At the same time, Grant was warning Burr that poachers were stealing mahogany and that the 1860 mahogany-cutting company was so hopelessly insolvent that Burr and Grant would wind up suffering financially if steps were not taken to sell the land. Colonization of freed blacks on the land was the only way out, Grant wrote to Burr. Burr wrote to Carroll, and Carroll to the president, proposing a colony in British Honduras.[59]

Carroll presented the colony as attractively as possible. It was close to the United States and had a direct trading track by sea, easy access, a friendly government, a tropical climate, and fertile soil. There was an added and perhaps overstated attraction: that the government of British Honduras wanted "to develop its vast resources of wealth, by receiving upon a social and political equality, the very class of persons which it is the interest of this country to furnish." It was also a way for the United States, she wrote, "to remove the colored race and make them useful to themselves," while still retaining them "as friends of the whites."[60]

The formal proposal was finally made by Burr himself on 6 May 1862 to the Department of the Interior, which was in charge of all colonization projects. For seventy-five thousand dollars, Burr would transfer title, found a settlement colony named the "Lincoln Colony," and if the government so desired, would "receive these freedmen as they are transported, and superintend their location upon the land, upon whatever principle may be determined by the government." On 13 May Carroll wrote to Secretary of the Interior Caleb Smith with a full account of the improvements on the land and included a map of Scotland Town, the main settlement. The matter was laid before Lincoln by the nineteenth.[61]

At this point, there may have been a meeting between Carroll and Lincoln regarding the colonization project. Reminiscing late in life, Carroll recalled a touching scene in which Lincoln asked her what he should do about the matter of colonization.

I was perfectly charmed with his cordial and simple remarks, free from every semblance of ambition. He, in the most exalted office upon earth, deferring as humbly to another, as if he had no power or aim! He was patient and gentle as a woman could be, nothing brusque about him. He got up and took a large map which he hung in the room and sat down on a small low stool by the fireplace, spread the map on his knees, and asked me to point out the place I recommended for the colonization of the freedmen. I pointed to British Honduras, in Central America, and gave all the reasons for this as the then proper locality to act to this nation as a friendly power.[62]

Such a domestic scene may have been fact, or fancy created by the passage of time and presidential martyrdom. At any rate, Carroll did continue to write Lincoln. In a letter on 19 May, she argued against Liberia as a colony: transportation costs were too great, and the reluctance of freed blacks to leave the United States for Africa was too strong. Haiti, another suggested site, was just as objectionable. The island was too small for freed slaves used to the vastness of the North American continent and who were now four million in number. No doubt a "few, shrewd" colonists would succeed, but only by "sinking their Americanism and becoming thoroughly European in their caste . . . [while] the majority . . . would be held only as laborers and producers. . . ." In addition, the government of Haiti would not provide colonists any more chance to elevate their social or political position than they had had in the United States. British Honduras was the answer. Large enough to establish a colony of millions, it was, she argued, the only country in Central America that would not require civil and military support and protection from the United States for its colonists. Life, liberty, and property were secure in British Honduras, and its government would not interfere with colonization.[63]

It is difficult to tell exactly when Lincoln rejected the choice of British Honduras as a possible colonization site, if he did indeed consider it seriously. Carroll sent him a box of "Central American goods" to convince him of the plenty that awaited colonists, and she thought it was still alive as a choice on 30 August. She wrote to Burr telling him she had heard that the Chiriqui colonization project, another Central American site in competition with her suggestion, was defunct. She may not have known about Lincoln's recommendation to a delegation of free blacks on 14 August that they go and live at Chiriqui.[64] But Carroll was correct in her perception that Lincoln was moving toward emancipation of slaves with or without colonization. Lincoln could see a way to accomplish emancipation either way. Much as she hated slavery, Carroll could not wield such a two-edged sword. In her opinion, emancipation had to include colonization. Without it, the border states would be lost, and in the end, the Union itself would die.

In a 13 September meeting with Senator Samuel C. Pomeroy, head of the Chiriqui project, Carroll discovered Chiriqui was still lively, and the British Honduras colonization project was still-born. Disappointed, she wrote Burr, the "Chiriqui property will be bought & fortunes made for the *white* speculators through the poor Africans who will hew the wood & draw the water." In fact, the Chiriqui site was not the final choice, and, on 21 October, Carroll made a last-ditch effort to meet with Lincoln as "a sincere friend of the colored" to argue once more for the British Honduras site. If she met with him, her arguments failed to sway him, for the announced site was the Haitian island of Ile A'Vache.[65] Meanwhile, the administration's two-pronged attack on slavery continued with the issuance of the Preliminary Emancipation Proclamation on 22 September. Although this proclamation included provisions for compensation and colonization, the deadline of 1 January was a setback for moderation that no doubt angered Carroll.

The extent of Carroll's access to Lincoln as well as the degree of attention he paid her ideas is difficult to ascertain. Certainly he knew who she was. One letter to Carroll from the president survives: in August 1862 he had thanked her for an address she had made to the people of Maryland calling for more volunteers, which he had read "with a great deal of pleasure." Lincoln's Attorney General Bates was on good terms with her and wrote to her cordially during the war, but Bates and Lincoln were not that close, and if she tried to reach the president through Secretary of State Seward, no evidence survives of her attempts.[66] While Carroll may have occasionally enjoyed Lincoln's attention, she was only one of many people trying to influence him.

What is important, however, even as Carroll failed to convince Lincoln to follow her course of advise, is that she did articulate soundly the concerns of the border states regarding emancipation and colonization. Lincoln recognized and spoke to those concerns, if not in direct reply to her. In September 1862, for example, he pointed out his fear to a visiting interdenominational delegation of Christians from Chicago that "fifty thousand bayonets" from the border states might be turned against the Union in consequence of a radical emancipation proclamation they supported. This was the argument and the figure that Carroll had used in her letters to Lincoln the previous April and July.[67]

Fragmentary evidence in Carroll's papers suggests she accepted the presence of free blacks in society after the war, and once emancipation was a fait accompli she turned her attention to other matters. Besides writing in support of Maryland anti-secessionists and the president's war measures, and her work on behalf of Burr for the proposed Lincoln Colony, one other issue interested Carroll greatly. In the fall of 1861, Anne Carroll turned her eyes to the war in Tennessee and her hand to military strategy, thus beginning the most legendary and the most controversial endeavor of her long political career.

FIVE

Carroll Stakes Her Claim

In the summer of 1862 Anne Carroll met with President Lincoln and presented him with a bill for the pamphlets she had written, as well as a proposal that she travel to Europe to write for the Union. He dismissed her idea with such vigor that she did not discuss her second proposal: that he pay her for her work as a military strategist. She had written out the introduction of the idea to Lincoln—"Now, Mr. President, there is another subject, which I desire to bring to your attention"—but her audacity seems to have deserted her.[1] Not for long. The fantastical legend of Anna Ella Carroll, "Lincoln's Lady Strategist," the "Great Unrecognized Member of Lincoln's Cabinet," "The Originator of the Tennessee Campaign," and, at its fullest flight of fancy, "The Woman Who Saved the Union," was about to spring forth.[2]

In early October 1861, so the legend goes, shortly after making her oral agreement with Assistant Secretary of War Thomas A. Scott to write pamphlets for the War Department, Carroll left the comparative safety of Washington to discover for herself the state of the Union in the western theater of the war. She went first to Chicago, then to St. Louis, where she met her old friend and close companion, Lemuel D. Evans, who had been sent to St. Louis on a secret mission by Secretary of State Seward.[3]

To her dismay, Carroll found St. Louis a hotbed of Confederate sympathizers and discouraged Unionists. She decided to continue writing pamphlets arguing for the Union cause and went to the Mercantile Library in St. Louis to do research. There she met the librarian, Edward Johnston, cousin of Confederate General Albert Sidney Johnston. She engaged him in a warm discussion, for he was a Confederate sympathizer and expressed surprise that, as a Southern lady, she should be so avid a supporter of the Union cause and should be using her literary talents in such a losing venture. Sensing his disbelief that her convictions were firm, Carroll flattered and charmed her way into Librarian Johnston's confidence and took note of all he said. She also took note of what all those around her said and eventually decided to share the information she had gathered with the Union authorities. She went to see General John C. Frémont, who was in charge of the Western Department, but he was absent and, she snidely wrote, only "his wife was in command."[4]

Not deigning to share her information with Jessie Frémont, Carroll kept all these things to herself. She knew that President Lincoln had decided that the Mississippi River must be controlled by the Union in order for the North to win the war. But all with whom she spoke assured her of the strength of Confederate fortifications down the river and of the impossibility of opening it. Furthermore, after witnessing the disheartening effects on Union sympathizers when they saw the injured and dead Federal soldiers after the Battle of Belmont on 7 November, she was determined to find a safer way for Union troops to invade the South, a way that bypassed the fortified Mississippi.[5]

There were two other rivers besides the Mississippi that afforded possible invasion routes into the Confederacy: the Tennessee and the Cumberland. Carroll reasoned that if she could talk to a riverboat pilot familiar with these rivers, she might be able to learn if the rivers would be navigable by Union gunboats. Fortunately, in the same hotel where Carroll was staying, there resided one Anna Scott. Mrs. Scott's husband, Captain Charles M. Scott, was a riverboat pilot and, in fact, had piloted the transport *Memphis* at the recent Battle of Belmont. Carroll sent for him immediately upon his arrival in the city.[6]

Questioning Captain Scott intently on the characteristics of the Tennessee and Cumberland rivers, Carroll discovered that the Tennessee was always deep enough for gunboats; the Cumberland was deep enough most of the time. At that moment, Carroll had a flash of inspiration. She knew in an instant that an invasion route that used these two rivers was the solution to the strategic problem that had puzzled the military leaders in the West and planners in the East and had kept the army frozen in its tracks, fearful of another raid with the death toll, disarray, and failure of Belmont.[7]

Lemuel Evans called to see Carroll just then, and Carroll turned to him with her idea that the Federal troops should be transferred from the Mississippi to the Tennessee River and should use that route to invade the Confederacy. Since Evans had been born near the Tennessee River and had lived near Muscle Shoals in Alabama most of his life, Carroll trusted his opinion. He concurred with the value of her plan of invasion, and they went to Captain Scott to glean as much information from him as possible. Carroll then wrote immediately to Attorney General Edward Bates, who had first suggested using gunboats, but on the Mississippi, not the Tennessee, then to Assistant War Secretary Scott, and then to President Lincoln himself, detailing her plan and promising to return to Washington to explain it in person.[8]

Carroll then left St. Louis and traveled to Ohio, to Covington, Kentucky, and then on to Buffalo, New York, where she met with her old friend Millard Fillmore. Everywhere she went, the talk was all about the necessity of controlling the Mississippi by storming its defenses. In Buffalo, Fillmore listened to Carroll's new plan and agreed that it was a wonderful discovery. He urged her to waste no time, but to present it to President Lincoln at once.[9]

She arrived in Washington in late November and began work immediately. On 30 November, her maps drawn and her papers finished, she called on Colonel Thomas Scott at the War Department with a detailed plan of attack.

The civil and military authorities seem to be laboring under a grave mistake in regard to the true key of the war in the Southwest. It is not the Mississippi, but the Tennessee River. It is well known that the eastern part or the farming interests of Tennessee and Kentucky are generally loyal, while the middle and western parts, or what are known as the planting districts, are in sympathy with the traitors, but except in the extreme western part the Union sentiment still lives.

Now, all the military preparations made in the West indicate that the Mississippi River is the point to which the authorities are directing their attention. On that river many battles must be fought and heavy risks must be incurred before any impression can be made on the enemy, all of which could be avoided by using the Tennessee River. This is navigable for first-class boats to the Mississippi line, and is open to navigation all the year, while the distance is only two hundred and fifty miles by river from Paducah, on the Ohio.

The Tennessee River offers many advantages over the Mississippi. We should avoid the most impregnable batteries of the enemy which cannot be taken without great danger and great risk of life to our forces, from the fact that our boats, if crippled, would fall a prey to the enemy by being swept by the current to them and away from the relief of our friends. But even should we succeed, still we will only have begun the war, for we shall then have to fight to the country from whence the enemy derives his supplies. Now, to advance up the Tennessee River would avoid all this danger, for if our boats were crippled they would drop back with the current to their friends and escape all damages. But an advantage still would be a tendency to cut the enemy's lines in two by reaching the Memphis & Charleston Railroad, threatening Memphis, which lies about one hundred and fifty miles due west, and no defensible point between; also Nashville, only ninety miles northeast, and Florence and Tuscumbia, in North Alabama, forty miles east. A movement in this direction would do more to relieve our friends in Kentucky, and inspire the loyal hearts in East Tennessee than the possession of the whole Mississippi River. If well executed it would cause the evacuation of all those formidable fortifications on which the rebels ground their hopes of success; and in the event of our fleet attacking Mobile, the presence of our troops in the northern part of that State would be of material benefit to the fleet. Again, the aid our forces would receive from the loyal men in Tennessee would enable them to crush the last traitor in that region, and the separation of the two extremes would do more than one hundred battles for the Union cause.

The Tennessee River is crossed by the Memphis & Louisville Railroad [the Memphis & Ohio] and the Memphis & Nashville Railroad [the Nashville & Decatur?] at Hamburg, where the river makes the big bend to the east and touches the northeast corner of Mississippi, entering the northwest corner of Alabama, forming the arc of a circle to the south, enters the State of Tennessee at the northeast of Alabama, and if it does not touch the northwest corner of Georgia comes very near it.

It is but eight miles from Hamburg to the Memphis & Charleston Railroad, which road goes through Tuscumbia, and only two miles from the river, which it crosses at Decatur, thirty miles above, intersecting with the Nashville & Chattanooga road at Stephenson, Alabama.

The Tennessee River never has less than three feet to Hamburg on the shoalest bar, and during the fall, winter and spring months there is always water for the largest boats that are used on the Mississippi River.

It follows from the above that in making the Mississippi the key of the war in the West, or rather in overlooking the Tennessee River, the subject is not understood by the superiors in command.[10]

Carroll read the paper aloud to Scott, slowly and carefully. Greatly excited by the brilliant strategy conceived by the lady from Maryland, Scott begged her to allow him to take her plan to the president, who had already read her earlier letter and who was eager to see her final draft. If it would be of aid to her country, Carroll would leave it. So assured, she left the plan with Colonel Scott.[11]

Lincoln embraced the plan with enthusiasm. He fired Secretary of War Simon Cameron because he was too old to carry out this new strategy and brought in the unpopular but young and energetic Edwin Stanton. Stanton sent orders immediately to General Henry Halleck who had taken command of the Western Department. Halleck ordered General Ulysses Grant up the Tennessee River to the Confederates' Fort Henry and, carrying through Carroll's strategy, continued the Union advance toward the rail junction of Corinth, Mississippi. Lincoln then sent Assistant Secretary of War Scott west to ensure that Halleck and Grant understood the overall strategy and carried out the plan faithfully.[12]

Carroll's Plan ➤➤➤➤ Union Move ➤ Scale 12 Miles ▲▲

© Micaela C. Ayers, 1989

Carroll's plan called for Union troops to move up the Tennessee River to Muscle Shoals, Alabama, near Decatur. Such a movement would cut the Memphis & Ohio Railroad near Fort Henry and the Memphis & Charleston Railroad as it crossed at Decatur. This, she thought, would drive the Confederates out of Bowling Green, Nashville, and eastern Tennessee, and would give the Union control of the railroads in that region.

The Union forces under Grant moved up the Tennessee and captured Fort Henry on 6 February 1862, and took Fort Donelson on 16 February. Nashville surrendered on 25 February. By March, Grant had moved up the river to Pittsburg Landing, near Shiloh Church. He defeated Albert Sidney Johnston's troops at the Battle of Shiloh, 6–7 April.

The importance of the successful campaign in Tennessee cannot be over-estimated. Because of Carroll's plan, the Confederacy was cut in two, Confederate fortifications on the Mississippi were evacuated, the enemy was driven inland from the outer borders of the Confederacy, European intervention on behalf of the South was prevented, the Northwest remained in the Union, the national credit was revived, Unionist sentiment in the border states was reinforced, Union contact with the slave population turned them against the Confederacy and toward support for the Union cause, Missouri stayed in the Union, Vicksburg was captured, and the Union was saved.[13]

Shortly after the fall of Forts Henry and Donelson in February 1862, legislators in both houses of Congress sought to reward the brilliant general whose strategy had saved the Union. Major General Halleck, Brigadier General Grant, Brigadier General Don Carlos Buell, and Flag Officer Andrew Foote were all mentioned. Anne Carroll sat in the galleries, listening to the debates with a secretive smile on her face. Lincoln, Stanton, Scott, and Evans all knew the secret, as did Benjamin Wade, chairman of the recently formed Committee on the Conduct of the War. But they all knew as well the danger of allowing the identity of the author of the plan to be known. As Lincoln said, "The officers would throw off their epaulets if they knew they were acting on the plan of a civilian; and good God, if they knew it was a woman, the whole army would disband!"[14]

So silence reigned, and those who searched for a hero eventually gave up their search and resumed the business at hand. The woman whose work had saved the Union turned her hand to other matters, not the least of which was trying to obtain payment for her pamphlets from the War Department. Only years later did Carroll reluctantly allow herself to be pulled forth from her feminine obscurity to be presented to the American people as a true hero to be recognized and liberally rewarded.

Against this incredible legend stands the more commonly accepted version of events that culminated in the Tennessee River campaign. The Union was in dire straits after the Battle of Bull Run in July 1861. Months of inaction by his generals had driven Lincoln to despair. General-in-Chief Winfield Scott had conceived of an overall strategy at the beginning of the war that would surround the Confederacy with an army on land and a naval blockade. With a move down the Mississippi to the Gulf of Mexico to cut off interior trade added to the external pressure, the "Anaconda Plan" would gradually squeeze the life out of the South. Control over the Mississippi was essential. It would cut the Confederacy in two, block food, supplies, and contact from the agricultural states of Texas and Arkansas, and block importation of war materiel from the Northwest as well.[15] But Scott's plan would take far too long. The political situation demanded a quick end to the war.

East of the Mississippi River were the Tennessee and Cumberland rivers, part of which courses ran northward through Tennessee, emptying into the Ohio River. These rivers were the natural highways of the region, and the Confederates were quick to fortify them. Primary fortifications were Fort Henry on the Tennessee and Fort Donelson on the Cumberland.

By September 1861 General Grant, under command of Major General John Frémont, head of the Western Department, established his headquarters at Cairo, Illinois, on the Mississippi. He seized and reinforced the cities of Paducah, at the mouth of the Tennessee, and Smithland, at the mouth of the Cumberland. By mid-October Union gunboats were reported thirty miles below Fort Henry, and the Confederates feared a Union push up both rivers. The Cumberland was "in fine boating order and rising quite fast," and would stay deep enough for gunboats through the fall and winter. William W. MacKall, assistant adjutant general to General Albert Sidney Johnston, urged Confederate General Leonidas Polk to hurry and finish reinforcing Fort Donelson, telling him that "the necessity of interrupting the Cumberland is urgent." If the Union forces were to invade Tennessee by water, they would be able to push on to the Memphis and Ohio Railroad which ran from Memphis to Bowling Green, and cut this important rail connection.[16]

The Union forces under Grant were quite cognizant of the Confederates' fear of their designs. On 8 November Brigadier General Charles F. Smith wrote Grant from Paducah that Confederates at Fort Henry had "been under apprehension of attack from here for the past two weeks." Lieutenant S. Ledyard Phelps of the Union Navy was "constantly moving his vessel [the wooden gunboat *Conestoga*] up and down the Tennessee and Cumberland" to ascertain Confederate positions and strength. On 20 November Colonel Charles Whittlesey of the Corps of Engineers suggested to Halleck that a joint land and water move up the Cumberland and Tennessee rivers, "the most passable route into Tennessee," would threaten Confederates in Columbus, force Brigadier General Simon Bolivar Buckner to retreat, and provide a water route halfway to Nashville, all of which would drive the Confederates out of central Tennessee.[17]

If, contrary to Carroll's assertations, the military minds in the West were aware of the strategic importance of the Tennessee and Cumberland rivers, and if, contrary to what she reported, preparations were being made to invade the South by these rivers rather than concentrating Union forces solely on the Mississippi, then why was there no action in the late fall and early winter of 1861? Carroll would always believe that it was her letter to the War Department on 30 November that informed the Western Department of the value of the rivers and that her plan prodded the Union forces into action—the action that eventually led to the capture of Forts Henry and Donelson in February, 1862. But Carroll, as a civilian and an outsider, did not have the complete picture of the state of affairs in the western theater. It was not a lack of intelligence or strategic understanding that kept the Union forces immobile, but rather supply shortages, battling commanders, lack of cooperation between army and navy, inexperienced troops and sailors, and nominal support from Washington that all contributed to the Union's failure to move rapidly on the western rivers.

At the time of President Lincoln's proclamation of the naval blockade of the South, the United States Navy consisted of forty-two commissioned vessels. These were deep-water ships, totally unsuited for use on the inland waters of the war's western theater. Navy Commander John Rodgers was sent west in May 1861 to establish naval forces on the river. First under the command of Major General George B. McClellan, head of the Department of the Ohio, in July Rodgers fell under General Frémont's command when the Western Department was organized. Rodgers worked hard, purchasing three river steamers in Cincinnati and pushing for their conversion into armed gunboats. Still, it was 12 August before the alterations resulted in three low-lying wooden gunboats. These gunboats, though usable, were not armor-plated. So in August as well, a contract was made with James B. Eads of St. Louis to build seven armor-plated gunboats to deliver down-river to Cairo. Eads had volunteered his knowledge of the Mississippi, Tennessee, and Cumberland rivers to the government in April 1861. "Once close them," he wrote, ". . . and starvation is inevitable in six months." The gunboats built by Eads's company were promised for 10 October.[18]

By September Rodgers had been relieved by Captain Andrew H. Foote for exceeding his authority in buying the first gunboats and for being too busy to pay proper obeisance to General Frémont. General Grant, at Cairo by September, employed the wooden gunboats provided by Rodgers in taking Paducah and Smithland, but it was not until 12 October that the first ironclad was launched and available for Union use. Short of money and supplies for both the wooden and the ironclad gunboats, Captain Foote pleaded with Secretary of the Navy Gideon Welles, Quartermaster General Montgomery Meigs, and Secretary of War Cameron for help. "The officers and crews of the three gunboats already in commission are clamorous for their pay," he wrote. Tired of being continually embarrassed by poor government financing, Foote nevertheless performed miracles, drafting crew members from steamboat men, Great Lakes sailors, and even the army, promising payment for supplies, hounding his superiors, and occasionally fighting the Confederates with skirmishes and raids on their positions along the rivers.[19]

One of Captain Foote's problems was his rank. As a captain in the navy, he was the equivalent of a colonel in the army. He finally requested Frémont to recommend that the Navy Department appoint him flag officer of the western flotilla, a rank designed to prevent a situation whereby "the gunboats are liable to be diverted from the service which I know you might wish, even by a volunteer colonel of a single regiment, should he happen to be in command in the vicinity of the gunboats." Secretary Welles gave him the appointment he requested on 13 November 1861; Frémont had been removed and replaced by General Henry Halleck on 2 November.[20]

Since the beginning of the war, there had been three different army commanders, two different naval commanders, a frantic dash to buy, convert, build, equip, and staff as many gunboats as possible, all while dealing with a shortsighted and occasionally recalcitrant government incapable of paying its bills on time. The wonder was not that the Union forces had not moved by late November, when Carroll presented her plan that had supposedly enlightened them as to the "true key to the west." The wonder was that they moved at all—which they did with decisive victories after the gunboats were available. Grant and Foote both sent messages to Halleck on 28 January 1862 that they wanted to move upriver to take Fort Henry. Halleck approved their request on 30 January. On 3 February Foote led his seven gunboats up the Tennessee, followed by Grant's troops on transport ships. Fort Henry fell on 6 February. Grant marched overland to Fort Donelson, which fell on 16 February. Ironically, the gunboats for which the Union forces had waited were almost superfluous. Fort Henry had been practically abandoned by the Confederates. Still, it was so quickly reduced by Foote's fire that Grant's troops were not needed. Fort Donelson's batteries, on the other hand, nearly destroyed Foote's squadron, which retreated to let the army have its day.[21]

If the strategy of invading the Confederacy by way of the Tennessee and Cumberland rivers was well established prior to Carroll's trip to St. Louis, if actions had been delayed due to logistics instead of strategic incompetence, how did the legend of Carroll as "Lincoln's Secret Weapon" begin, and how did it maintain itself in what has become one of the most thoroughly studied and documented periods of American history?[22]

The legend began with Carroll herself. As always, whenever an event occurred in which she could legitimately claim a small part, Carroll soon enlarged her contributions to monumental proportions. Thus, she wrote Lincoln in the summer of 1862, "I became satisfied that the effort then making to open and hold the Mississippi by an expedition downward could not succeed, and that the true key, was the Tennessee river. . . . I impressed these views upon military men, wherever I met them, until I returned to this city, the latter part of November, when I gave the result of my observation to the Government. . . ." As far as Carroll was concerned (and as a civilian untutored in military matters it was not an unreasonable belief on her part), that campaign in Tennessee in the winter of 1861–62 had come from her ideas presented on 30 November. "If this expedition was planned . . . upon any other suggestions," she wrote, or "if it originated with any one else, I am not aware of it." More important, she pointed out, "if the plan of the Western campaign was based upon the facts, furnished by me, to the Secretary of War . . . I ought now to have a substantial and liberal recognition of this service."[23]

Herein lay the crux of the matter. As always, Carroll was trying to make a living. The war provided her with an unprecedented opportunity as a writer, and apparently her agreement with Colonel Scott prompted her trip to St. Louis. Since her military strategy was presented in written form, no doubt Carroll had decided that any intellectual labor, particularly one with such monumental results for the Union, was compensable under her agreement with Scott. Much of Carroll's difficulties lay with Scott. By July 1862, six months after her second pamphlet supporting the president's policies had been issued, Carroll had not yet been paid for her work. The handsome Scott, whom Postmaster General Montgomery Blair had once characterized as a "corrupt lobby-jobber from Philadelphia," had overstepped his authority when promising Carroll payment for her approved pamphlets. Still, Scott did admit to the oral contract, saying that all of his interviews with Carroll were in his official capacity as assistant secretary, and he believed she should be paid for her work. Her bill had been partially paid, but that payment was out of Scott's own pocket, not from the War Department. "Reply to Breckinridge" had been circulated at a cost of $1,250, which Scott had given Carroll; *The War Powers* and "Reply to Sumner" would cost the government $5,000 more. While a bit steep, the bill for the pamphlets was not outrageously so, and, moreover, Carroll had done the work and deserved payment despite a price which was high enough apparently to startle the War Department and the president.[24]

What Scott could not have foreseen was the rapid rise of inflation. *The War Powers,* Carroll declared to Lincoln, "was destined to stand, as long as the Declaration of Independence. . . ." Accordingly, when she "considered the time and labor the document had cost me . . . I thought, fifty thousand dollars a small sum." Carroll had mentioned this mind-boggling sum earlier in a letter to Scott's replacement in the War Department, Assistant Secretary John Tucker (Scott had been sent west early in 1862 not to supervise implementation of Carroll's plan but to ascertain the condition of troops and railroads for the new Secretary of War, Edwin Stanton). By July, when she met with Lincoln and read a paper concerning her claim aloud to him, she had modified her bill somewhat by including a proposal that she make a trip to Europe to disseminate Union propaganda. Lincoln, whose own salary was but twenty-five thousand dollars per annum, told her he thought her proposition " 'the most outrageous one ever made to any government on earth,' " to which Carroll responded stiffly that "the difference between us, was in our views, upon the value of intellectual labor, in the administration of government."[25]

The interview was private, but the story got out and Carroll was mortified to hear her proposition and Lincoln's reply discussed "at a public dinner table in a Washington Hotel. . . ." It was clear, she wrote the president, that he had misunderstood her proposition. The sum was vast, but considering the five thousand dollars already owed her, the cost of journeying to Europe, finding a place to stay, keeping herself (with no doubt at least one servant to keep house while she wrote), and then arranging for the publication and "circulation of my documents among the millions" in Europe, fifty thousand dollars was "a very reasonable sum." She warned the president, scattering commas needlessly, that ". . . physical force, *alone,* however strong it may be, can never bring this war, to a successful termination; unless, you avail yourself, of intellect, to make clear to the popular mind, the *issue,* about which, the country, is now, at war." There was not any "fair minded man" alive who would call her bill "absurd, or unjust." If it was too high, the error was not hers, "but that of the friends of yourself, and of the country," since she had written to a number of prominent lawyers, describing her work and the amount of her bill (excluding the fifty thousand dollar demand). All had thought her work intellectually sound and politically useful, and all approved her bill for her writing. But (and her martyr's crown gleamed again), if he could not bring himself to admit the value of her noble service to the Union cause, she would continue with love of country in her heart, "to labor for the salvation of our liberties to the very extent of my ability, as heretofore without any pecuniary reward, or the hope of any."[26]

Carroll did not include in this letter to Lincoln her proposition to bill the government for her services as a strategist. In truth, her conscience may have been nagging at her, however briefly. For the Tennessee campaign, the most long-lasting claim to fame Anne Carroll ever possessed in her constant search for power and recognition, was not solely her idea. While denying Carroll's claim as a military strategist in terms of timeliness was common among her critics, few realized that the plan's most salient features were lifted from the ideas of her contact in St. Louis, Charles M. Scott.[27]

Charles Scott was a Mississippi riverboat pilot who, unlike the vast majority of his colleagues, stayed with the Union in 1861. He had fled New Orleans at the outbreak of the war and made it up the Mississippi to Memphis, where he was captured by Brigadier General Gideon Pillow. Refusing to swear allegiance to the Confederacy, he escaped from custody and made his way to Cairo, Illinois, by 19 June. He described the Confederate batteries he had seen in the Memphis area to Union officials, then went on to St. Louis to escort his family to safety in Ohio.[28]

Scott's version of the events that led to the plan to invade the South by using the Tennessee and Cumberland rivers differed substantially from Carroll's story and, naturally enough, made him the hero instead of Carroll. When Scott heard Grant had been given a command in Cairo, he later wrote, he returned to the area in late September 1861 and volunteered his abilities as a pilot. He knew the topography of the area well, having been a keel-boatman on the Tennessee and having hunted in the area around the Cumberland as a boy. He often discussed the usefulness of the rivers as invasion routes with loyalist friends, but did not discuss the strategy with Grant because he thought Grant soon would be removed from command. He was, however, willing to share information on the river defenses with the general, and served Grant as a pilot of one of the transports at the Battle of Belmont on 7 November. His proximity to that deadly raid bothered him enough that, suffering from insomnia, he betook himself to write a letter to his wife who had come back to St. Louis to be nearer Scott. Mrs. Scott received the letter 10 November and shared it with the other ladies at the hotel's dining room. One of the ladies present was Anne Carroll.[29]

Why Carroll was in St. Louis is unclear. She may have gone there, as she claimed, to survey the territory and report back to Colonel Scott in the War Department. She did have relatives in St. Louis, but clearly was not staying with them (purportedly her sister-in-law's family, first cousins of Carroll's, were secessionists). She may have merely come along with Lemuel Evans, whom Seward sent on a mission in September to talk to Frémont about invading Texas.[30] At any rate, Carroll talked to Evans about the letter Mrs. Scott received, and Evans requested a meeting with the pilot. The following Sunday, 17 November, Scott met both Carroll and Evans.

One conversation led to another, and before long Scott was telling Evans and Carroll (after assurances both were "agents of the government") that the "true key to the West" was the Tennessee River and that the Mississippi was too heavily fortified to allow an invasion downstream. Evans knew enough about the topography of the area to value Scott's opinion. He urged Scott to communicate it to the authorities, but Scott protested that he "was not a good writer anyhow." Carroll, an almost silent partner to the conversation because of her deafness, was leaving the next day with dispatches for Washington. Scott, said Evans, could write to her, and she would place his plan before the War Department.[31]

Scott wrote to Carroll twice, sending the first letter about 23 November, the second about 15 December. By mid-December his opinion of Grant's staying-power improved, and he decided to share the plan with him as well in hopes "it might lead to something, perhaps to a command [by Grant] of the expedition." By 4 February, he wrote his wife that the Union forces were "in sight of Fort Henry. . . . I think that this move is the beginning of My Plan that I wrote to Miss Carroll at least it looks so." After the fall of Fort Henry on the sixth, he was convinced that "we will continue on untill we reach the State of Mississippi when I think we will end the War by taking the Memphis and Charleston Rail Road." Scott's optimism was premature, but Union forces did continue to move south toward the railroad center at Corinth, Mississippi. Scott continued to write to Carroll as well as to his wife. Carroll passed along ideas and strategy to Stanton. Scott's brother, E. A. Scott, also corresponded with Carroll. Through him, she gained access to Charles's letters to his wife, with their descriptions of battles and army life.[32]

Charles Scott wrote vividly and well of his experiences, in spite of his brother's opinion that he saw in his work a "deficiency in grammar, that causes him to smother his writings." His letters portray a man who loved his country and sought to serve its interests. He sent a detailed account of the navigability of the Illinois River to Representative Frank P. Blair, along with the promise of more information on western waterways if it was needed. But, he wrote Blair, "I wish you to distinctly understand that I am not an Applicant for office direct or Indirect but am only Influenced by the hope that I may do some good by giving the facts to you." In fact, when Carroll proposed she use her influence to get him a position, Scott told her he was "unfit by Education for any office in . . . Government but that of the Lowest," and he did not want to take jobs away from those more competent, or from those more needy, such as wounded Union soldiers.[33] His job as pilot, while not as lucrative as he could wish, nevertheless provided what he needed.

Scott wrote to Carroll throughout 1862, sending her his opinions of military strategy. He thought delaying the Union move up the Tennessee to take Fort Donelson was an error that delayed the capture of Vicksburg unnecessarily, a view that failed to take into account the obvious threat posed to Union forces by Confederate troops from the fort if left unreduced. He also thought that a Union victory in the eastern theater would send Confederates fleeing into Arkansas, Louisiana, Texas, and eventually Mexico. Gunboats at the mouths of the Red and Arkansas rivers and in the Yazoo River would help control the area. Carroll passed along his comments to the War Department. Sometimes she credited him, as in one letter to Stanton in which she praised Scott's "incalculable service" and requested Stanton to promote him to the surveyorship of New Orleans (a post for which Scott may have been qualified but would not likely have wanted with his family in Ohio).[34] Sometimes she did not credit him, as with the 30 November letter that first set out the Tennessee Plan, and in the letters to Lincoln in which she first wrote of her skills as a strategist in developing that plan.

The cordial relationship Carroll and Scott enjoyed may have been what kept Carroll from pushing herself too strongly as sole author of the plan. While the two letters she wrote to Lincoln in late June and early July 1862 made no mention of Scott as the source of her information, a safe assumption might also be that Carroll never read to Lincoln the second half of the letter wherein her claim as sole strategist was laid out. A Lincoln angry at Carroll's propositon to be paid fifty thousand dollars for her literary services was not a man to be given an additional bill for strategic services rendered. Carroll quite possibly might have stopped her reading at Lincoln's evaluation of her demand as "outrageous" and left his presence. Hot-tempered as she was, she was politically prudent enough to know when to retreat temporarily from an unpopular cause. As for Scott, he made no mention of feeling slighted, if indeed he knew of her attempts, and expressed no desire to be paid for his services as a strategist.

Carroll had also written to Colonel Scott and to John Tucker in the War Department in the spring and summer of 1862, seeking payment for her pamphlets, and none of those letters mention her military claim; her demands are for payment "for time, labor and means expended" in producing her pamphlets. Given Lincoln's reaction to her literary claims, Carroll probably simply decided she would be pushing her luck to demand payment for a plan of military strategy in the summer of 1862. Being a civilian and a woman would guarantee her little support should she choose to stake such a claim, particularly without Lincoln's support, and particularly if she chose to ignore Scott's role, since she had already mentioned his work to the War Department. Thus, in a letter to Stanton in September 1862 she made no mention of her strategy of the previous year, but instead concentrated on her past pamphlets and on future sales: "I believe in my work on the War Powers of this government I was the first writer who succeeded in placing the power of the government to make arrests for political offenses and to suspend the writ of Habeas Corpus on its true foundation!" This claim to premiership, Carroll argued, not only should be liberally rewarded, but she would be pleased to expand the circulation of *The War Powers,* or, "better still . . . write a *new paper,* specially on the powers of the Executive to suspend the Writ . . . and to arrest political offenders."[35]

Thomas Scott, largely responsible for Carroll's monetary predicament, was avoiding her by October of 1862. He had left the War Department in June and was back full-time as vice-president of the Pennsylvania Railroad. After she had tracked him down in Philadelphia, he wrote that if he had known where to find her he would have called. He was pleased to learn that her pamphlets had been deemed useful to the cause, but he continued to put her off, hoping she would be able to work with Tucker to resolve the matter. By this time, Carroll's financial worries were exacerbated by the collapse of her colonization plans with Aaron C. Burr for the Lincoln Colony in British Honduras. But in spite of her straitened finances, and in spite of her tentative attempt to bill the government for her military strategy, Carroll thought better of making her claim as a military strategist an issue. By the end of the war, in fact, she wrote a letter in the *National Intelligencer* praising both Charles Scott and Thomas Scott, deeming it

> a pleasant duty to make known to the American people how much they are indebted to Captain Charles M. Scott for the crowning victory which now thrills with joy every patriot heart. For when the history shall be correctly written it will be obliged to treat the campaign up the Tennessee River as the turning point which decided the triumph of the Union over treason and rebellion, and that this campaign was the result of the information herewith submitted [by Scott] was fully confirmed by . . . Thomas A. Scott, Assistant Secretary of War, to whom the country is incalculably indebted for inaugurating the movement.[36]

Carroll's letter not only recognized Charles Scott's role in developing the plan, but also (mistakenly) credited Thomas Scott with the plan's implementation because of his trip west shortly after she sent the plan to the War Department. But by 1876, when Carroll and Charles Scott faced each other in a congressional hearing on her claim to be the sole author of the Tennessee Campaign, Carroll's apparently gracious attempt to give credit where credit was assumed due began to acquire a character of deviousness.[37]

Claims against the government for services rendered during the Civil War were heard by various committees throughout the 1860s and 1870s and beyond. Scott and Carroll appeared before the House Committee on Military Affairs in 1876, both claiming authorship of the Tennessee Plan and both desiring payment for their work. Scott, unlike Carroll, had never thought of billing the government when the war ended. According to his testimony, he went to Washington in April 1865, a day or so before the letter praising him was printed, to ask for help from General Grant or anyone else with influence to help him obtain a tax exemption from a 25 percent duty on one thousand bales of cotton he was trying to sell. Scott lost money in the war: he worked for a lower salary to serve the Union, and when captured by General Pillow in the summer of 1861, he had received a certificate of valuation for his steamer that his partners traded for cotton. If he could get the cotton through the lines and sell it duty-free, he decided, that would even things up. He wrote to Carroll and called on her and Lemuel Evans, two persons who had given him the impression they had considerable influence with various high-ranking officials in Washington. There with Carroll, Evans wrote out a permit, Scott testified, that gave him permission to bring in not one thousand bales, but ten thousand bales duty-free. Scott handed the permit back, but Evans assured him that "everybody else was doing it" and proposed that Scott should give him an interest in the cotton: half of the profit from the extra 9,000 bales would go to Evans— and half of that to Carroll. Scott refused the permit "in toto" and left.[38]

A few days later, the letter signed by Carroll praising Scott appeared in the *National Intelligencer.* The author's motivation might have been the highly noble one of honest praise. More likely, though, it was an attempt to bribe Scott with recognition in hopes of getting him to return for the ten-thousand-bale permit or, at the least, to keep him from disclosing Evans's dishonesty. Apparently the article attracted Scott's attention, for the three met again. Carroll, Scott said, "began to soft soap me," telling him that she and Judge Evans had written the article so they could garner public support for a claim to Congress that would pay Scott for his military strategy. They would "engineer it through" in Scott's name, and Scott would divide the proceeds with them. "I told them I had only done my duty and all I asked was the privilege of bringing in my cotton. . . ." The "thing dropped right there," and Scott returned to the West. His cotton claim was lost in the shuffle of bureaucracy.[39]

Carroll's version of the circumstances which had prompted her generous letter disclosing Scott as the author of the Tennessee Plan was a bit different. She granted that Scott had come to Washington for help in bringing in his cotton, worth about thirty thousand dollars. But, she testified, Scott had offered her one-fourth of that amount for her help. She refused the payment, since aiding Scott merely consisted of going to the Treasury Department to get a copy of the regulations. She then sent them to Scott, telling him when he complied with them he could get his cotton duty-free. She had asked for nothing and received nothing for her favor to him. As for the article in the *National Intelligencer,* Carroll had not even written it; Lemuel Evans had, even though her name was printed as author. And Scott had paid the paper thirty-five dollars to guarantee its insertion.[40]

Evans, testifying on behalf of Carroll's claim, said Scott had asked him for a permit for his cotton. This he said in spite of Carroll's assertion moments earlier that "no papers were drawn; none were needed." Confronted with Scott's accusation that he had written a permit, Evans admitted that he might have suggested the proper form for Scott's permit, but that would have been only to Carroll and would have been in her handwriting, an admission that might explain Carroll's letter which, Scott claimed, told him she had sent him the authority he needed. As for the article in the *Intelligencer,* Evans wrote it "not only to do Captain Scott justice, but also to give him prominence and standing, as he complained of injustice having been done him."[41]

Scott's sense of injustice had been building for a long time. Of 128 St. Louis and New Orleans pilots, he was one of only five Union men. He had to take a pay cut during the war from $300 to $250 per month. After the war, when he tried to return to work as a pilot, he had trouble getting work: "A steamboat agent in New Orleans told me he would not ship freight on a boat that I was connected with, and would use his best influence to prevent others also." He lost his steamer to the Confederates, lost his cotton that was the steamer's exchange, and lost his temper when he discovered in the late 1860s that Carroll had begun promoting herself as "claimant for remuneration for originating the Tennessee campaign."[42]

In 1871 Scott and Carroll had met in St. Louis. She "found him after money and wanting me to pay him, for the information," she wrote her uncle, but by that time she had convinced herself that she was the sole author of the Tennessee Plan. "I have never assumed to have discovered the fact," she continued, acknowledging Scott's contribution. But her work was invaluable "in perceiving how these facts could be made available to the salvation of the Union. There are certain classes of mind who cannot distinguish between the knowledge of a fact and the uses [to] which it may be applied." Carroll was furious at Scott's interference. "While the pilot, Mr. Scott, can do himself no good, he can invite the enemies of my claim to try and defeat it."[43]

By 1872 Carroll's claim had acquired newspaper, congressional, and pamphlet support. Scott decided to try his luck before Congress as well. Carroll had failed him, both on the cotton permit and on finding him a patronage position after the war, but his overall motive was not revenge. A mutual acquaintance, L. S. McCoy, reinforced Carroll's impression that Scott was after money. He had "little faith in the generosity of Claim grants," or whether his petition would work, but financial woes and a pushy brother-in-law (a "Mr. Fish") had convinced him to take his claim to the government. He "would prefer to have your & the Judge's [Evans] cooperation if it can be conveniently had," wrote McCoy. Scott reassured Carroll that "I do not believe that I will injure your claim, but rather strengthen it. . . . [I]f you like the idea I think you can make more out of it (my claim) than you can out of your own," presumably referring to the three-way split Evans had allegedly offered in 1865.[44]

Scott underestimated Carroll's ability to make something momentous out of something miniscule, however. By 1876, while Scott's claim had gone nowhere, Carroll had turned her original $5,000 claim into a request for $250,000 "as compensation for originating the Tennessee Campaign."[45] An angry and embittered Scott faced Carroll in that congressional hearing and lost.

Both Carroll's and Scott's claims to be the authors of the Tennessee campaign rest primarily on circumstantial evidence. While Carroll would continue to build on her shaky foundations until her elaborate tale hid its questionable core, as will be shown, Scott retired from the fray. Only in 1889 was he again driven to make public his part in the Tennessee campaign, when he published a pamphlet regarding Carroll's "Fradulent" [*sic*] claim. He deemed it his duty, he wrote in his introduction, "to prevent this raid on the Treasury that I am sure is being prepared for during the present administration." Scott included selected portions of the House document that had been published after the 1876 hearing, letters of endorsement for his "valuable information" from both Grant and Acting Rear Admiral S. P. Lee in support of his contention that the strategy was his rather than Carroll's, and a letter in which he had promised Carroll that if she did not desist in her claim, he would "take means to explode it." To make his position appear as disinterested as possible, Scott even included a petition submitted by his friends some years previous to the 1876 hearing when they had requested a pension for him for his inventions of a signal system used by passing boats and a device to protect boilers on board boats, as well as for his "valuable information to those in charge of the Tennessee Campaign." The pension request had never passed and Scott swore he had had no part in getting it up. Moreover, he had only mentioned it before the hearing "to show the standing in which I have been held." In fact, however, Scott had told the House committee in 1876 that, while he had not come before them "expecting pay for doing my duty as a loyal man," justice demanded that he should be given credit as the campaign's originator, "and if your honorable body think that any compension is due the author, I claim that that compensation is due to your petitioner."[46]

As far as Scott, Evans, Carroll, and the cotton claim were concerned, Scott printed only his version of events in his pamphlet, but with Carroll's history of self-puffery, pretensions to influence, and the lingering rumors of deception that survived from her days in New York, Scott's accusations seem sound. Given Carroll's constant need of money, if Scott's offer of one-fourth the value of the cotton (seventy-five hundred dollars) for her help had been made, as she claimed it had, she would have taken it. Since she swore she did not, "nor did I ever think it worth while to inquire," the greedier version of Scott's claim that Evans had offered to obtain a tax exemption for him ten times his original request in exchange for a half share of the profits to split with Carroll certainly seems more likely. And Scott's departure from Washington in April 1865 did not end Carroll's attempts to make a profit on the cotton trade. She contacted John Tucker in the War Department, but by May, he advised her that "the decline in Cotton &c has . . . largely diminished the margin for profits."[47]

There is no question that both Scott and Carroll had an equal share in developing what each called the Tennessee Plan. Scott was an experienced pilot and a strong Unionist who took every opportunity to help the war effort. No doubt he did discuss the western waterways with Grant or other Union men. And Carroll did have enough access to Colonel Thomas Scott in the War Department to present the well-written and strategically sound plan she, Scott, and Evans had developed, as well as enough initiative to write to Stanton and Lincoln to pass along Scott's information and tell them how to run the war. But as far as either one of them materially affecting the outcome of the war by the submission of the Tennessee campaign plan, both strategists were too late in their actions. General Grant made that clear in a letter to his friend, Representative Elihu B. Washburne, written during the congressional search for a hero to reward after the successes of Henry and Donelson:

> I see the credit of attacking the enemy by the way of the Tennessee and Cumberland is variously attributed! It is little to talk about it being the great wisdom of any Gen. that first brought forth this plan of attack.
>
> Our gunboats were running up the Ten. and Cumberland rivers all fall and winter watching the progress of the rebels on these works. Gen. Halleck no doubt thought of this route long ago and I am shure [*sic*] I did.[48]

The Union leaders knew of the importance of the Tennessee and Cumberland rivers. The Confederates had built Forts Henry and Donelson because of the strategic importance of those rivers. The army knew their importance, the navy knew their importance, even the *New York Times* had printed a letter that not only detailed the importance of the rivers as alternate routes to the Mississippi, but mentioned the possibility of cutting the Charleston and Memphis Railroad by going up those rivers. That letter was published 17 November 1861, before Carroll had even returned to Washington. As for her comments regarding the importance of relieving loyalists in Tennessee and Kentucky, they were hardly original either. Lincoln was well aware of the importance of those areas to the Union cause by September 1861. Simply put, given the time constraints within which Carroll and Scott both placed their actions, neither one can be taken seriously by military historians as unsung heroes who saved the Union with their brilliant strategy.[49]

But Carroll took herself very seriously as precisely such a figure, and that is part of her story as well. Obsessed with a desire for recognition and payment, once again twisting and turning the truth until it fit her perception, Carroll sought the recognition of the world for her claim. From the fall of Forts Henry and Donelson in February 1862 until her death thirty-two years later, Carroll's other interests gradually faded until her desire for recognition became her consuming passion.

SIX

The Search for Vindication

Gratified by the success of the federal armies in the western theater moving in apparent response to her plan, Anne Carroll continued to make suggestions of military strategy to the War Department in the spring of 1862. On 2 May she gave the government information Charles Scott had sent her that skiffs and canoes were being sent to the Yazoo River. Fearing that Confederates would flee down the Yazoo to the Mississippi and thence to Texas and Mexico, Scott suggested the Yazoo be watched with Federal gunboats. On 14 May Carroll wrote again, reiterating Scott's comments on the necessity of guarding the Yazoo and recommending the occupation of Vicksburg. General Henry Halleck was creeping toward Corinth, and the "impending battle in North Mississippi" would force the enemy to retreat to Vicksburg, she reasoned, so they could take the railroad from there to escape into Texas.[1]

Carroll's continued assumption that the Confederates would flee west of the Mississippi rather than retreating south from Corinth by either the Tombigbee River or the Mobile and Ohio Railroad, might have been due to the influence of her Texan friend, Lemuel Evans. Evans is an important but shadowy figure in Carroll's life. They probably met when he took office as an American party congressman in 1855; they traveled together to St. Louis in October 1861 and corresponded frequently when separated from each other, but only a few of Evans's letters survive in Carroll's papers. Though she remained "Miss Carroll" to him until his death in 1877, the nineteenth-century formality did not hide the intimacy of their friendship. Whether they were lovers is difficult to judge. Carroll had told Thurlow

Weed that she would go to Mexico with Evans if he was appointed minister. Her journey with him to St. Louis was apparently with no other companion or chaperone, but that was not unheard-of even in the early days of the war. She traveled with him to Texas and cared for him during an illness. Their relationship was public enough for her to discuss him with her family, including her father, and for former Connecticut Senator Truman Smith to tease Evans to "give my love to Miss Carroll if you dare!!"[2] Either Carroll presumed her age and her known political activities would protect her from gossip regarding Evans, or she did not care what rumors flew. She had found a man who shared her political views, championed her cause, and probably helped assuage her pain at the death of John Causin.

Evans had gone to Texas just prior to his trip to St. Louis with Carroll to find out if Confederates were receiving supplies from Mexico. Discovering that the Union had no plans to attack Texas, and being thus satisfied he had done all he could, he resigned his State Department commission of August 1861, and by March 1862 had returned to Washington where he remained near Carroll for most of the rest of the war. Carroll continued to write for the war effort, but her attempts to contribute were soon rejected. Although Evans told the new Secretary of War Stanton that an agreement existed between Carroll and the War Department, Thomas Scott left 1 June 1862, and Carroll now dealt with the new Assistant Secretary Peter H. Watson, who proved less than amiable regarding her work. In July and August she resubmitted her bill for $5,000 for work already done; on 9 September she suggested another pamphlet for the department's consideration. In January 1863 she submitted her bill again, this time adjusted upward to $6,250, noting that Thomas Scott had directed her not to credit $1,250 she had received from him since he had paid that out of his pocket and, when the whole bill was paid, she would return that amount to Scott.[3]

By September 1862 Watson had decided to pay Carroll off by giving her $750 as "reasonable compensation . . . for the public service" she had rendered. Carroll had taken the money and signed a receipt as a payment "in full for the above account and of all demands against the United States government." Watson considered the case closed, but Carroll, having found a source of income that enabled her to pursue her favorite activities of writing and politicking, interpreted Watson's payment not as a way to end her importunities but as a confirmation that the oral agreement she had made with Scott was still in force. Accordingly, when Carroll wrote another pamphlet on the rights of the seceded states and submitted it to the department in October 1863, she no doubt expected a continuation of the account.[4]

When Carroll followed up her pamphlet with another letter that suggested a paper on emancipation, Watson had had enough. While he had been willing to pay at least a part of Carroll's bill, she was, he said, " 'entirely mistaken in assuming that I have undertaken to employ you to write for this Department or to compensate you for writing.' " Carroll was greatly surprised at his refusal. Watson, she insisted, had asked her to call on him. Obviously, he must have wanted her to continue to work for the War Department. Now, she wrote, if he would simply do his duty and lay her ideas before Stanton, "I cannot doubt that, could the Sec. give his *attention* to the proposition, he would at once concur in the *utility* of such a production as mine would be." In a frigid reply to her request, and "to avoid all misunderstanding and all necessity for further correspondence on this topic," Watson wrote, he was "authorized to state that the Secretary of War has never employed a public writer, on any subject whatever, and the department accordingly cannot avail itself of your services."[5] Carroll was only momentarily dissuaded by this icy dismissal; she would take up her cause again late that year. In the meantime, though, the presidential election of 1864 captured her attention.

Carroll did not care much for Lincoln's policies as president, particularly after his failure to follow her counsel regarding emancipation and colonization. As early as the off-year elections of 1862 she became certain that it had "ever been the purpose of the President and the faction, with whom he acts, to abolish slavery, in the entire South, and to restore the States upon no other condition." Lincoln's removal of General George McClellan from the command of the Army of the Potomac in the fall of 1862, after McClellan failed to capitalize on the Union victory at Antietam by pursuing the Confederates, was, according to Carroll, Lincoln's way to gain control of the army so he could establish emancipation by force. Although Carroll maintained a cordial relationship with Lincoln's Attorney General Bates, and included a pipe for Lincoln in a gift of tobacco pipes she sent to Bates, by 1864 she was convinced that Lincoln had to be defeated to save the country from a military despotism.[6]

In June, Carroll attended the Republican nominating convention in Baltimore; in August, she went to the Democratic convention in Chicago. While she would later write Salmon P. Chase that she believed "an irreparable mistake was committed" when he was passed over for the Republican nomination, for Carroll, the Republican party was a lost cause regardless of the nominee. The president, the growing power of the Radicals and the momentary candidacy of John Charles Frémont all required supporters to accept the emancipation of slaves. Carroll was convinced that the Republicans were too intransigent to compromise on the question of slavery. That intransigence would destroy the Union if the party prevailed in the upcoming election.[7]

Even though Carroll perhaps began to sense the inevitability of forced emancipation, telling Chase she had "no sympathy with a dominant race, insolent & oppressive, who violate all the conditions of liberty and then claim to be the authors of freedom," most likely she supported Democratic nominee George B. McClellan. His platform called for the restoration of the Union without regard to slavery. The *Washington National Intelligencer,* to which Carroll contributed various articles, supported McClellan for reasons echoing Carroll's dislike of Lincoln. Lincoln's "despotic assumptions under the specious plea of 'military necessity' " made clear his intention, according to the *Intelligencer,* "to change the character of the war from the single object of upholding the Government to that of a direct interference with the domestic institutions of the States." McClellan, on the other hand, "promised to look with a single eye to the restoration of the Union under the Constitution," and would not "be jostled from his purpose by extraneous influences."[8]

The *National Intelligencer* reflected Carroll's opinions throughout the Civil War, and in November 1864 she wrote Thurlow Weed, Edward Bates, and Lemuel Evans that its editor, Colonel William W. Seaton, had asked her to assume the editorship of the paper. To Weed she explained that Seaton would be forced to shut down if Lincoln were reelected because of Seaton's longtime opposition to the administration. "Even if Mr. L—— is not elected, he will have to sell it all the same. . . ." She invited Weed to take part of the paper in a joint stock company to raise the necessary one-hundred-thousand-dollar purchase price. Seaton would give Carroll twenty thousand dollars of that "to carry on the paper." "I have no earthly doubt," she wrote, "about my power to conduct the editorial department. . . . I could make it a great lever & I think, with due modesty, you will not dissent from this opinion."[9]

Weed turned her down. Edward Bates appreciated her "talents and acquirements" but cautioned that she might not understand fully "the arduous labor required" to run the paper. Lemuel Evans, however, urged Carroll to accept. "I have thought for some time that your vocation is *editorial."* He wrote from Chicago with the election results. Lincoln's reelection, he thought, meant a "consolidated centralized *Despotism,"* in which Washington City would become like the Rome of old. "Henceforth," he warned, "all success depends on the ability to be . . . a part of the governing power . . . or a *flatterer* of the governing power." Carroll could achieve that status more easily, Evans thought, if she were editor of the *Intelligencer.*[10]

As is true of many events in Carroll's life, there is no corroborative evidence to support Carroll's claim that Seaton offered her the paper. It is possible. Josephine Seaton, the colonel's surviving daughter, thought enough of Carroll's talents as a writer to consider carefully her offer to write his biography and to suggest that Carroll edit a collection of her father's letters or a "political history of my Father . . . or *leaders* of the Intelligencer, which would no doubt be valuable, and *take.*" The editorship seems a bit of a farfetched proposition for Carroll to have invented out of thin air. But if it was offered to her, it came to naught by December 1864. Seaton retired, a new editor took over, and Carroll began to dun the War Department again to pay her claim.[11]

After the war ended in April 1865, times were hard for Carroll, and she kept constant pressure on the War Department to pay her the rest of the money she believed it owed her. She cut expenses by moving in with her brother Harry in Baltimore and searched for other sources of income, asking Seward to send her on a tour of the Southern states "in some confidential capacity for the Govt." in order to ascertain "their feelings, sentiments and aims" as the country moved toward reconciliation. She moved back to Dorchester County with her father for a short time and worked on a history of the war, asking for reports from such primary sources as Seward and Navy Secretary Welles. She filed a formal claim with the War Department's Board of Claims, still making no mention of any work but her pamphlets, and convinced Thomas Scott to endorse her bill for her writing again. He agreed, telling the government that since "all she asks is but a small matter . . . if under my control I should have no hesitation in allowing it." She briefly looked for work as a teacher in New York City and, pen ever at the ready, continued her prewar activities of seeking patronage positions for friends. Her fortune had changed little in the interim: though she told her colonization ally Aaron Burr, for whom she lobbied nearly two years for a post in Tripoli, that the senator she lobbied would "do anything" for her, "and he *has,*" no appointment was forthcoming. She also continued to write on political questions of the day and revised old articles for resale.[12]

In the winter of 1868–69, Carroll traveled to Texas with Lemuel Evans to report on the Texas Constitutional Convention, in which he took part. She met the famous former spy Belle Boyd on the boat from New Orleans to Galveston and found her "just the bold forward creature you may suppose . . . disgusted every one. . . . [T]alks of nothing but herself—what great men she met . . . &C." She wrote a long report on the Texas convention to President-elect Grant, suggesting Texas be divided into several new states to destroy the power of secessionists. Evans was a leader of the "divisionists" in the convention, and Carroll supported his position enthusiastically. When the convention successfuly voted to send a delegation to Washington for congressional help in dividing Texas, Carroll rejoiced. As usual, she took full credit for the success of an event in which she was only marginally involved. Boasting to her father, she wrote that the new constitution and "the division are both successes, that I can prove, I have been the means under Providence of bringing about. . . ." Providential blessing on the divisionists proved momentary. Congress did not aid them, and the idea of making three or more states out of Texas soon died.[13]

Although Carroll originally planned to return home as soon as the convention ended, Evans became seriously ill, so she stayed to care for him. "When he got alarmed," she wrote her sister, "he proposed to turn over all his effects & money to me at once," another indication of the intimacy of their long relationship. Fortunately, Evans recovered. In the meantime, Carroll amused herself during his recuperation with a visit to a lunatic asylum ("almost all the females are so from the *War*—loss of friends or property or both") and otherwise enjoyed a "*glorious* country."[14]

But always in Carroll's life there was her claim. On 10 May 1869 Carroll withdrew all her papers from the War Department's files. On 31 March 1870 she petitioned the United States Senate to award her "compensation commensurate with the service" she had provided the government with her pamphlets which "communicated throughout the struggle important facts and suggestions," and her military observations which induced the government "to adopt the Tennessee River instead of the Mississippi. . . ."[15]

There are several possible reasons why Carroll chose to enter the public forum with her claim instead of continuing her pleas and petitions to the War Department. Edwin Stanton, whom she believed had been kept uninformed of her claim and therefore had been unable to aid her, left office in 1868 and died in December of 1869. Recently elected President Grant, whom she may have believed would support her claim in order not to appear unchivalrous before his public, was in a position to wield considerable power in her favor. And Benjamin Wade, retiring from the Senate to Ohio, had written her on 1 March 1869 that:

> I cannot take leave of public life without expressing my deep sense of your services to the country during the whole period of our national troubles. Although a citizen of a state almost unanimously disloyal and deeply sympathizing with secession, especially the wealthy and aristocratical class of her people, to which you belonged, yet, in the midst of such surroundings, you emancipated your own slaves at a great sacrifice of personal interest, and with your powerful pen defended the cause of the Union and loyalty as ably and effectively as it has ever yet been defended.
>
> From my position on the Committee of the Conduct of the War I know that some of the most successful expeditions of the war were suggested by you, among which I might instance the expedition up the Tennessee River. . . . I also know

in what high estimation your services were held by President Lincoln; and I cannot leave this subject without sincerely hoping that the Government may yet confer on you some token of acknowledgment for all these services and sacrifices.[16]

Wade continued to write letters in favor of Carroll's claim. In February 1872 he wrote the Committee of Military Affairs considering Carroll's claim that President Lincoln had told him "that the merit of this plan was due to Miss Carroll" and that both Lincoln and Stanton had told him they wanted the government to reward her for her plan.[17] He repeated his praise of Carroll's accomplishments and worth throughout the 1870s.

Wade's most supportive letter in Carroll's behalf, however, was not published until 1881, three years after his death. In that letter, dated 4 April 1876, Wade claimed credit for convincing Lincoln to use Carroll's plan in spite of its origin. "It was a great work to get the matter started; you have no idea of it," he supposedly wrote her. "We almost fought for it." The need for secrecy at the time had precluded recognition of Carroll then, but "if ever there was a righteous claim on earth, you have one."[18]

At first glance, Wade's letters seemed to remove all doubt regarding the legitimacy of Carroll's claim. As the chairman of the Committee on the Conduct of the War, Wade's approval of her claim was powerful support. But there is no evidence that the committee ever discussed the movement up the Tennessee River. Most of their published hearings concerning the western theater during the time Carroll set her claim (the winter of 1861–62) dealt with Frémont's difficulties in supplying his men and with the confusion in command at the Battle of Fort Donelson.[19] No evidence exists to suggest that Wade and his committee ever dealt with the strategy of the Tennessee campaign.

Moreover, Caroline Wade, the senator's wife, was on close terms with Carroll, and it was through Mrs. Wade that Carroll corresponded with Benjamin Wade. Considering Carroll's penchant for bypassing middlemen, it would hardly seem likely she would use an intermediary to approach Wade on such a vital matter as establishing her claim. It would seem logical, therefore, to assume that Wade had at first simply written a nice letter of thanks to a loyal citizen who had told his wife and him what she deserved credit for. And, as the years went by, Carroll no doubt convinced the aging senator she deserved more than thanks for her work. Wade, who like many others responded favorably to the idea of Carroll as a heroine, saw in her claim a chance to thank all the women of the war. He continued to support her with letters of increasing fulsomeness. But the letter claiming he had fought for her plan, the one dated 1876 and not published until after Wade's death, was almost certainly a forgery.[20]

Wade's endorsement of Carroll's claim in 1869, however, clearly had convinced her she had enough evidence to bring her claim to the public forum and pursue it through Congress beginning in 1870. She started slowly, couching her petition for payment with feminine delicacy and in the mildest of terms. Carroll knew she was treading on dangerous ground, but reassured those who cautioned her, writing that "in pressing my claim . . . I cannot by any possibility detract from our brave and heroic commanders to whom the country owes so much and so far from opposing me I believe that as a class they would be gratified to see me or any one properly rewarded acc. to the part performed in this mighty drama."[21]

As her petition failed to attract notice, she determined she would strengthen it with more favorable testimonies. She wrote to John Tucker, former assistant secretary of war and still associated with Thomas Scott, to see if Scott would support her claim. He was sure the colonel would, Tucker wrote, but Scott was out of town. He would give him the papers when he returned. At the time, Scott was in Texas, trying to develop the Texas and Pacific Railroad. Lemuel Evans was there too, newly appointed as chief justice to the Texas Supreme Court. And Carroll had a railroad charter to offer Scott for his support.[22]

When Scott returned, he did indeed write a letter to Senator Jacob M. Howard, chairman of the Committee on Military Affairs, supporting Carroll's claim. But since Scott's letter referred only to Carroll's pamphlets, which Scott thought "were valuable at that time and served a good purpose," Howard asked Carroll why Scott had not mentioned her military strategy. Scott hadn't because she didn't ask him to, Carroll said. And she didn't because Scott told her she "had better not," Carroll explained, "because military men were very tenacious & jealous." A few days after that conversation between Howard and Carroll, Scott wrote a second letter of support. This time, and for the first time, he included a specific mention of Carroll's Tennessee Plan, "which plan I submitted to the Secretary of War, and its general ideas were adopted. . . . Through the adoption of this plan the country had been saved millions," Scott wrote, entitling Carroll "to the kind consideration of Congress."[23]

With additional proof of her service provided by Scott along with the support of Ben Wade, Carroll thought victory was certain. "I have wonderful friends," she wrote her father from Washington in January 1871. "All my labours here brought me friends." The Committee on Military Affairs reported favorably on her claim and recommended she be paid for her "highly meritorious services."[24]

There the matter rested. Read, passed to a second reading and printed, the bill never moved out of Congress. Maryland Senator George Vickers thought it might be due to Carroll's anti-Republican sentiments. Perhaps if she had come forth immediately after the war, he wrote, she might have succeeded. Carroll blamed inaction on the bill on Massachusetts Senator Henry Wilson. Wilson, a former Know-Nothing and chairman of the Committee on Military Affairs throughout the course of the Civil War, failed to shepherd Carroll's bill through the Senate. And Chairman Howard himself had "proved a traitor & would have done me injustice," Carroll claimed to her sister. "You have no idea how false he played."[25]

Defeated but momentarily, Carroll worked to gather more letters of support and to increase her visibility as claimant. She made friends with Samuel Hunt, secretary to Henry Wilson, back as chairman of the Committee on Military Affairs, and did all she could to curry Hunt's favor. As an insider, Hunt suggested she use publicity to help her claim and obtain as many supportive letters as she could. Carroll wrote to Millard Fillmore, who remembered their meeting in November 1861 on her way back from Tennessee but could remember none of the specifics of the conversation. Besides, he wrote, he was sure she would prevail in Congress regardless of his faulty memory. Carroll did add support to her claim with copies of complimentary letters received from such men as Edward Bates, Edward Everett, Reverdy Johnson, and Horace Binney. She included as well a statement on the value of the Tennessee strategy from Chief Justice Lemuel Evans, by now possessed of his more impressive title.[26]

Pressing Hunt to use his influence on Wilson that winter, however, Carroll confronted two immovable individuals. Hunt was not willing to jeopardize his future. He had to be cautious, he later wrote Carroll. Appearing to be her advocate would diminish his usefulness. Wilson would not place the bill on the calendar and would not discuss it with Hunt at all. Apparently he wanted more proof.[27]

Wilson received additional proof of a sort in the form of a pamphlet published to support Carroll's claim. Although issued anonymously, the author was Lemuel Evans. Carroll, he wrote, "had the genius to grasp the situation and perceive that the fall of Richmond could not destroy the rebellion, and the Mississippi river could not be opened on its waters; that the Government must seize a strategic position within the cotton States, and if a fatal blow could be inflicted, it must fall there." To Carroll, alone, "therefore, must be given the credit of having solved the problem of the military destruction of the 'Southern Confederacy.' "[28]

In his pamphlet, published in the winter of 1871–72, Evans added another laurel to Carroll's wreath by including a letter which she supposedly had written to Assistant War Secretary Tucker regarding Vicksburg, pointing out that the city was too heavily fortified to take from the river. The Federals had discovered that in the spring of 1862 when Admiral David G. Farragut had failed to take the town. Carroll recommended that the town be taken by a land route. Going down the Mississippi Central Railroad from Memphis to capture Jackson, Mississippi, and thus to cut off Vicksburg from the east was a plan that would save the Union millions of dollars.[29] Grant had in fact made such a move, which Evans cited as clear evidence of Carroll's military genius. Her letter, dated October 1862, however, was almost certainly a post facto creation. The original, if there was one, did not survive, and no evidence exists of its fortuitous receipt by anyone connected with the Vicksburg campaign.

Saving the government money became part of Carroll's claim to fame in Evans's pamphlet. After all, she saved the government "three thousand millions" of dollars, Evans estimated, by her work in the war. Surely Congress would not begrudge her what he suggested she ask for: the pay and rank of a major general retroactive to 30 November or 1 December 1861. He thought this form of request might be more appealing than a specific dollar amount would be.[30]

Hunt agreed with Evans's idea. He viewed Carroll's method of asking for money as "rather pretty and practical" and no doubt befitting her womanly nature. Her claim, he thought, was more valuable because as a woman, Carroll could serve as a symbol of all the women of the war. It was becoming painfully apparent to Carroll, however, that her continued push for recognition and payment of her claim was meeting with considerable disapproval from the public, particularly among her female acquaintances. She dismissed it, however, writing her sister that "women . . . are as a class jealous & envious of their sex. None are allowed to come around me, except that Miss Munroe who is a great bore & I have no doubt would at heart rejoice, if she could have seen me defeated."[31]

By May 1872 Carroll was convinced once again that she was winning the battle. "My enemies have fought me desperately to defeat me or rather my claim," she wrote her father. "We fought them and contested every inch on the battle field and the Lord being my Helper in His own good time has given me great extraordinary victory!" But Carroll spoke too soon. The bill for her relief, read and referred to the Committee on Military Affairs, died. "You can't trust a professional politician," Carroll told her sister. But she had hope nonetheless. "It is wonderful with what strength & energy Our Father in Heaven endows us in such peculiar trying times. . . ."[32]

In August Carroll was ready to do battle again. She went to New York City to work for the Republicans in the presidential election of 1872, though she was less interested in getting Grant reelected, "so narrow and selfish his nature," than in working for Henry Wilson as his vice-president, no doubt deciding Wilson's gratitude for her support would help her cause in Congress. The vice-presidential candidate, "a respectable man," she wrote, "will carry the ticket." In November, anxious over a new round of

© Micaela C. Ayers, 1989

Carroll's plan to reduce Vicksburg, which she later claimed she had sent the War Department in October 1862, suggested a move down the Mississippi Central Railroad and the Mobile & Ohio Railroad to control the cities of Jackson and Meridian. Control of these two towns would force the Confederates to move east of the Tombigbee River and to evacuate Vicksburg.

After five futile attempts, one of them down the Mississippi Central Railroad, Union forces under Grant moved down the western bank of the Mississippi, thus avoiding the Yazoo Delta east of the river. By May, Grant had crossed the Mississippi below Grand Gulf and was headed for Jackson. From that town he would move to take Vicksburg from the east by siege. The city surrendered on 4 July, 1863.

hearings on her claim, she contacted Hunt, who remained with Wilson after his election. She asked if he could "think of any one in this city who has more than ordinary influence with Wilson? One whom I could approach by an offer of money if successful. I would allow any per centage at all could I find the party of the right status. . . ." With Grant returned to office, Carroll thought, the Republicans could "surely now be magnanimous" and concede her claim, since Grant, after all, had never bothered to claim that he had conceived the Tennessee campaign. Carroll finally appealed to Vice-president Wilson himself, telling him that "President Grant as long ago as [18]67, *advised me to claim the service in history,"* and Ben Wade had told her that the president would stand by her regarding her claim. Give justice now, she pleaded, for "if I am not successful now after all, I shall not live I fear ever to be."[33] Because Wilson's access to Grant was considerably greater than Carroll's, he certainly would have known what Grant desired regarding her claim. But Congress adjourned with no action taken.

Immediately after the new year, Carroll reached out for public support again with a new pamphlet. She restated her claim and added the argument that because historians could not agree on whose idea the campaign was (they credited Halleck, Grant, Foote, Buell, McClellan, and Frémont variously), it was clear that the plan came from none of the generals and was therefore unknown when Carroll submitted it. Wade had written another supporting letter, telling the committee that Lincoln had informed him *"that the merit of this plan was due to Miss Carroll."* Secretary Stanton had agreed, and *"fully recognized"*—on his deathbed, according to Wade— *"Miss Carroll's service to the Union in the organization of this campaign."*[34]

Throughout 1873 Carroll gathered letters of support for her next assault on Congress. Cassius M. Clay, out of the country as United States minister to Russia in 1861, endorsed her claim, telling her he saw "no reason why officers and soldiers who fought in the field should be more entitled to honor and emoluments, than the many eminent women, who showed great patriotism and rendered essential aid. . . ." George Vickers promised his vote the next time around, but advised her she should condense her claim to make it easier reading for busy politicians. Carroll also wrote to Civil War historians J. T. Headley and Dr. D. W. Draper, correcting their histories of the war. Lemuel Evans still supported her in this new round, warning her to keep her claim above politics if she could, "by extreme circumspection— remaining wholly in the background." Get the appropriation first; then she could "write or visit or mix in any movement. . . ."[35]

In September everything stopped for Carroll as her beloved father fell ill. He died on 3 October. Carroll was devastated. "I have lost the best Father, the most perfect of all the race, not in my judgment only, but in that of all who had the fortune to know him," she wrote to her old friend, Millard Fillmore. Her deep grief did not blind her to practicalities, however; shortly after her father's death she questioned his former lawyer in Somerset County to see if the sale of her father's home in 1837 had been proper. If the estate was entailed, for instance, she might be able to get it back for her brother Harry. No, wrote Isaac Jones, "I have never heard any question of the absolute title in the grantee of your father." All Carroll would inherit was her father's good name. Her uncle comforted her: his brother might have had "the usual Carroll-infirmity of great lack of the faculty of making money," he wrote, but "he had all their nobility of character, kindness of heart and sympathy of nature," loving "his family and children with almost feminine fondness. . . ."[36]

By 1874 Carroll was back at work. Her publication of another pamphlet had attracted the notice of Charles M. Scott, who defended himself as true author of the Tennessee Plan in a letter to the *New York Daily Tribune.* Questioned once again by the Committee on War Claims about the lack of contemporaneous proof regarding the official nature of her mission to Tennessee, Carroll replied that she realized she had omitted any statement in her early claims that she had told Colonel Scott she would visit the West. She had written to Scott when she was there and at his official request, she insisted, reporting on "any thing that I might deem important to the cause." But he had not written to her because he was afraid his letters would not arrive in time and because he knew she would be returning to Washington soon. The lack of correspondence did not mean, she reassured the committee, that she had undertaken her mission on her own. All her work was done under the authority of the War Department. Another pamphlet came out in December 1874. In that one, however, Carroll at last responded to the political resistance to her military claims and made her literary services a separate claim from the more controversial military service.[37]

Charles Scott's attack in the press had an effect. The *New York Times* wondered if Carroll had bothered to press her claim while Halleck was still alive, since he was the obvious author of the plan. Carroll's defense of her claim and her assertion that she had started her petitions prior to Halleck's demise were not printed in the *Times,* but she was given the chance to respond in public at last on that hot July day in 1876 when the two claimants, Scott and Carroll, faced each other in the Committee on Military Affairs hearing in Washington. Carroll, with Evans by her side, wore down her accuser, who retired from the fray. The field was hers, and with Scott more or less consigned to the oblivion of the Midwest once again, she renewed her battle.[38]

But the battle would soon be hers alone. Lemuel Evans died in Washing-

ton 1 July 1877. The *Galveston Daily News* took note of his passing, surprised that it seemed "to have been an event less noted by the press of the
State than would have been anticipated. . . ." Evans had supported Carroll from the earliest days of her claim. He gave both Thomas Scott and
Charles Scott credit for their role, but Carroll was the "versatile genius"
who had devised a plan, based on the idea obtained from Charles and given
to Thomas. Captain Scott, he wrote, deserved the credit "for suggesting to
you, and to me, the Tennessee river. Yours is the *merit* of [planning?] *how*
that suggestion would be *made available.*" Evans continually made a crucial distinction between having an idea and using it. "Col. Scott got the *idea*
from you—& he had the *idea* executed by Halleck."[39]

Carroll went on without her close friend. Another memorial was introduced in October, shortened to eleven pages and asking for compensation
for her work "somewhat in proportion to its value to the country." In 1878
a poetical version was filed in the 45th Congress that confronted the public's reluctance to accept the validity of Carroll's claim. This massive
memorial, which reprinted all the petitions, documents, memorials, reports, and pamphlets that had previously been issued in the case, praised
the intelligence and discernment of the American public and asked Congress to put the matter before them. "Let the people grasp the merits of this
case, and understand what results followed the adoption of this plan, by
which the unity of the United States stands to-day, and we can trust them
to . . . place the reward . . . so as to connect it fairly with the benefits
the nation itself received," Carroll wrote. After all, changing the invasion
strategy from the Mississippi to the Tennessee River, for which she was
responsible, "was the greatest military event in the interest of the human
race known to modern ages. It was nothing less than the beginning of a new
and higher civilization. . . ." Perhaps, but the memorial still was referred
to the House Committee on Military Affairs where it languished unto
death.[40]

At long last, on 18 February 1879, came an answer to a congressional
petition. The Senate Committee on Military Affairs, in reply to Carroll's
memorial of 1877, finally issued its report, deciding against her. Every
Congress since the Civil War, the committee argued, had had a chance to
reward her and none had. "There must have been," the committee argued,
"some very grave and important reasons underlying the non-action of these
Congresses in these premises. . . ." Carroll had been paid $1,250 by
Thomas Scott and another $750 by Assistant Secretary Watson. Two thou-
sand dollars for her pamphlets was plenty. As for her military strategy,
well, all civilized nations honored the names and deeds of women like Florence Nightingale and Clara Barton "because they are heroines who have
risked their lives in the cause of humanity." But if they, like Carroll, applied

for a monetary reward, why, "it would destroy much of the poetry and grandeur of noble deeds" and smack of "hucksterism" and barter. Carroll should be satisfied with the monies received, and should she want more, "the deficit should be supplied from the large store of gratitude which . . . republics should bestow upon their citizens."[41]

Carroll must have been crushed or, more likely, infuriated. Perhaps it was the condescending and patronizing tone of the committee that implied womanly deeds ought to be self-sacrificing enough to pay the printer that brought Carroll's case to the interest of the woman suffrage movement. The suffragists had been aware of Carroll and her claim since 1873, when Carroll had sent copies of her early petitions and memorials to Matilda Joslyn Gage at the National Woman Suffrage Association's annual convention in Washington. She thought, perhaps, it might interest Gage, "inasmuch as it may serve in some degree to furnish evidence in behalf of the cause you so ably represent."[42]

Gage took up the cause, publishing a pamphlet with the combative title, *Who Planned the Tennessee Campaign of 1862? or Anna Ella Carroll vs. Ulysses S. Grant,* giving a brief synopsis of the case. She painted Carroll's claim in the light of injustice of "man toward woman." Carroll, a "young girl of Maryland, full of a patriotic spirit," had developed a plan which had saved the Union. Nowhere in the world had there ever existed "a person possessed of the transcendant [*sic*] military genius of Anna Ella Carroll." Yet Grant was feted and honored and reelected, while Carroll, the plan's true author, "in unregarded solitude," sought from Congress but a simple pension to support her in her sunset years. "Had she not been a woman would she have met this injustice?" Gage thundered rhetorically.[43] Actually, if Charles Scott's experience were taken into consideration, the answer might well have been yes. But no matter. Here was a cause worth fighting for.

Carroll's choice to seek support from the National Woman Suffrage Association (NWSA) instead of the state-based and more conservative American Woman's Suffrage Association (AWSA) made sense considering their respective constituencies. Unfortunately for Carroll, however, in 1873, when she first wrote to Gage, the NWSA was still suffering public censure for the radical free-love ideas publicized by member Victoria Woodhull in 1871 and 1872. The outcry against Woodhull cost the four-year-old organization much of its support and public approval. It was not an effective organization to mount such a campaign as Carroll required, especially considering the controversial nature of Carroll's military claim.[44] By the 1880s, however, when the suffragists began to champion Carroll's cause, members from both the NWSA and the AWSA would write on Carroll's behalf.

Gage's article was printed first in the *National Citizen,* NWSA's monthly newspaper, then brought out as a pamphlet in 1880. One more petition by Carroll to Congress followed. Carroll asked Thomas Scott for help once again, but Scott had suffered a stroke two years previously, and though his mind was clear and he continued his presidency of the Pennsylvania Railroad, he was, his assistant wrote Carroll, "too broken down by overwork" to be of any help. Ben Wade, her other constant support, had died in 1878.[45] Carroll was truly on her own this time.

Called before the Committee on Military Affairs in January 1881, she was momentarily at a loss when they asked her to talk about her claim rather than read it. But then she spoke for an hour and a half. As had been true throughout her life, her forceful personality and speech seemed to impress those with whom she dealt much more than did her written work. On 3 March 1881 Representative Edward S. Bragg, a former Union general and now chairman of the committee, reported a bill for her relief, finding that the evidence unquestionably established Carroll as author of the Tennessee Plan that gave "mastery of the conflict to the national arms. . . ." The "thanks of the nation" were due Carroll, and the committee recommended that she be given a pension "as a partial measure of recognition for her public service. . . ." The pension, Carroll hoped, would date from 30 November 1861, but she would take whatever she could get, "as *time* is important. . . ."[46]

Time was very important. In 1881 Anne Carroll was sixty-six years old. Contemporaries who had supported her were dead. She was forced to rely on new sources of support, and those took time to cultivate. She had written to James Abram Garfield after his Republican presidential nomination in 1880, for instance, offering a manuscript on Maryland's colonial history for his perusal, warning him about an alliance between Democrats and the Pope, and asking for five hundred dollars or so to publish an anti-Catholic pamphlet; in short, repeating all the activities which thirty years previously had established her relationship with Millard Fillmore and the Know-Nothing party. She congratulated Garfield on his election, finding it "so remarkable that I do not see how any true Christian can doubt that God rules and controls the governments of men." When she came to Washington, she would call on him, she promised, but in the meantime, she enclosed the March 1881 report on her claim, "sure it will be gratifying to you, that this measure of success has been attained. . . ."[47]

But success was short-lived. Garfield, whose brief, polite answers to Carroll's letters encouraged her into considering him a good friend and ardent supporter, was assassinated in the summer of 1881. Carroll suffered a paralytic stroke in early September, and Congress adjourned without passing the bill for her relief.[48]

A woman suffering from injustice at the hands of the male-dominant national government provided the suffragists with a cause which could be made only more glorious by that woman's frailty, illness, and poverty. Matilda Gage had included Carroll's story in detail in the massive *History of Woman Suffrage,* published in 1881. In an article the following year, lawyer Phoebe Couzins, whose mother, incidentally, had nursed the wounded in Tennessee throughout the Civil War, was able to portray a woman "unhonored, unsung and paralyzed." Carroll lay dying "within the shadow of the capitol," where the Committee on Military Affairs did its work, awarding pensions to the far less deserving. The "silence and selfishness of men" were permitting Carroll's great deeds to "pass into oblivion," wrote Couzins. In truth, one man did seem to be all that stood between Carroll and her pension, which, if the War Department refused to pay the bill for her pamphlets, was the least she deserved. The determined opposition to Carroll's claim by Francis Cockrell, former Confederate brigadier general now Missouri Democratic senator, kept the bill from a final vote. Added to his opposition, wrote Democratic Representative Edward S. Bragg, was that of the War Department as a whole. It stood firmly against the claim, considering it "absurd . . . that a woman's knowledge of topography and strategic lines led the advance of the warriors. . . ."[49]

The support from suffragists was a double-edged sword. While Carroll gained organized and widespread publicity, her attorney wrote her, members of the Committee on Military Affairs manifested "very strong opposition to woman's rights, suffrage, etc. which was made to prejudice [the] claim, though having no direct connection with the case, of course."[50] Carroll was not a suffragist, but her invitation in 1873 to them to take up her cause did form a connection and, for better or worse, she was inextricably linked with the political movement for woman suffrage. Republican Representative John D. White of Kentucky pointed out the connections in his speech on 7 February 1884, comparing Carroll's claim with that of Fitz John Porter.

Union Major General Porter had been cashiered from the army for disobeying an order in 1863 and had spent many of the ensuing years petitioning Congress to clear his name. He had, according to White, suffered wrongs which Congress had taken weeks to consider. Carroll, on the other hand, had suffered far greater wrongs, but, White argued, "because she is a woman and can not help herself, and because she has no political power to bear. . . . for twenty years her claim has been dishonored." "Does any one doubt for one moment," White asked, "that had Miss Carroll possessed the powerful political influence of Fitz John Porter . . . she long ago [would have] received every dollar" of her claim?[51]

That was the question asked again and again by the suffragists. Where Congress had failed, perhaps public opinion could succeed in gaining Carroll justice. While the suffragists prepared the matter for the public, Carroll worked within the system one more time. On 29 January 1885 William W. Warden, a Washington attorney, filed a claim for Carroll in the United States Court of Claims.[52]

Anna Ella Carroll v. The United States was decided by 1 June 1885. Time was of the essence, her attorney argued, for although Carroll's health had improved, she was still ill and had no income save a pension from a group called the "National Woman's Aid Association." Carroll's sister Mary had placed her in a private boarding home in Baltimore, and expenses were high. Using his son Clifford's position as editor of a Washington newspaper to gather support for Carroll and thoroughly embarassing her sister and the rest of her family with the publicity, Warden claimed to have gained a favorable decision. "The Court of Claims today decided the Carroll Case in your sister's favor," he wrote to Mary. "Receive my congratulations accordingly."[53]

But Carroll had not won. The court decided that there was simply no legal evidence to support her claim of military services. "Until that fact be shown (for it is certainly susceptible of proof)," Justice J. Nott wrote, "no court would be authorized in deciding that the strategy was not original with the military authorities who apparently planned that advance, and who were morally and officially responsible for its success." As for her claim for literary services, while the documents she used for proof might "morally satisfy the judgment of the individual," they were not evidence "which can be received or considered by a court." As impressive as her letters from notables were, "as a court we must pronounce these certificates as valueless as blank paper . . . they establish no judicial fact." The court transmitted its opinion as such to the House committee. The only "victory" of which Warden wrote might be considered the court's remark that Congress was not circumscribed by legal evidence to justify its actions. It could, if it desired, base its reward to Carroll on the morality of the claim. It did not so desire. Another bill introduced in 1890 for ten thousand dollars for Carroll once again met its fate in a referral to the Committee on Military Affairs.[54]

As Carroll went before the courts, the suffragists continued their literary campaign of support. By July 1885 Carroll had recovered from her stroke enough for a personal interview with journalist Mr. H. R. Shattuck. Carroll's appearance—blue-eyed, bespectacled, white-haired, short and stout but still animated—impressed Shattuck. "Taking both my hands in hers, she held them tightly, while she looked into my eyes with an expression of such ingenuous truth and honesty, that if I had ever any doubts of her story they could exist for me no longer." Until she began to speak, though, one might suppose she was a "simple old lady." But relating her tale (which had grown grander as the years had passed), he wrote, "she became the wonderful woman to whom some day our country will do honor."[55]

Carroll told her story of planning the campaign with appropriate gestures and "eyes as bright as stars." She explained how she had talked to Grant after the war: " 'He was like a child,' " she said. 'He asked me all about it, and how I came to think of it; and until I described my plan to him, and showed how success came from its consummation, I am convinced that he had no conception that it was this that brought us victory.' " Carroll, wrote Shattuck, "was God's agent in the nation's day of peril." And now, simply because she was a woman, she could get no recognition or reward, "another instance of the ingratitude of republics."[56]

Shattuck's article was followed a few months later by one written by suffragist Mrs. C. C. Hussey, and in 1886, Carroll herself took pen in still-crippled hand to rewrite her story for the *North American Review*. Mary Livermore included Carroll's story in her bestselling history, *My Story of the War,* in 1889. Again, as did the other suffragists, she emphasized that Carroll's sex, "a fact for which she is not responsible," led men to ignore her claim. In 1891 the first volume of a short biography of Carroll and her cause appeared, written by suffragist Sarah Ellen Blackwell and titled *Life of a Military Genius.*[57]

Blackwell had been corresponding with the Carrolls since the mid-1880s. She saw Carroll's case, she wrote, as a "brilliant exemplification of the treatment of women all the world over." Publicity would help Carroll's case, she wrote, so Blackwell placed letters that asked for a subscription drive for Carroll's benefit in the pages of the *Woman's Journal, Woman's Column, Century Magazine,* and other periodicals. She was joined in her letters on behalf of the "Carroll Fund" by Hussey, Abbie M. Gannett, and Lucy Stone. Susan B. Anthony wrote a note to Mary Carroll, urging her to trust the suffragists' support. *"No man ever has—or ever will* put heart and soul & brain into the work of getting this justice done for Anna," she told her, adding, "only an earnest & true woman can succeed."[58]

The 1890 congressional bill for ten thousand dollars failed, beaten by Senator Cockrell again. Carroll, cared for in Washington by her youngest sister, Mary, was at times destitute, in spite of contributions from the suffragists. Mary had taken an appointment in the Treasury Department in 1886 thanks to the intercession of President Cleveland's sister Rose and, possibly, her sister's letters to the president on her behalf. She suffered a pay cut in 1888 and again in 1892, along with a year's absence from work due to nervous prostration, followed by a dismissal for absenteeism. Her troubles prompted frantic letters from Mary to the Clevelands on behalf of her own position and her sister's needs. "Today I have not marketing for tomorrow," she wrote, and, "I have no means even for required medicine from day to day and am well nigh desperate." Her sister was ill, her own health was failing, and her family was of no help. The Catholic Carrolls had long memories and did not forgive Anne for her early anti-Catholic writings; the secessionist Carrolls did not forgive her for her Unionism; the rest of the family was angry at having family matters continually put on public display and were too poor to help the sisters even if they had wanted to. The sisters clung to each other in their small Washington home on Twenty-first Street, buoyed by visits from supporters, but financially "in great distress."[59]

Rallying for a short while after a case of pneumonia and what was probably a second stroke in the summer of 1893, Anna Ella Carroll declined in health in the fall and winter and finally died on 19 February 1894. Partially paralyzed for thirteen years, she had succumbed in the end to old age and Bright's disease, a failure of the kidneys due to circulatory problems common in the chronically bedridden. Her death certificate listed her occupation as "authoress," and she did write until the end of her life, scratching out questions and answers when she could not speak, reading her visitors' answers and questions when she could not hear. Her body was taken by her sister to Dorchester County, Maryland, where she was buried near her beloved father in the Old Trinity Church yard. Her stone bears the true inscription, "A Woman Rarely Gifted—An Able and Accomplished Writer."[60] But below that inscription, her death is misdated as 1893, in fitting irony for a woman who spent much of her life trying to set her historical record straight.

SEVEN

Carroll as Cause

Anna Ella Carroll's story did not end with her death in Washington in 1894. The suffragists' campaign had portrayed Carroll as a woman denied recognition because of her sex, and with her paralysis and then her death in poverty, Carroll's campaign for recognition took on an added poignancy. Her story took on added details. Over the next one hundred years, the legend grew of a noble and self-sacrificing woman who had saved the Union through her brilliant military strategy. The shaky foundation upon which it rested collapsed only under the force of scholarly investigation of her claim.

But the historians who investigated Carroll's life did not try simply to sort out Carroll's story and its connection to the truth. Most also tried to use Carroll's history to make their own comments about history and the role of women. What Carroll had done became less important to both her supporters and critics than what Carroll symbolized. The interpretation of Carroll's work provided a battleground where feminists and antifeminists could score points under the guise of scholarly inquiry or getting at the truth. But the truth seemed to change as often as the position of women in American society changed. Almost without exception, those who wrote about Carroll used her and her story to make statements about women, regardless of any lofty claims of objectivity. Following the history of Carroll's story might even be seen as an overview of women's place in American society and of the regard in which women's history was held throughout the twentieth century.

At first, it seemed as if the suffragists would win their cause. Carroll's story did not die, a fact that in itself was remarkable, considering how many notable women's accomplishments have been lost to American history. She was listed as a military strategist in the *National Cyclopedia of American Biography,* for instance, and President Lincoln was quoted, supporting her claim, though no source for the quotation was given. A year later, in 1895, former Representative Albert Gallatin Riddle mentioned her case in his *Recollections of War Times,* again quoting Lincoln as her supporter. Riddle's portrayal of a "short, stout, middle-aged maiden lady, intently listening through an ear trumpet" to debates in Congress, helped support the suffragists' drive to have Carroll recognized as a valid contributor to the war effort. Riddle had been informed of Carroll's plight by suffragists, or the "strong-minded" as he jocularly referred to them, but he failed in his attempt to persuade Congress to reward her. His interest was not particularly keen; he misdated her death as 1893.[1]

The "strong-minded" continued to fight for Carroll. Sarah Ellen Blackwell published her second volume on Carroll in 1895. The first had dealt with Carroll's formative years; the second reprinted all her writings. The small book, which sold for one dollar at the offices of the Woman Suffrage Society, contained all of Carroll's Civil War pamphlets and a touching rendition of the scene at her deathbed. Subscriptions to the volume were sold through advertisements in the feminist *Woman's Journal.* The less-radical *Godey's Magazine* of September 1896 put Carroll on the cover as "The Woman that Saved the Union." Author Lucinda Chandler retold much of what was in Blackwell's biography, but included a hint of skulduggery by those determined to block Carroll's claim by disclosing the alleged theft of her papers twice from the Committee on Military Affairs. The current Congress, she suggested, could "redeem their sex" from the "amazing cowardice" of preceding Congresses by placing Carroll's portrait and a plaque commemorating her deeds in the Capitol. Since Carroll was dead, there was little sense in pursuing a monetary reward, but Chandler proposed recognition at the very least.[2]

In 1910, however, a defense of congressional inaction regarding Carroll was published. The suffragists had argued for years that Carroll had not been fully recognized because she was a woman operating in the male sphere of politics and war. But Ida M. Tarbell saw Carroll and her supporters as an example of the unreasonable demands of suffragists. In an article on how American women were changed by the Civil War, antisuffragist Tarbell argued that Carroll's work during the war had been duly recognized by the two-thousand-dollar payment she had received for her pamphlets and by the notice Congress had taken of her military claims when it had congratulated her on her work in 1881. The failure to compensate Carroll for her role as strategist, a role which Tarbell accepted unquestioningly, was due to the plan having come from a civilian instead of a military person, and Carroll's sex had nothing to do with it. The recognition for her military labor was "emphatic and generous"; she was just never paid.[3]

Tarbell argued that the suffragists were incorrect in their basic assumption that Carroll's gender excluded her from proper recognition. She saw a parallel between the suffragists' inability to accept congressional inaction on Carroll's claim and their inability to accept congressional opposition to suffrage. Because suffragists continued to demand recognition for Carroll, rather than accepting the decision of Congress as appropriate, they were treading where they did not belong. In the same way, because suffragists demanded voting rights, instead of accepting the decision of Congress and other institutions denying them those rights, they were doomed never to receive the right to vote. Carroll had been amply rewarded, at least in Tarbell's eyes, and nothing would ever come of any further demands. So, too, had women been amply recompensed for their lack of voting rights by the special commission, provided by God and maintained by Congress, of maternity and the rule over the woman's sphere.[4]

While Tarbell was perfectly willing to admit that the Civil War, as was true of all wars, had necessarily changed the place of women in American society, she was not willing to let the transformation continue into the field of politics. It was duty, in the form of necessity, that had moved women into the workplace during the Civil War. Carroll had done her duty, and she had been recognized. To ask to be treated as a man would be treated in the same circumstances, that is, to receive a pension or promotion to major general, would be to try to move into the male sphere. But the war had not broken down the separate spheres of male and female, it had merely enlarged the number of activities within the female sphere, and that only for the duration of the war. Tarbell's argument against Carroll's attempt to demand recognition for her work outside her God-ordained sphere, even if duty to the nation had led her there, was an example of the separate-but-equal repudiation of natural rights that was common among the anti-suffragists.[5]

The argument over what Carroll had actually done, in either sphere, was never completely answered, and her story never completely faded from public view. She was mentioned in a county history as "the most distinguished and brilliant woman Maryland ever produced." In 1925 the *Baltimore Sun* described her as a precursor of the "modern woman." It is difficult to decide if the reporter was more interested in reassuring her female readers that they could have new interests and still be ladies, or in reassuring her male readers that women have stepped outside their sphere before and the world had still gone on. Blackwell's and Chandler's articles on Carroll were clearly the sources used for the piece, but Lincoln was said to have gone to St. Louis to implement Carroll's plan, an invention that would presumably lend needed male credibility to her claim. In an unconsciously patronizing article in 1934, Dr. Milton Shutes, a California attorney whose avocation was Lincolnania, defended Carroll's trespass on the *"verboten"* domain of the military "that has always been jealously reserved for the brilliant male!" "Somewhere a little monument is missing!" argued Shutes, because Carroll was a "civilian and—a woman!"[6]

In 1940 Anne Carroll's story finally appeared in the popular press. *Woman's Home Companion,* with a circulation of over three million readers, published a two-part serialization of Carroll's career as a strategist. The story of the "unhonored general of the Civil War" again accepted the validity of Carroll's tale, again misdated her death, and again argued that her sex was the reason her work had not been properly rewarded. The piece, based on research by Marjorie Barstow Greenbie, added a twist to the last argument. Four years after the publication of the great Civil War novel, *Gone With the Wind,* Greenbie reasoned that had Carroll been a romantic feminine figure who had defied Southern soldiers at the door, spied for the Union in the dead of night, or been a "federal Scarlett O'Hara" she would have been long remembered and greatly honored. But "hers was a man's role throughout." Because Carroll wrote for the Union, advised President Lincoln and his cabinet, and designed military strategy, she did not fit into the acceptable romantic portrayal of women's work during the Civil War.[7] Her work was too cerebral, her figure too corpulent, her age too advanced to permit men to allow her to become a national heroine.

Greenbie's research for the article went far beyond the repetition of the congressional documents, Blackwell's biography, and the other suffragist writings upon which earlier defenders of Carroll's claim had relied. She had found a treasure on the Eastern Shore of Maryland in one of Carroll's nieces, Nellie Calvert Carroll, who remembered her "Aunt Anne," and in Pikesville, Maryland, where she found Katherine Cradock, another niece, who had kept her aunt's papers in the attic. (Greenbie later persuaded her to place them in the keeping of the Maryland Historical Society.) Shortly after Greenbie's magazine article was released, her book on Carroll, *My Dear Lady,* was published. Although she had had time to use only a few of the documents she had discovered in her first book, Greenbie would be joined by her husband Sydney twelve years later in a second biography of Carroll that promised to use all the documents. The Greenbies were a team determined to put their version of Carroll's story into the appropriate place in the history of America.[8]

The Greenbies were not really historians. Marjorie had a doctoral degree in philology from Yale; Sydney was what might be euphemistically termed a "popular" writer, the author of such books as *Furs to Furrows: An Epic of Rugged Individualism,* an apologia for Manifest Destiny. He also wrote a whole series of travelogues on South and Central America as the "sister republics" of the United States. Historians deemed his works stylish, but insubstantial and evincing a distressing lack of attention to detail. The writing styles of both Greenbies were similar, not only to each other, but to Carroll's own work as a writer for the politically paranoid Know-Nothings as well. Hyperbole, exclamation points, and paranoia abound. "Could it be," Marjorie Greenbie began in *My Dear Lady,* "that there was a body of fact about the Civil War, fact intimately concerning . . . Lincoln and General Grant, which had been deliberately concealed? Could it be that much of the history of the Civil War is, in effect, untrue . . . and has been allowed to remain so?"[9]

My Dear Lady suffered from the rush to publish. It is replete with errors: incorrect dates, names (one of Carroll's pamphlets, *Union of the States,* is mistitled *The American Union*), and events. Even the epigraph taken from Carroll's massive tome on the Know-Nothing party, *The Great American Battle,* was misquoted. Greenbie gave Carroll numerous imaginary beaux, including both Millard Fillmore and James Buchanan. Family legend, it is true, had mentioned both. But in her letters to Fillmore, Carroll obviously chose to regard him as a father figure; as for Buchanan, there is no evidence she ever met him. Lemuel Evans was married off by Greenbie, though there is no evidence he ever married. He became Carroll's military attaché to prevent any hints of scandal or impropriety on Carroll's part. Greenbie also gave Carroll an access to Lincoln unimagined of by any of her previous biographers. Mary Livermore had written in *My Story of the War* that Carroll saw Lincoln frequently and that he had kept a "special file for her communications," but few biographers were willing to suggest that Carroll could simply walk in and see Lincoln as she wished. His papers, in fact, contain an angry letter from Carroll demanding either an appointment or a reply after she had been waiting to see him for over a month.[10]

Greenbie stressed Carroll's femininity constantly, although it proved difficult for her to comply with niece Nellie's request that the biography be written in such a way as to "remove the false sense of strong-mindedness conveyed by her works."[11] Carroll was to be feminine, sociable, ladylike. She could work hard, even in the male sphere, as did many women in Depression America, but she had to maintain her femininity. Any suggestion of Carroll without the protective shield of the image of the Southern lady was inconceivable to her genteel niece. Greenbie began nobly, but faced with the contradiction between the niece's demands and Carroll's work and personality, she soon gave up trying to assert her subject's femininity in hopes of convincing the reader of Carroll's overall worth in spite of her imperious and independent nature.

She succeeded to a degree. Reviews of *My Dear Lady* carefully noted that Carroll's intelligence and hard work for the Union had not interfered with her femininity. As was true a half century before, however, those who heard the story of Carroll's claim had a difficult time accepting it. They reviewed the work cautiously, granting its readability but awaiting more conclusive evidence before accepting the validity of the claim.[12]

Greenbie believed the Carroll story completely. Hurrying into print with *My Dear Lady,* she had not used many of Carroll's papers she had retrieved from her niece's attic. She wanted more time for research and promised her public that a closely documented, less speculative work would follow that would prove Carroll's claim beyond any doubt. World War II intervened after fifteen hundred copies of *My Dear Lady* had been run, and the book quickly disappeared from print. The story, however, did not disappear. A radio play based on Greenbie's book was broadcast in June 1941, starring Agnes Moorhead as Anne Carroll. Movie offers came from several studios. Greenbie, in the South Pacific with her husband Sydney for the duration of the war, left the story behind and returned to it about 1946.[13]

At the same time the Greenbies began their work on a more substantial biography, newspaper reporter Hollister Noble was finishing a novel based on the life of Anne Carroll, *Woman with a Sword,* published by Doubleday in 1948. Noble's novel, which shaved fifteen years and twenty pounds off Carroll, incorporated the romantic ideas the *Woman's Home Companion* article had found lacking in her story. Carroll became a secret agent paid by the War Department and under the direct supervision of Lincoln, Stanton, and Benjamin Wade, chairman of the Committee on the Conduct of the War. Lemuel Evans became Carroll's fiancé whom she would never marry because of what Noble delicately referred to as her "psychological problem." Noble's opinion that Carroll never found a man who could measure up to her father was a reasonable interpretation of her single state. He added, however, that career demands also limited her freedom of action. Those demands were not confined to simple personal fulfillment, though. Noble wrote during an era that was busily reviving the feminine mystique that woman's God-given role was home and family, to be set aside only when duty to God and country called.[14]

Noble's novel was romantic and dashing and fairly well written. It was also historical fantasy of the bestselling sort, with just enough sex and violence to make it interesting without being offensive. Reviewers praised the portrait of the "petite, lovely and completely charming lady," whose "ingenious and brilliant mind" had saved the Union. *Life* magazine told her story, calling Carroll "Lincoln's Lady Strategist" and only briefly mentioning that the work was fiction. Adaptations of the novel were performed on *Cavalcade of America* and on the *Playhouse 25* broadcast of the Armed

Forces Radio Network. The more times the story was told, the greater Carroll became: a spy, a major-general, a "secret war tactician." She met with Lincoln and Stanton often to mastermind Union strategy. She deserved the country's gratitude, but she had nobly kept her secret, so as not to denigrate the country's heroes. She died in penury (with dates as various as April and February; 21, 19, 18, 16; 1893 and 1894),[15] an unsung heroine foiled by an ungrateful Congress and sexist historians, and all that had happened to her was important and destructive and romantic because she was a woman.

A lone woman, fighting for recognition and payment for her work, yet managing to retain her attractive femininity throughout the battle, had enormous appeal for the public. Anne Carroll would have been thrilled. At last her story had been told. Granted, some of the biographers' embellishments were inaccurate (a point which would have concerned her not at all) but all accepted unquestioningly the central issue: Anna Ella Carroll had designed and presented the plan for the Tennessee campaign to the United States government during the Civil War and that plan had been directly responsible for winning the war and saving the Union.

After the first flush of literary excitement at such a discovery in American history died down, however, critical reviews and articles began to appear. F. Lauriston Bullard, who had reviewed *My Dear Lady* favorably but reservedly in 1940, published a critical analysis of Carroll's congressional claims. A contributing editor to the *Lincoln Herald,* Bullard argued that claims made by and for Carroll were so incredible and so excessive that they demanded dispassionate and scholarly investigation. Bullard concentrated on the inconsistencies and changes in text found in Carroll's congressional petitions, the fortuitous additions, and the credit that Carroll had willingly given to the helpful riverboat pilot, Scott, in 1865, but had tried to belittle in a later memorial to Congress. In the end Bullard accepted Carroll as the one who had brought the Tennessee Plan to the attention of military authorities in Washington, but claimed pilot Scott, "an able and honest man" as its true author. His conclusion, while somewhat logical as far as the source of the information, neglected Carroll's ability to use information received to formulate military strategy. Of course, Bullard was also writing during an era when female veterans of World War II were not regarded as "real" vets by either the armed forces or the government. Service to the military by women was not awarded by pension or even a burial allowance.[16]

A few months later, Carroll's Civil War pamphlets came under scrutiny by lawyer Walter Armstrong. He found them to be the "best and most persuasive contemporary rationalization of the theory upon which Lincoln acted." As for the military plan, while Armstrong did not deny the validity of Carroll's claim outright, he pointed out that Lincoln's dismissal of her 1862 proposal that she be given fifty thousand dollars to go to Europe to continue writing propaganda for the Union made it clear that the president probably would have been unsympathetic to Carroll's military claims. Armstrong ignored any limitations Carroll's sex might have placed upon her. The problem with recognizing her historical worth came, he implied, when, as a civilian, she stepped into the military sphere.[17]

In 1950 Kenneth P. Williams, working on a multivolume history of the war, considered Carroll's story in both his history and a journal article. Her claim, "seemingly settled" by congressional inaction and her death, had been revived by Greenbie and Noble to such an extent that Williams was determined to rule on its veracity once and for all. His interest was not entirely academic: Williams, whom Sydney Greenbie later referred to as "the bull in General Grant's pasture," admired Grant, and any attack on the general's abilities and accomplishments was automatically suspect.[18]

Williams used the *Official Records* to trace the actions in the western theater to disprove Greenbie's and Noble's versions of Carroll's claim. Greenbie had not consulted the *Official Records* and had mistakenly credited Carroll, Assistant Secretary of War Scott, and Lincoln with informing Grant of the plan in February as General Halleck ordered Grant up the Tennessee. Noble had explained the same event with a secret order from Lincoln to General Don Carlos Buell and Halleck. In fact, Williams argued, that move upriver was suggested by Grant and Admiral Foote to Halleck. Further, since ingratitude was certainly uncharacteristic of Lincoln, he wrote, the fact that Lincoln turned down Carroll's propaganda proposal with such vigor further showed that she could not have been the author of a successful campaign undertaken such a short time prior to her proposal.[19] As for her defenders, such as Wade and Scott, they were politicians and notably inconsistent in their statements on her behalf.

In the end, Williams was not even willing to grant that Carroll had presented the same plan to Scott as had been printed in her congressional claims, because the original document had never been found. In the light of his analysis of the inaccuracies of both Greenbie and Noble, his caution was reasonable. However, he did not examine Carroll's papers for the plan, merely the War Department records. Since Carroll claimed to have read her paper to Scott, it would not have been in the register of letters received anyway. Be that as it may, there was and is still no proof that the copy of the plan now in Carroll's papers was the one she claimed to have presented to Scott at the War Department.[20]

Williams did an excellent job of analyzing Carroll's claim to prove the errancy of her assumptions regarding the effect of her plan. He also did an excellent job of provoking Sydney and Marjorie Greenbie, who had been hard at work on a follow-up biography of Carroll. *Anna Ella Carroll and Abraham Lincoln* was due to be published in 1952, and a friend of Williams wrote to the University of Tampa Press for a pre-publication copy for Williams. At that time, the press was run by Sydney Greenbie, and the Carroll biography was its first publication. Williams's attack on *My Dear Lady* had roused Sydney Greenbie's wrath, and the polite request for a copy of the new biography was met with a childish refusal. "We don't give a whoot what Mr. Williams says or whether he sees it," Greenbie wrote. "In due course we will still take him on and show him a thing or two."[21] This was the first shot in a series of nasty exchanges between Williams and the Greenbies on the validity of Carroll's claim, on the scholarly credentials of her biographers, and on the scholarly elitism prevalent in American higher education.

While the Greenbies' second volume made use of Carroll's papers and benefited from interviews with family members, their extravagant and unsupported claims detracted from Carroll's reputation as a legitimate historical figure. The Greenbies were convinced that Carroll's help was essential to Lincoln. They accepted her pamphlets and petitions as prima facie evidence that their interpretation was correct, that she had been denied recognition solely because she was a woman, and that "wicked and malicious historians" were conspiratorially determined to negate her importance to the conduct of the war and to history.[22]

The Greenbies' book was embarrassingly defensive in tone. It portrayed a fantastical version of events: Carroll supporting Lincoln as early as Lincoln's Cooper Union speech in February 1860, which the Greenbies claimed she attended as a member of the committee that selected lecturers for the platform; Lincoln, Stanton, Wade, and Carroll meeting together nightly in the War Department's telegraph office to plot strategy; Carroll so close to Lincoln and so much a part of his cabinet that the empty chair in Francis B. Carpenter's painting of the cabinet at the time of the Emancipation Proclamation was for her. Aside from these insupportable conjectures, the Greenbies' inattention to historical detail provided a field day for reviewers. Secretary of War Simon Cameron was "Simeon Cameron" throughout the text; photographer Mathew Brady was "William F. Brady." President Andrew Jackson's famous toast at the Jefferson Day dinner in 1830 was misquoted, as was Samuel Morse's biblical telegraph message that inaugurated the use of his invention. Even literary nuances suffered as magnolia trees burst "into waxy bloom" in March in Washington, three months prior to their normal blossoming.[23]

Most damaging of all to the Greenbies' text and to their version of Carroll's claim was the inventive terminology within their footnotes. Practically every controversial claim about Carroll that the Greenbies made had a footnote. But practically every one of those footnotes included the phrase: "This scene is synthetic." Where evidence was missing, the Greenbies argued, "psychology must step in and, with sleuth-like determination, reestablish the facts."[24]

The Greenbies met criticism of their book with little grace. In the *Journal of Southern History,* which was the only major historical journal that reviewed *Anna Ella Carroll and Abraham Lincoln,* they accused the reviewer of exaggerating and distorting the few errors that existed "for his own ends." But Sydney Greenbie saved his most acidulous replies for the criticism Kenneth Williams presented in the *Lincoln Herald.* For the Greenbies (at least for Sydney, since Marjorie tended to let her husband fight the battles), Carroll and her claim had by now become less a symbol of man's inhumanity to woman than the failure of "distinguished egg-heads," "subterreanean" pundits, and "academic gauleiters" to appreciate the work of outsiders in the academic provinces.[25] As Carroll had been an outsider in the nineteenth century, striving for recognition and legitimization by those in power, so the Greenbies fought for the recognition of the value of their work by legitimate scholars.

In large part, that recognition was denied. James G. Randall mentioned Carroll and the Greenbies' work favorably; Allan Nevins mentioned Carroll's claim as well, but pointed out the additional evidence that she was not the first nor the only one to conceive of the Tennessee River campaign. Roy P. Basler included a letter from Lincoln to Carroll praising her "address to Maryland" in his nine-volume edition of Lincoln's papers. But overall, the academic community found Williams's refutation of Carroll's claim convincing and substantially supported by the *Official Records.* Even Williams's additional, somewhat specious, argument was accepted: it was unnecessary to give Carroll credit for the Tennessee Plan because even if she had thought of it, it was so obvious it had doubtless occurred to every military mind.[26]

Resigning themselves momentarily to the lack of scholarly appreciation, the Greenbies returned their attention to the popular press, where praise for Noble's work was still strong. A *Hallmark Hall of Fame* television production, based on his novel and starring Jayne Meadows, had been broadcast in February 1952. Noble had also made a distribution agreement with Sears, Roebuck and Company. Thousands of copies of *Woman with a Sword* were sold through Sears' People's Book Club. If the Greenbies could not obtain scholarly regard, they were determined to protect their version of Carroll's story from pirates such as Noble who were making a fortune. On 21 July 1954 the Greenbies filed a copyright infringement suit against Noble, his publisher Doubleday, Sears and Roebuck, and those who had sponsored the shows based on Noble's book: Dupont, the National Broadcasting Company (NBC), Hallmark Cards, *Cavalcade of America;* Batten, Barton, Dunstine & Osborne, who had produced a 1949 radio show; and Foote, Cone and Belding, producers of the *Hallmark Hall of Fame* version.[27]

The civil case was before the courts for nearly three years and produced over one thousand pages of testimony. Noble committed suicide just prior to the suit's filing, and eventually only his publisher and Sears remained as defendants. The judge ruled against Marjorie Greenbie, finding that Carroll's story could be derived from commonly available historical sources. Since historical facts contained in government publications were not subject to copyright, and since Greenbie had failed to prove that Noble had copied from her book rather than using the original source material available on Carroll, no copyright infringement existed. Furthermore, since Greenbie's first book had not been a commercial success and had been out of print for six years before Noble published the novel, Greenbie had not been harmed financially and could recover no damages. As for Noble's "parallel language, incidents, ideas and juxtaposition of words and events" that Greenbie had exhibited as clear evidence of Noble's plagiarism, the judge ruled that similarities in phraseology did not amount to a copyright infringement.[28]

"Against this Janus-faced decision" the Greenbies appealed, but withdrew after a settlement offer, citing the cost of pursuing an appeal. Infuriated by the loss, Sydney Greenbie wrote a book about the writing and plagiarizing of the story of Anna Ella Carroll. The book is valuable for additional information of Carroll's life as it recounted the interviews held with her family. Greenbie was more interested, however, in revealing that Noble's "sole original contribution to the life of a very great person was to falsify her position and her American ideals by making her and her distinguished associate, Judge Evans, into communists."[29]

Noble's book, ranted Greenbie, was a collaboration by "communists" at Doubleday to "propagandize 'old man Marx' " and to make money. Evidence of the second was a given. Evidence of the first was circumstantial. Noble did have a jarring reference to Carroll reading Marx's Civil War essays, and he had persisted in referring to the Radical Republicans as the "red Republicans." He had also included a scene wherein Evans called for a restructuring of American capitalist society away from the "feudal strangle" of Southern planters that had rested on the "exploitation of man by man" in the form of racial slavery. But such minor incidents of communist philosophy tended to be buried by the sweeping romance of Noble's novel. The book was not, as Greenbie preferred to view it, "a case of cultural adultery. . . . the rape of one of the great stories of American history by communists for communist ends."[30]

Such vituperation kept any publisher from bringing out Greenbie's manuscript, so he had it privately printed. But the Greenbies' championship of Carroll's cause might have had some effect on the scholarly world, for even though Williams had essentially destroyed their version of her claim, her story did not disappear from view entirely. She appeared again, tale intact, in a history of women in the war and in a juvenile biography. One of her Civil War pamphlets was reprinted in a scholarly collection of such publications, and she was listed in the major reference work in American women's history, the biographical directory *Notable American Women.*[31] Finally, in the 1970s, as women's history began to achieve acceptance as a legitimate field of historical inquiry, her entire career was given scholarly attention, somewhat freer from the partisanship and literary vindictiveness that had characterized earlier work.

Historian Charles McCool Snyder discovered approximately fifty letters between Carroll and Millard Fillmore and presented his findings about Carroll's career during the 1850s, characterizing her accurately as a political strategist for the Know-Nothings, but dismissing her somewhat by calling her a "gadfly." Jean Baker, historian of Maryland politics in the nineteenth century, analyzed Carroll's writings in two of her texts, including a quantitative textual analysis of Carroll's *The Great American Battle* as a leading example of Know-Nothing literature. E. B. Long, research director for Civil War historian Bruce Catton in the 1950s and 1960s, took on Carroll's military claim once again, but with a less condescending and hostile attitude than Kenneth Williams had evinced. He fully expected, he wrote, that his attempt would "undoubtedly arouse the same acrimonious controversy that has surrounded this Maryland lady for over a century," but he was willing to take his chances. Long granted that Carroll had written the paper that Williams had dismissed, and that she had presented the plan to the War Department. While he also pointed out that those "with political and social axes to grind" had used Carroll's story for their own purposes, he reasoned, as had Williams, that the design of the plan was so obvious that giving any one person credit was a bit absurd. The validity of her claim aside, Long did not think Carroll was a "maliciously hidden" figure in history, but merely a "competent, capable woman," a "minor figure with a fascination all her own, but with slim importance."[32]

This last assessment of Carroll must be reconsidered, however, for two reasons. First, earlier writers tended to define Carroll in terms of her victimization, just as the early stages of women's history as a discipline tended to concentrate on women as victims of men's injustices. Carroll was a victim in that she did provide the government with a number of writings for which she should have been paid, something Roy Basler pointed out in an article on Lincoln's difficulties in dealing with professional women. But

Carroll was not simply and only a victim of injustice. Her work outside her claims of military strategy moves her beyond victim to a notable historical persona. Carroll's pamphlets promoting Lincoln's position, for instance, were some of the earliest printed during the war. They provided some of the best-argued rationales for Lincoln's actions, using the same points that Lincoln himself used. Evidence of their value to Lincoln is clear: Carroll's pamphlets were printed and distributed to Congress in the first year of the war, when much of what Lincoln did came under virulent attack.[33] The fact that such competent, if not brilliant, legal reasoning came from a woman in the nineteenth century would be cause for study in itself.

But there was more to Carroll's work than her pamphleteering. For most of her life, she was able to work outside the woman's sphere. Carroll used her skill as a writer to do the work she wanted in a field she loved. As a woman, her options in politics were limited. So, in the beginning of her career, Carroll developed a compromise methodology to fulfill her goal of participating in political activity. Writing was one of the very few socially acceptable activities outside the home for upper-class women, particularly Southern women, and even that activity was limited by the cult of the "Southern lady." The pervasiveness of that image meant that to achieve social acceptability for any activities outside the norm, the woman working had to do so within the cultural framework that existed. Carroll accepted the validity of the dominant assumptions of her culture at first: the importance of politics, of ambition and achievement, and of the idea of the woman's sphere. Her writings reflected those assumptions rather than doing battle against them, and because of that, Carroll achieved one of her major goals: to have her work read and taken seriously by politicians.[34]

At the same time, the cultural imperative of the Southern lady demanded that she present her work in a very specific manner. The image demanded ladies who were selfless and voiceless and who listened to those who had something to say worth listening to (that is, to white male politicians and preachers). For Carroll, the cultural demands of that image would be met instead by anonymity. Her unknown voice could present ideas important to her in a manner that was designedly nonthreatening. Carroll's method of presentation, as she began her career, did not threaten to challenge the male-dominant power structure or to change it. Nor did it threaten her own sense of feminine self. She was well aware that she was a female operating in a male sphere. But with the ladylike quality of duty as her motivation and anonymity or, later, self-effacement and apology part of her by-line, she reassured her readers. Perhaps Carroll knew claiming a right to participate fully in politics would raise a backlash that could shut her out completely.[35]

Carroll communicated her ideas through print and personal contact, through petitioning rather than confrontation. These three characteristics of her style are typical of what historian Linda Kerber has labeled "pre-political" behavior: the acknowledgment of inferiority (the apology), the rhetoric of humility (the assurance that only duty had drawn Carroll into political matters and away from her more appropriate role), and the individual nature of the act of petitioning (Carroll wrote alone, even when the ideas she presented were shared by many).[36] But for Carroll, her actions as writer, lobbyist, critic, hostess, traveler, saleswoman, or strategist were unquestionably political acts with political goals in mind, be they publication, patronage positions, or simple acceptance of the value of her opinions and intelligence.

Carroll combines the images found in three specific nineteenth-century roles for white middle-class women that historians of women have delineated. The imagery she employs in her writings for the Know-Nothings is that of the Republican Mother who raises her children to be good citizens of the Republic. The cult of domesticity, the second image, compelled Carroll to justify her intrusion into the political world by citing financial necessity or duty to God, country, and paternal ancestry. The third image, that of the Southern Lady, limited Carroll's activities to writing, about the only acceptable activity exclusive of the church in which she could participate without danger to her femininity. The Civil War did not destroy the force of those roles, as Carroll discovered when she began writing under her own name with no apology, filed for her claim against the government, and gathered support from suffragists. By entering the public sphere, Carroll confronted the institutions and cultural imperatives that had proved so hostile to her desire for recognition, and discovered the power that could be turned against a former lady who had stepped outside her proper sphere.

To place Carroll into a historical category is difficult because of the individualistic nature of her work. She was not a reformer, abolitionist, or a protofeminist of the type identifiable from 1830 to 1860. She did not join voluntary associations. She was not a suffragist, although she did not hesitate to use their strengths to support her cause. She was not an upper- or middle-class family-oriented woman preserving the hearth for hard-working husband and embracing the cult of domesticity. Nor was she an unmarried daughter working until she was married and thus properly taken care of.[37]

If categorized at all, Carroll was a bit of a Victorian bluestocking, albeit a sociable one, but enraptured by books and education. A prescriptive writer, her works reflected the assumption that universal moral principles could be conceptualized, understood, and acted upon in the same manner as the natural sciences. Feeling free to write on all sorts of subjects, Carroll exemplified the lettered women and men of the Victorian era in America who were amateur experts and believed learning and scholarship were inclusive rather than exclusive, and should be shared with others, whether as commentary or advice.[38]

The fact that Carroll never married was not that surprising. She was an attractive and vivacious woman of a distinguished family, but she never seemed inclined to give up the relative freedom a single woman could have over a married one in nineteenth-century America. Her work as a writer supported her adequately through most of her career and enabled her to care for her father, a "congenial presence [which] seemed to be all-sufficient for her."[39] By caring for her father, she could fulfill the domestic role which society demanded of her, while retaining her independence. She was not without men in her life, but her work was her passion. Her surviving letters to politicians and family alike contain little of the domesticity that was the usual lot and focus of most women during this period, when the proper sphere of womanly activity became the cult of domesticity. Instead, her letters and those she received were full of political news and gossip, reports and opinions, rumors and plans, articles and editorials. She was treated by the vast majority of minor politicians who wrote to her as a woman with a great deal of political and legal acumen and a certain amount of influence. The former was evidenced in her published work as well; the latter was a less tangible and certainly overestimated quality.

Defining Carroll's historical importance has been limited to one-sided stands taken in support of or in opposition to her claim to authorship of the Tennessee campaign, stands that tended to parallel societal views on women and even women's history. As women's history has matured in the last twenty-five years, however, it has become a field ever more complex. Within that complexity, Carroll begins to assume her place more clearly. She becomes not a simplistic figure of downtrodden womanhood but rather a woman of active political involvement, laboring for causes she believed in, using the methods available to her. As a historical persona, Carroll has become what she called for in *The Great American Battle:* not a Joan of Arc, but a faithful and true woman, neither heroine nor fool, but an American woman who could stand in her own shoes.[40] Those shoes might be a different size than she had planned, a different style, planted in a different place, but they are at last her own.

Notes

Chapter 1

1. Elias Jones, *Revised History of Dorchester County, Maryland* (Baltimore: Read-Taylor Press, 1925), 296–97; *Appleton's Cyclopedia of American Biography*, ed. James Grant Wilson and John Fiske, 6 vols. (New York: D. Appleton, 1886–91), 1 (1891): 536–38; Anna Ella Carroll, *The Great American Battle, or the Contest Between Christianity and Political Romanism* (New York: Miller, Orton and Mulligan, 1856), v (hereafter cited as *GAB*).

2. Hester Dorsey Richardson, *Sidelights on Maryland History with Sketches of Early Maryland Families* (Baltimore: Williams and Wilkins, 1913), 156; Jones, *Revised History*, 297–98; *A Biographical Dictionary of the Maryland Legislature, 1635–1789*, ed. Edward C. Papenfuse, Alan F. Day, David W. Jordan, and Gregory A. Stiverson, 2 vols. (Baltimore: Johns Hopkins Univ. Press, 1979–85), 1 (1979): 200; Thomas King Carroll Folder, Biographical Folders Collection, University of Pennsylvania Archives, Philadelphia; Sarah Ellen Blackwell, *Life of a Military Genius: Anna Ella Carroll of Maryland* (Washington, D.C.: Judd and Detweiler, 1891), 4. Blackwell's biography benefits from having been written while Carroll was still alive and could provide the author with an interview. Carroll was deaf and in poor health, however, and evidence indicates most of the interviewing was conducted by note-writing and through Carroll's sister Mary, who took care of Carroll during the last years of her life. Most of the biographical information on Carroll's early years available in other sources appears to have been taken from details provided in Blackwell's two books on Carroll, *Military Genius* and *Life and Writings of Anna Ella Carroll* (Washington, D.C.: Judd and Detweiler, 1895).

The familial relationship between the Carrolls of Somerset County and the more famous Carrolls of Carrollton is difficult to determine. Jones's book on Dorchester County, where the Carrolls moved in 1843, is less than accurate and therefore must be used cautiously. Anna Ella Carroll's great-grandfather claimed cousinship to Charles Carroll of Carrollton, a claim thus far undocumented. Carroll herself claimed a common ancestry and mentioned the connection with considerable pride and frequency, particularly when justifying her involvement in activities outside the woman's sphere. See chap. 2. Sally D. Mason, associate editor, Charles Carroll of Carrollton Papers, to author, 6 Dec. 1985.

3. *Biographical Dictionary of Maryland Legislature* 2 (1985): 513; Blackwell, *Military Genius*, 5–9.

4. Blackwell, *Military Genius*, 5–7; Jones, *Revised History*, 297–98; *Biographical Directory of the Governors of the United States 1798–1978*, ed. Robert Sobel and John Raimo, 4 vols. (Westport, Conn.: Meckler Books, 1978), 2:659; newspaper clipping enclosed with letter, Anna Ella Carroll to James Abram Garfield, 11 Sept. 1880, James Abram Garfield Papers, Library of Congress; *Biographical Dictionary of Maryland Legislature* 2:513; Mark H. Haller, "The Rise of the Jackson Party in Maryland, 1820–1829," *Journal of Southern History* 28 (Aug. 1962): 323; *Tercentenary History of Maryland*, comp. Henry Fletcher Powell, 4 vols. (Baltimore: S. J. Clarke, 1925), 4:48; Frank F. White, *The Governors of Maryland, 1777–1970* (Annapolis, Md.: The Hall of Records Commission, 1970), 96–99; Blackwell, *Military Genius*, 25–26. Unless otherwise indicated, all letters to or from "Carroll" will refer to Anna Ella Carroll.

5. W. Wayne Smith, "Politics and Democracy in Maryland, 1800–1854," in *Maryland: A History, 1632–1974*, ed. Richard Walsh and William Lloyd Fox (Baltimore: Maryland Historical Society, 1974), 282, 243, 269; James S. Van Ness, "Economic Development, Social and Cultural Changes: 1800–1850," in *Maryland: A History*, 191–97. Between 1826 and 1840 Maryland incurred a debt of nearly fifteen million dollars by promoting various transportation projects.

6. *Tercentenary History* 4:48; Richardson, *Sidelights*, 156–57; P. J. Staudenraus, *The African Colonization Movement, 1816–1865* (New York: Columbia Univ. Press, 1961), 70, 111. Penelope Campbell, *Maryland in Africa: The Maryland State Colonization Society, 1831–1857* (Urbana: Univ. of Illinois Press, 1971), does not mention Thomas King Carroll, but *Tercentenary History* 4:48 states his pro-colonization position. Although several sources cite family reminiscences that the Carrolls had 150 slaves at Kingston Hall, this figure is greatly exaggerated. The 1800 census listed only 29 slaves at Kingston Hall; Thomas Carroll's father, Colonel Henry James Carroll, had only 14 on his estate. Slaves were not listed in the 1810 census. Thomas King Carroll had 47 slaves and 4 free black males at Kingston Hall in 1820. The 1830 census for Somerset County has not survived. Given the small number of young slave children in the census of 1820, there were probably about 45 slaves when Carroll received his inheritance five years earlier. *1800 Census Index*, ed. Ronald V. Jackson et al. (Bountiful, Utah: Accelerated Indexing Systems, 1976), 22, 76; *Population Schedules of the Third Census of the United States, 1810*, roll 16, Maryland (Washington, D.C.: National Archives and Records Service, 1959), 4:263; *Population Schedules of the Fourth Census of the United States, 1820*, roll 45, Maryland (Washington, D.C.: National Archives and Records Service, 1959), 6:146.

7. "Anna Ella Carroll," *Notable American Women 1607–1950*, ed. Edward T. James, 3 vols. (Cambridge, Mass.: Harvard Univ. Press, 1971), 1:289–92; Obituary Clipping File, Maryland Historical Society, Baltimore; *Portrait and Biographical Record of the Eastern Shore of Maryland* (New York: Chapman Publishing, 1898), 219–20; gravestones at Old Trinity Church, Church Creek, Maryland. Information about Carroll's immediate family is difficult to obtain and difficult to verify.

8. Blackwell, *Military Genius*, 15; Carroll to Thomas King Carroll, 17 Feb. 1830, cited in Blackwell, *Military Genius*, 18.

9. Blackwell, *Military Genius*, 19; Caspar Harris, M.D., *Memoir of Miss Margaret Mercer*, 2d ed. (Philadelphia: Lindsay and Blakiston, 1848), 27, 102–3. Miss Mercer's father was Maryland governor John Francis Mercer. See James Mercer Garnett, "John Francis Mercer, Governor of Maryland, 1801–1803," *Maryland Historical Magazine* 2 (Sept. 1907): 191–213. Miss Mercer's teaching career at West River is mentioned in J. Reaney Kelly,

"Cedar Park, Its People and Its History," *Maryland Historical Magazine* 58 (Mar. 1963): 47–52. An 1831 list of scholars includes "Ann Carroll" and "Julia Carroll" among those from Maryland's Eastern Shore. Presumably this was Anna Ella and her sister Julianna.

10. Harris, *Memoir*, 113–14, 130–33; Blackwell, *Military Genius*, 25–26; Carroll to Gerrit Smith, 26 June 1854, Gerrit Smith Collection, George Arents Research Library, Syracuse University, Syracuse, N.Y.; *Tercentenary History* 4:48.

11. Somerset County Tax Assessment Ledger, 1817–22, 1823, 1830, Hall of Records, Maryland State Archives, Annapolis.

12. Somerset County Tax Assessment Ledger, 1833 and 1835; Somerset County Chancery Court Records, 21 Jan. 1836; Somerset County Deed Book, 19 Oct. and 29 Dec. 1835, Hall of Records, Maryland State Archives, Annapolis; Jones, *Revised History,* 298; Blackwell, *Military Genius,* 19–27; Charles McCool Snyder, "Anna Ella Carroll, Political Strategist and Gadfly to President Fillmore," *Maryland Historical Magazine* 68 (Spring 1973): 37; White, *Governors,* 99; Paul Touart, Architectural Historian, Somerset County Historical Trust, MS Chain of Title to author, 25 June 1986.

13. *Population Schedules of the Sixth Census of the United States, 1840,* Somerset County and Dorchester County, Maryland (Washington, D.C.: National Archives); Somerset County Tax Assessment Ledger, 1840.

14. Somerset County Tax Assessment Ledger, 1841–52; Blackwell, *Military Genius,* 23–24; Carroll to John Young Mason, 6 Nov. 1848, Mason Family Papers, Virginia Historical Society, Richmond. Carroll was a member of the Second Presbyterian Church of Baltimore in 1845. Dorothy E. Milliken, church secretary, to author, 20 Nov. 1985. Date of death from Julianna Carroll's gravestone, Old Trinity Church, Church Creek, Md. For more information on this period in Carroll's life, see the family reminiscences cited by Marjorie Barstow Greenbie in *My Dear Lady: The Story of Anna Ella Carroll, the "Great Unrecognized Member of Lincoln's Cabinet"* (New York: McGraw-Hill, 1940). Greenbie interviewed surviving relatives about "Aunt Anne" but used considerable poetic license in her biography of Carroll. Her book must be used with great caution and considerable skepticism. See also Sydney Greenbie, *Suit with Red Lining* (Penobscot, Maine: Traversity Press, 1958), 25–30.

15. *Population Schedules of the Seventh Census of the United States, 1850,* Maryland (Washington, D.C.: National Archives and Records Service), Baltimore City, 11th Ward, 187; Carroll to John M. Clayton, 13 Apr. 1849, John M. Clayton Papers, Library of Congress; Snyder, "Anna Ella Carroll," 38.

16. Carroll to John M. Clayton, 13 Apr. 1849, Clayton Papers.

17. Millard Fillmore to Carroll, note at top of letter from Carroll to Fillmore, 27 Apr. 1852; Carroll to Fillmore, 26 May 1852, Millard Fillmore Papers, Buffalo and Erie County Historical Society and Penfield Library, State University of New York, College at Oswego, Oswego, N.Y.

18. Carroll to Millard Fillmore, 28 May 1852, Fillmore Papers.

19. Carroll to Millard Fillmore, 21, 26, and 28 June 1852, Fillmore Papers; Snyder, "Anna Ella Carroll," 38–39.

20. Carroll to Thomas Corwin, 15 Feb. 1853, Thomas Corwin Papers, Library of Congress; Carroll to Millard Fillmore, 7 Mar. 1853, Fillmore Papers. A manuscript sketch of Corwin survives in Carroll's papers, indicating she met Corwin prior to 1850. While most of their surviving correspondence dealt with patronage and political matters, one letter from Corwin in particular stands out as evidence of the intimacy of their friendship. He sadly recounted to her that he was a failure at life, unable to accept happiness in his own life or manifest joy "at the happiness of others." See "Sketch: Senator Corwin of Ohio," Anna Ella Carroll Papers, Carroll, Cradock, Jensen Collection, Maryland Historical Society, Balti-

more (hereafter cited as Carroll Papers, CCJ); Corwin to Carroll, 28 Sept. 1854, Anna Ella Carroll Papers, Maryland Historical Society, Baltimore (hereafter cited simply as Carroll Papers).

21. Carroll to William Marcy, 27 Mar. 1853, William Learned Marcy Papers, Library of Congress.

22. Carroll to William H. Seward, 15 Sept. 1852, William Henry Seward Papers, Rus Rhees Library, University of Rochester, Rochester, N.Y.; Allen Nevins, *Ordeal of the Union: A House Dividing, 1852–1857* (New York: Charles Scribner's Sons, 1947), 23–32.

23. Carroll to William H. Seward, 15 and 27 Sept. 1852, Seward Papers.

24. Carroll to Millard Fillmore, 15 Apr., 12 Oct. 1853, Fillmore Papers; Carroll to William H. Seward, 6 and 28 Apr. 1853, Seward Papers.

25. Carroll to William H. Seward, 28 Apr., 23 May 1853, Seward Papers.

26. Records of Thomas King Carroll's sale of family slaves are in the Chattel Records of Baltimore City, Liber E.D. Folio No. 6 and the Manumission Records, 1806–64, Department of Legislative Reference, Bureau of Archives, Baltimore City Archives, Baltimore, Maryland, n.p. See 28 Apr., 14 and 18 May 1854. Seven slaves originally owned by Carroll were mortgaged to John B. Pinney and freed in 1854, presumably after the mortgage was paid.

27. Carroll to Gerrit Smith, 26 June 1854, 18 Nov. 1873, Smith Collection; Gerard Halleck to Carroll, 19 Dec. 1853, Carroll Papers.

28. Baltimore City Superior Court Records, case no. 94, 29 Oct. 1855, Hall of Records, Maryland State Archives, Annapolis; *Hatchett's Baltimore Directory, 1855–1856* (microform) in *American Directories through 1860* (New Haven, Conn.: Research Publishers, 1969), 65.

29. Carroll to Millard Fillmore, 31 Mar., 21 and 23 Apr., 5 and 15 May 1855, Fillmore Papers; Snyder, "Anna Ella Carroll," 42–43.

30. Carroll to Millard Fillmore, 15 May 1855, Fillmore Papers.

31. Carroll to Millard Fillmore, 28 May, 7 July 1855, Fillmore Papers; Snyder, "Anna Ella Carroll," 44.

32. Carroll to Millard Fillmore, 16 Jan. 1856, Fillmore papers.

Chapter 2

1. David M. Potter, *The Impending Crisis,* ed. Don E. Fehrenbacher (New York: Harper and Row, 1976), 249–56; Joel H. Silbey, *The Partisan Imperative: The Dynamics of American Politics Before the Civil War* (New York: Oxford Univ. Press, 1985), 127–65; William E. Gienapp, "Nativism and the Creation of a Republican Majority in the North Before the Civil War,"*Journal of American History* 72 (Dec. 1985): 529–59; Michael F. Holt, "The Antimasonic and Know Nothing Parties," in *History of U.S. Political Parties,* ed. Arthur M. Schlesinger, Jr., 4 vols. (New York: Chelsea House Publishers, 1973), 1:569, 594–95, 610–11; Frederick J. Blue, *The Free-Soilers: Third Party Politics, 1848–1854* (Urbana: Univ. of Illinois Press, 1973), 284; Ludwell Johnson, *Division and Reunion: America 1848–1877* (New York: John Wiley and Sons, 1978), 21; David Brion Davis, "Some Ideological Functions of Prejudice in Ante-Bellum America," *American Quarterly* 60 (Summer 1963): 121; Harry J. Carman and Richard H. Luthin, "Some Aspects of the Know-Nothing Movement Reconsidered," *South Atlantic Quarterly* 39 (1940): 217, 222; Michael F. Holt, *The Political Crisis of the 1850s* (New York: John Wiley and Sons, 1978); [Friedrich Anspach] *The Sons of the Sires* (Philadelphia: Lippincott, Grambo, 1855), 99, 189; Michael F. Holt, "The Politics of Impatience: The Origins of Know Nothingism,"*Journal of American History* 60 (Sept. 1973): 323;

Daniel Walker Howe, *The Political Culture of the American Whigs* (Chicago: Univ. of Chicago Press, 1979), 9, 349; William J. Evitts, *A Matter of Allegiances: Maryland from 1850 to 1861* (Baltimore: Johns Hopkins Univ. Press, 1974), 59–67.

2. Jean H. Baker, *The Politics of Continuity: Maryland Political Parties from 1858 to 1870* (Baltimore: Johns Hopkins Univ. Press, 1973), 14; Evitts, *Allegiances,* 96, 102; W. Darrell Overdyke, *The Know-Nothing Party in the South* (Baton Rouge: Louisiana State Univ. Press, 1950), 12; Carman and Luthin, "Aspects," 216–17; Holt, "Antimasonic and Know Nothing Parties," 1:596–97; W. Dean Burnham, *Presidential Ballots 1836–1892* (Baltimore: Johns Hopkins Univ. Press, 1955), 504; Anna Ella Carroll, *Which? Fillmore or Buchanan!* (Boston: James French, 1856). Most historians hold New York as the key state in the contest and argue Clay lost because his status as a slaveholder cost him Whig votes that went to the abolitionist Liberty party. Lee Benson's study of New York State voting patterns in *The Concept of Jacksonian Democracy: New York as a Test Case* (Princeton, N.J.: Princeton Univ. Press, 1961) is cited by Silbey as proof of the decline of the Liberty party in 1844 and the primacy of ethnoreligious factors in the election. This argument validates, at least in part, Carroll's contention that Clay lost the election because of the ethnic vote. See Silbey, *Partisan Imperative,* 4–5.

3. Thomas Holmes Walker, *One Hundred Years of History, 1802–1902: A History of Second Presbyterian Church* (Baltimore, 1902), 94–142; Dorothy E. Milliken, church secretary, to author, 20 Nov. 1985; Carleton Beals, *Brass-Knuckle Crusade: The Great Know-Nothing Conspiracy, 1820–1860* (New York: Hastings House Publishers, 1960), 172. Breckinridge was pastor from 26 Nov. 1832 until 4 May 1845. Carroll joined the church on 12 Apr. 1845, just prior to Breckinridge's departure. Carroll remarked upon the distinct impression Breckinridge made with "the few discourses it was my fortune to hear from your pulpit"; "by your writings I became an early disciple of yrself in opposition to *Roman Catholicism. . . .*" Carroll to Robert J. Breckinridge, 29 Nov. 1864, Breckinridge Family Papers, Library of Congress.

4. Silbey, *Partisan Imperative,* 71–75; John Hope Franklin, *From Slavery to Freedom: A History of Negro Americans,* 3d ed. (New York: Vintage Books, 1969), 77–78; Evitts, *Allegiances,* 2–3; Smith, "Politics and Democracy," 305; Howe, *Political Culture,* 164.

5. Carroll, *GAB,* 69.

6. Richard Hofstadter, *The Paranoid Style in American Politics and Other Essays* (New York: Alfred A. Knopf, 1966), 29–40.

7. Carroll to Millard Fillmore, 28 Feb., 8 May 1856, Fillmore Papers.

8. Carroll, *GAB,* 22, 18, 20. See also Daniel Walker Howe, "Victorian Culture in America," in *Victorian America,* ed. Daniel Walker Howe (Philadelphia: Univ. of Pennsylvania Press, 1976), 9, 21–26.

9. Carroll, *GAB,* 26, 34, 31, 56.

10. Carroll, *GAB,* 56, 61.

11. Beals, *Brass-Knuckle Crusade,* 178; Evitts, *Allegiances,* 71–73; Laurence F. Schmeckebier, *History of the Know-Nothing Party in Maryland,* Johns Hopkins University Studies in Historical and Political Science, ed. Herbert B. Adams, series vol. 17 (Baltimore: Johns Hopkins Univ. Press, 1899), 15–16; Jean H. Baker, *Ambivalent Americans: The Know-Nothing Party in Maryland* (Baltimore: Johns Hopkins Univ. Press, 1977), 18.

12. Carroll, *GAB,* 72.

13. Carroll, *GAB,* 82, 32.

14. Carroll, *GAB,* 115, 120, 123, 109, 104 [Mother]. Carroll was particularly offended by the appointment of Catholic James Campbell as postmaster general. See Carroll to Thomas King Carroll, 26 May 1856, Carroll Papers. See also Nevins, *Ordeal of the Union,* 47, 324, 403.

15. Carroll, *GAB,* 178; Hofstadter, *Paranoid Politics,* 36.

16. Carroll, *GAB,* 274–89, 127; Charles Oscar Paullin, *Paullin's History of Naval Administration, 1755–1911* (Annapolis, Md.: U.S. Naval Institute, 1968), 238–43. See also Charles Stewart to Carroll, 18 Apr., 11 May 1857, Carroll Papers. The reference was to Catholic Campbell's position in Pierce's cabinet. The Crimean War was still raging as Carroll wrote, but the peace conference in Paris had begun by the time *GAB* was published.

17. Carroll, *GAB,* 341.

18. Carroll, *GAB,* v, 13–14, 18.

19. Carroll, *GAB,* 16, 20.

20. Carroll, *GAB,* 28.

21. Carroll, *GAB,* 92.

22. Carroll, *GAB,* 98, 238, 223.

23. Carroll to Thomas King Carroll, 23 and 26 May 1856, Carroll Papers. This was a common charge of Carroll's; see also Carroll, *GAB,* 212–27; Anna Ella Carroll, *Review of Pierce's Administration; Showing Its Only Popular Measures to Have Originated with the Executive of Millard Fillmore* (Boston: James French, 1856), 24, 28–29. A second edition of *GAB* was issued in 1859; see Walter P. Armstrong, "The Story of Anna Ella Carroll; Politician, Lawyer and Secret Agent," *American Bar Association Journal* 35 (Mar. 1949): 199n. 2.

24. Kenneth Rayner to Carroll, 7 Mar., 12 May 1856, Carroll Papers.

25. Millard Fillmore to Daniel Ullmann, 12 Dec. 1856; Carroll to Fillmore, 26 June 1856, Fillmore Papers; Fillmore to Isaac Newton, 3 Jan. 1855, in *Millard Fillmore Papers,* ed. Frank H. Severance, 2 vols. (Buffalo: Buffalo Historical Society, 1907), 2:347–49; Fillmore quoted in Anna Ella Carroll, *The Union of the States* (Boston: James French, 1856), 62–63; Snyder, "Anna Ella Carroll," 44; Fillmore to American Party Nominating Committee, 21 May 1856, in *Fillmore Papers* 2:358–59; Carroll to Fillmore, 23 May 1856, Fillmore Papers.

26. Carroll, *GAB,* x, 154, 156, 198–207, v, viii, vi, 120.

27. Overdyke, *The Know-Nothing Party,* 213.

28. Kenneth Rayner to Carroll, 7 Mar., 12 May 1856, Carroll Papers. In like manner, Republicans incorporated anti-Catholic rhetoric in their campaign to attract Know-Nothings to the party, hoping to capture voters who were both anti-Catholic and anti-slavery extension, since the Know-Nothings had not taken as clear a stand in the slavery issue. See Gienapp, "Nativism," 542–45.

29. Mayor Eli Perry of Albany quoting Fillmore in an 1856 speech, quoted in Carroll, *Union,* 60; Baker, *Ambivalent Americans,* 47; Overdyke, *The Know-Nothing Party,* 142; Carman and Luthin, "Aspects," 218. Carroll's *Union* and *Review* are considerably less anti-Catholic than *GAB,* as are her two other pamphlets of 1856, *Which? Fillmore or Buchanan!* and *Who Shall Be President? An Appeal to the People* (Boston: James French, 1856). A third pamphlet was a reprint of chap. 25 of *GAB: American Nominations Fillmore and Donelson, Being an Extract from a Work Entitled The Great American Battle; or, The Contest Between Christianity and Political Romanism* (New York: Miller, Orton and Mulligan, 1856).

30. Carroll, *Union,* 26, 54, 12, 28.

31. Carroll, *Union,* 49; Carroll to Thomas King Carroll, 23 May 1856, Carroll Papers, Snyder, "Anna Ella Carroll," 45.

32. Charles Vevier, "American Continentalism: An Idea of Expansion, 1845–1910," *American Historical Review* 65 (Jan. 1960): 323–35; Anna Ella Carroll, *The Star of the West; or, National Men and National Measures,* 3d ed. (Boston: James French, 1857), 162–86; Carroll, *Which?* 13–16, 34–35.

33. Carroll, *Review,* iii–iv.

34. Carroll to Millard Fillmore, 26 June, 6 Nov. 1856, Fillmore Papers; Snyder, "Anna Ella Carroll," 46–47; Carroll to Thurlow Weed, 17 Apr., 11 Dec. 1856, Thurlow Weed Papers,

Rus Rhees Library, University of Rochester, Rochester, N.Y.; Kenneth Rayner to Carroll, 14 Nov. 1856, Carroll Papers; J[osiah] F. Polk to Carroll, 25 Apr. 1856, Carroll Papers.

35. Carroll to Millard Fillmore, 19 July 1856, Fillmore Papers.

36. Carroll to Millard Fillmore, 27 July 1856, Fillmore Papers; Fillmore to Carroll, 30 July 1856, Carroll Papers.

37. Millard Fillmore to Carroll, 13 Aug. 1856, Carroll Papers; Carroll to Fillmore, 11 Sept. 1856, Fillmore Papers; Snyder, "Anna Ella Carroll," 48.

38. Carroll, *Star,* 232–77, vi, 122, 177, 148–49, 171–76; Paullin, *Paullin's History,* 241; Donald Dale Jackson, "Around the World with Wilkes and his 'Scientifics,' " *Smithsonian* 16 (Nov. 1985): 48–63.

39. Carroll, *GAB,* 28; Carroll, *Star,* 346–47.

40. Carroll, *Star,* 379, 384, 385, 378, 386.

41. William Walker to Carroll, n.d., Carroll Papers; Carroll, *Star,* 349.

42. Snyder, "Anna Ella Carroll," 50–52; Carroll to Millard Fillmore, 28 and 31 Oct. 1856, Fillmore Papers. In her 28 Oct. letter, Carroll enclosed a clipping of a pro-Fillmore article, presumably hers, signed "A Voice From Plymouth Rock."

43. Carroll, *Which?* 17.

44. Carroll, *Who Shall Be President?* 3, 4, 8. This was the only time she mentioned Frémont by name.

45. Carroll to Millard Fillmore, 31 Oct., 1 Nov. 1856, Fillmore Papers.

Chapter 3

1. Carroll to Millard Fillmore, 6 Nov. 1856, Fillmore Papers. Since Fillmore was the nominal head of a party that had split over the slavery question in the 1856 nominating process, and since Fillmore's embrace of Know-Nothingism was lukewarm at best, Carroll's observation was optimistic and inaccurate. While Fillmore stressed the Union in his campaign speeches, and seldom mentioned slavery, the party's decision to take the popular-sovereignty position regarding slavery extension split the party in convention and in the fall election. See Congressional Quarterly, *Guide to U.S. Elections* (Washington, D.C.: Congressional Quarterly, 1975), 13; Beals, *Brass-Knuckle Crusade,* 180–81; Ray Allen Billington, *The Protestant Crusade 1800–1860* (1938; rpt. New York: Rinehart, 1952), 428–29.

2. Carroll to Millard Fillmore, 6 Nov. 1856, Fillmore Papers.

3. Kenneth Rayner to Carroll, 14 Nov. 1856, Carroll Papers; Carroll to Millard Fillmore, 16 Nov. 1856, Fillmore Papers.

4. Carroll to Millard Fillmore, 16 Nov. 1856, Fillmore Papers. Of the three works Carroll mentions, presumably she was referring to *GAB* and *The Star of the West.* The third work may have been one of her campaign pamphlets, or perhaps a third, unknown work.

5. Daniel Ullmann to Millard Fillmore, 25 Nov. 1856, Fillmore Papers, refers to an earlier letter from Fillmore to Ullmann requesting information on Carroll. That letter apparently does not survive. Regarding the nineteenth-century practice of testimonial dinners, consider for example, the dinner offered Sterling Price by the alderman of Jefferson City, Missouri. Dinners like these could serve more than one purpose. This one was to honor Price's term as governor, to propitiate those who believed Price should have been nominated to the House of Representatives, and to keep Price's political profile high. Price, incidentally, refused the honor. Robert E. Shalhope, *Sterling Price: Portrait of a Southerner* (Columbia: Univ. of

Missouri Press, 1971), 133; Madeline B. Stern, ed., *Publishers for Mass Entertainment in Nineteenth Century America* (Boston: G. K. Hall, 1980), 93–96.

6. Daniel Ullmann to Millard Fillmore, 25 Nov. 1856, Fillmore Papers. Jeremy Diddler was a character in the 1803 farce *Raising the Wind* by Englishman James Kenney who borrowed money and failed to pay it back. See Snyder, "Anna Ella Carroll," 53n. 51.

7. Carroll to Millard Fillmore, 5 Dec. 1856, Fillmore Papers; newspaper clipping enclosed in letter, Carroll to Thurlow Weed, 11 Dec. 1856, Weed Papers; W[illiam] S[cudder] Tisdale to Fillmore, 8 Dec. 1856, Fillmore Papers.

8. Millard Fillmore to Daniel Ullmann, 9 Dec. 1856; Ullmann to Fillmore, 10 Dec. 1856, Fillmore Papers.

9. Carroll to Thurlow Weed, 17 Apr., 11 Dec. 1856, Weed Papers; Millard Fillmore to Daniel Ullmann, 12 Dec. 1856, Fillmore Papers.

10. Jacob Broom to Millard Fillmore, 15 Dec. 1856; W. S. Tisdale to Fillmore, 18 Dec. 1856; Daniel Ullmann to Fillmore, 18 Dec. 1856; Carroll to Fillmore, 18 Dec. 1856, Fillmore Papers. No book of this title has been found, but a form letter soliciting information and contributions does exist. The letter, signed by Tisdale and promoting Carroll as author of *The Great American Battle* (see chap. 2) as well as the proposed work, was apparently sent to a number of Know-Nothings and included the names of the leaders of the party. For a subscription price high enough to cover the cost of printing and engraving, participants could become a part of the book. See Undated Advertisement, MDHS 3655-703, Carroll Papers.

11. Samuel St. John, Jr., to Millard Fillmore, 18 Dec. 1856; Carroll to Fillmore, 22 Dec. 1856, Fillmore Papers.

12. Millard Fillmore to Carroll, 27 Dec. 1856, Fillmore Papers.

13. Carroll to Millard Fillmore, 1 Jan. 1857, Fillmore Papers.

14. Millard Fillmore to Carroll, 10 Jan. 1857, Fillmore Papers.

15. Carroll to Millard Fillmore, 16 Jan. 1857, Fillmore Papers. Later letters from Tisdale to Carroll make it clear that some sort of relationship survived this imbroglio. See Tisdale to Carroll, 23 Aug., 19 Sept. 1879, Carroll Papers.

16. The 1856 Minute Book of the City and County of New York Courts reveals nothing on Carroll; Joseph Van Nostrand, Archivist, Office of County Clerk and Clerk of the Supreme Court, to author, 8 Mar. 1985. For an examination of judges' reluctance to convict middle- and upper-class women of some crimes, see Elaine Abelson, "When Ladies Go A-Thieving: The Middle-Class Women in the Department Store, 1870–1914," paper delivered at "Facing the Future: Graduate Student Conference on Scholarship on Women," Yale University, New Haven, Conn., 13 Apr. 1985.

17. Carroll was emphatically not a woman's rights supporter (see chap. 2). The nineteenth-century cultural imperative that all women needed a man to watch over them, along with Carroll's occasional references on Fillmore as a father figure, would make it easy for Fillmore to assume a paternalistic attitude toward Carroll's actions. See, for example, Carroll to Millard Fillmore, 7 Mar., 12 Oct. 1853, Fillmore Papers. Little work has been done on Fillmore's life or his presidency. Robert J. Rayback, *Millard Fillmore: Biography of a President* (Buffalo: Buffalo Historical Society, 1959), is the best existing biography of this little-known president, and the only modern one, and a recent study of Fillmore's presidency can be found in Elbert B. Smith, *The Presidencies of Zachary Taylor & Millard Fillmore* (Lawrence: Univ. Press of Kansas, 1988). W. L. Barre, *The Life and Public Services of Millard Fillmore* (1856; rpt. New York: Lenox Hill, 1971), is a campaign biography, as is the only other full-length work on Fillmore, [Ivory Chamberlain], *Biography of Fillmore* (Buffalo, 1856). See also Glyndon G. Van Deusen, *Thurlow Weed: Wizard of the Lobby* (Boston: Little, Brown, 1947), 93, 151.

18. Carroll to Millard Fillmore, 16 Jan. 1857, Fillmore Papers; Snyder, "Anna Ella Carroll," 59n. 64; Carroll to Fillmore, 5 Sept. 1857, Fillmore Papers, Charles Stewart to Carroll, 18 Apr. 1857, Carroll Papers. The "cause" to which Stewart referred dragged on, prompting the *New York Times* to remark in April 1858 that, while they had occasionally flattered themselves that the country was rid of it, it would not die. "It would have been the cheapest and best way to have reinstated all the officers in the beginning, and then tried each of them in detail by a separated [*sic*] Court-Martial. It would have saved the country some hundreds of thousands of dollars, and been much better for the Navy." *New York Times,* 26 Apr. 1858. Regarding Carroll's book tour, see Carroll to Thurlow Weed, 11 Dec. 1856, Weed Papers; J[osiah] F. Polk to Carroll, 25 Apr. 1857, Carroll Papers. Book tours by women authors were not unheard-of; for another description see Kathryn Kish Sklar, *Catherine Beecher: A Study in American Domesticity* (New Haven, Conn.: Yale Univ. Press, 1973), 215. Carroll's petitioning for patronage positions was constant. See Carroll to Thurlow Weed, 11 June 1857, Weed Papers.

19. Kenneth Rayner to Carroll, 1 Oct. 1857, Carroll Papers; [Anna Ella Carroll], *Pope or President? Startling Disclosures of Romanism As Revealed By Its Own Writers. Facts for Americans* (New York: R. L. Delisser, 1859), vi. Carroll established her authorship of this book in a letter to the Rev. Dr. Robert Breckinridge, 29 Nov. 1864, Breckinridge Family Papers. She sent him a copy of her book by way of his nephew, John C. Breckinridge, while John was vice-president under James Buchanan. Conclusive proof of Carroll's activities on behalf of Hicks does not exist. Family tradition held it true, and it seems logical to assume Carroll would work to elect Hicks, a Know-Nothing and a former neighbor. See Greenbie, *My Dear Lady,* 75.

20. Carroll, *Pope or President?* 9–10; Nevins, *Ordeal of the Union,* 403–4.

21. Armstrong, "The Story of Anna Ella Carroll," 199n. 2; Carroll to Robert Kane, 5 Mar. 1859, Carroll Papers; Carroll to William Henry Seward, 23 Apr. 1859, Seward Papers. The outside of the Kane letter bears a note in Carroll's hand that her book on him was interrupted by the Civil War and never completed.

22. Thurlow Weed to Horace Greeley, 19 Oct. [?]; Anna Ella Carroll, "Editorial," *Louisville Journal,* signed "E. Puribus Unum," cited in letter, John Minor Botts to Carroll, 11 May 1858, Carroll Papers. The *Journal* was a Know-Nothing paper and printed a number of articles by Carroll.

23. John Minor Botts, *The Great Rebellion: Its Secret History, Rise, Progress, and Disastrous Failure* (New York: Harper and Brothers, 1866), frontis.; Anna Ella Carroll, "Editorial," 23 Apr. 1858, Carroll Papers. This was a rough draft, and no place of publication is indicated.

24. John Minor Botts to Carroll, 11 May 1858, Carroll Papers; Clyde C. Webster, "John Minor Botts, Anti-Secessionist," *Richmond College Historical Papers* 1 (June 1915): 10, 11–13; *Biographical Directory of the American Congress, 1774–1971* (Washington, D.C.: GPO, 1971), 614; Botts, *The Great Rebellion,* 66, 162–65, 127–28, 144–47; "John Minor Botts," *Dictionary of American Biography,* ed. Allen Johnson, 12 vols. (New York: Charles Scribner's Sons, 1964–73, 1 (1964): 472–73.

25. Webster, "Botts," 22–25; Anna Ella Carroll, "Sketch on John Minor Botts," n.d. [post-1869], MDHS 3649-93, Carroll Papers. Few of Carroll's papers from 1858 survive, but it is apparent she wrote Botts fairly often that year, as well as printing as many articles supporting him as she could. Publishing matters no doubt occupied most of her time.

26. Thomas H. Clay, Jr., to Carroll, 16 Apr. 1859, Carroll Papers.

27. N. Ranney to Carroll, 29 June 1859; Anna Ella Carroll, "Letter to Editors," *New York Express,* signed "Hancock," undated clipping found in an Oct. 1898 letter; [?] to Mrs. Thomas

Cradock, MDHS 3655-676, Carroll Papers. The "Hancock" pseudonym in the *Express* was referred to by Botts in a letter to Carroll, 29 June 1859, and in J. F. Polk to Carroll, 3 Aug. 1859, Carroll Papers.

28. John Minor Botts to Carroll, 30 May, 6 Aug. 1859, Carroll Papers.

29. John Minor Botts to Carroll, 9 Oct. 1859; J. F. Polk to Carroll, 11 Oct. 1859, Carroll Papers.

30. Jacob Broom to Carroll, 26 Oct. 1859; John Minor Botts to Carroll, 6, 12, and 16 Nov. 1859; Carroll to Botts, 18 and 20 Nov. 1859 (one letter), Carroll Papers. See also Reinhard H. Luthin, *The First Lincoln Campaign* (1964; rpt. Cambridge , Mass.: Harvard Univ. Press, 1964), 162. Corwin nominated McLean at the convention, supported Bates and Wade. Political reporter Murat Halstead remarked on Corwin's "covetous glances" at Wade's Senate chair as the real reason for Corwin's support of Wade's candidacy. See Allan Nevins, *The Emergence of Lincoln: Prologue to Civil War, 1859–1861* (New York: Charles Scribner's Sons, 1950), 53, 247–59; Murat Halstead, *Caucuses of 1860* (Columbus, Ohio: Follett, Foster, 1860), 140–44; Harriet A. Weed, ed., *Life of Thurlow Weed,* 2 vols. (1883; rpt. New York: Da Capo Press, 1970), 1:602.

31. John Minor Botts to Carroll, 16 Nov. 1859, 1 Jan. 1860, Carroll Papers.

32. O. B. Vienz [?] to Thurlow Weed, 27 Nov. 1858, Thurlow Weed Papers, Library of Congress (hereafter referred to as Weed-LC Papers); Glyndon G. Van Deusen, *William Henry Seward* (New York: Oxford Univ. Press, 1967), 67–71; Gienapp, "Nativism," 553.

33. Gienapp, "Nativism," 537. Gienapp forcefully argues this position, saying that "the political reality of the Know-Nothings' strength, if nothing else, dictated the necessity of seeking a fusion with antislavery supporters of the American organization." Simon Cameron, Nathaniel Banks, David Wilmot, Schuyler Colfax, and Edward Bates were all former Know-Nothings who became Republicans between 1856 and 1860. Even Thurlow Weed was willing to include some nativist remarks to attract Fillmore supporters in an attempt to prevent Democratic victories in off-year elections in New York. See pp. 540, 547–48, 556, 558–59. See also Eric Foner, *Free Soil, Free Labor, Free Men: The Ideology of the Republican Party Before the Civil War* (New York: Oxford Univ. Press, 1970), 248–60; Carman and Luthin, "Aspects," 229–30. W. Darrell Overdyke holds that the Know-Nothing party succumbed partly because of their failure to take a clearly sectional stand at a point when only sectional stands could attract mass allegiance to a political party. See *The Know-Nothing Party,* 294. For discussions of fusion attempts between Know-Nothings and Republicans, see Michael F. Holt, *Forging a Majority: The Formation of the Republican Party in Pittsburgh, 1848–1860* (New Haven, Conn.: Yale Univ. Press, 1969), 175–83; Holt, *Political Crisis,* 175–81; Stephen E. Maizlish, "The Meaning of Nativism and the Crisis of the Union: The Know-Nothing Movement in the Antebellum North," in *Essays on American Antebellum Politics, 1840–1860,* ed. Stephen E. Maizlish and John J. Kushma (College Station: Univ. of Texas at Arlington by Texas A&M Univ. Press, 1982), 166–98.

34. Kenneth Rayner to Carroll, 23 Nov. 1859; John Minor Botts to Carroll, 24 Dec. 1859, Carroll Papers; Emerson David Fite, *The Presidential Campaign of 1860* (New York: MacMillan, 1911), 237–40.

35. Edward Everett to Carroll, 12 Dec. 1859; John B. Fry to Carroll, 5 Jan. 1860, Carroll Papers. A note in Carroll's hand on a letter from Jefferson Davis, 22 Dec. 1857, indicates he sent her fifty dollars because of losses her family suffered in the panic of 1857. Presumably, it was this last disaster that sent her father to live with his son, Dr. Thomas King Carroll, in Dorchester County. Census records from 1860 indicate the Carroll household had four slaves, but it is unclear if they were Dr. Carroll's or four his father had held onto from his days in Baltimore. *Population Schedules of the Eighth Census of the United States, 1860* (Washington, D.C.: National Archives and Records Service, 1959), microscope reel no. 653, p. 192.

36. Carroll to Thurlow Weed, 27 Jan. 1860, Weed Papers.

37. Ollinger Crenshaw, "The Speakership Contest of 1859–1860," *Mississippi Valley Historical Review* 29 (Dec. 1942): 327; Carroll to Thurlow Weed, 27 Jan. 1860, Weed Papers.

38. Apparently, Carroll had either never been paid or been paid less than what she thought her work was worth by the Know-Nothings in 1856 (see chap. 2). She was determined not to repeat that mistake: "My ability as a writer is conceded by men of all parties and I don't mean ever to throw my time and talent away for any cause again," she wrote to Weed, after demanding she be "well & handsomely paid for my service by the opposition, by which I mean your Party." Carroll to Thurlow Weed, 20 Apr. 1860, Weed Papers. There is no evidence as to the result of her bill to Weed. Both Fry and Polk asked her to help them find positions; see J. B. Fry to Carroll, 5 Jan. 1860; J. F. Polk of Carroll, 5 Aug. 1859, Carroll Papers. Carroll's deafness came on gradually; by 1865 it was bad enough that one friend warned a senator in a letter of introduction to be sure to speak up, and by 1890 she was completely deaf. See R. W. Mundy[?] to Senator [?], 28 Sept. 1865, Carroll Papers; Blackwell, *Life and Writings,* 135.

39. Fernando Wood to Carroll, 30 Jan., 7 Mar. 1860, Carroll Papers; Carroll, Letter to Editor, *New York Daily News,* 27 Feb. 1860, signed "Madison."

40. Samuel A. Pleasants, *Fernando Wood of New York* (New York: AMS Press, 1966), 95–101; Carroll to Thurlow Weed, 24 Mar. 1860, Weed Papers.

41. Carroll to Thurlow Weed, 20 Apr. 1860, Weed Papers; Edward Everett to Carroll, 29 May 1860, Carroll Papers; Horace Greeley and John F. Cleveland, *A Political Textbook for 1860: Comprising a Brief View of Presidential Nominations and Elections: Including All the National Platforms Ever Yet Adopted: Also A History of the Struggle respecting Slavery in the Territories, and of the Action of Congress As to the Freedom of the Public Lands, with the Most Notable Speeches and Letters of Messrs. Lincoln, Douglas, Bell, Cass, Seward, Everett, Breckinridge, H. V. Johnson, etc., etc., Touching on the Questions of the Day; and Returns of All Presidential Elections Since 1836* (New York: The Tribune Association, 1860), 29.

42. John Minor Botts to Carroll, 1 May 1860; John Wilson to Carroll, 21 May 1860, Carroll Papers. Carroll had at least a nodding acquaintance (though undoubtedly she would consider it more intimate) with Edward Everett prior to his selection as John Bell's running mate, having written him regarding her antislavery activities in the early 1850s.

43. J. F. Polk to Carroll, 26 June, 6 July 1860; John Minor Botts to Carroll, 2 Sept. 1860; William Orton to Carroll, 1 Dec. 1860, Carroll Papers; [Washington] *National Intelligencer,* 6 Feb. 1861.

44. L. E. Barber to Carroll, 18 Feb., 12 Apr. 1861, Carroll Papers, CCJ; *Biographical Directory of the American Congress,* 719.

45. L. E. Barber to Carroll, 14 May 1861, Carroll Papers, CCJ.

Chapter 4

1. Carroll to Thomas H. Hicks, Nov. 1860, Carroll Papers.

2. Morgan Dix, son of Commander of the Department of Maryland John A. Dix, remarked on the importance of controlling Maryland for the Union, 23 July 1861. See Charles B. Clark, "Suppression and Control of Maryland, 1861–1865: A Study of Federal-State Relations During Civil Conflict," *Maryland Historical Magazine* 54 (Sept. 1959): 248. See also W. W. Brewer, "Lincoln and the Border States," *Journal of Negro History* 34 (Jan. 1949): 63–64.

3. Cited in William Cook Wright, *The Secession Movement in the Middle Atlantic States* (Cranbury, N.J.: Associated Univ. Presses, 1973), 35. Wright suggests, incorrectly, that Hicks

was a secessionist at heart. See also Smith, "Politics and Democracy," 298; Baker, *Politics of Continuity,* 13; Carl Degler, *The Other South: Southern Dissenters in the Nineteenth Century* (Boston: Northeastern Univ. Press, 1982), 146–52, 179–87.

4. Baker, *Politics of Continuity,* 48.

5. Thomas H. Hicks to Thomas G. Pratt, Sprigg Harwood, J. S. Franklin, Llewellyn Boyd, and I. [?] Pinkney, 27 Nov. 1860; Hicks to the Maryland People, 3 Jan. 1861; Hicks to Governor of South Carolina, 20 Nov. 1860, Governor's Letterbook, Hall of Records, Maryland State Archives, Annapolis.

6. Thomas H. Hicks to Carroll, 21 Dec. 1860; Carroll to Thomas H. Hicks, 16 Jan. 1861, Carroll Papers.

7. Thomas H. Hicks to the Maryland People, 3 Jan. 1861, Governor's Letterbook.

8. Carroll to Thomas H. Hicks, 16 Jan. 1861, Carroll Papers; Hicks to Carroll, 19 Jan. 1861, Carroll Papers, CCJ. See also Evitts, *Allegiances,* 164–65.

9. Carroll to Thomas H. Hicks, 24 Jan. 1861, Carroll Papers. Although Crittenden's compromise was not voted on until 2 Mar., it could be considered dead by 16 Jan. or so, something Carroll in Washington was far more cognizant of than was Hicks. See Nevins, *Emergence of Lincoln,* 392–402; David M. Potter, *Lincoln and His Party in the Secession Crisis* (New Haven, Conn.: Yale Univ. Press, 1942), 84–132.

10. Carroll to Thomas H. Hicks, 24 Jan. 1861, Carroll Papers.

11. Carroll to Thomas H. Hicks, 30 Jan. 1861, Carroll Papers; "Independent," *New York Morning Express,* 31 Jan. 1861.

12. Carroll to Thurlow Weed, 7 Jan. 1861, Weed Papers. The position was never specifically stated by Lincoln, but was rumored to be secretary of the navy or postmaster general. See Daniel W. Crofts, "A Reluctant Unionist: John A. Gilmer and Lincoln's Cabinet," *Civil War History* 24 (Sept. 1978): 231, 236–37, 241–42; Burton J. Hendrick, *Lincoln's War Cabinet* (Boston: Little, Brown, 1946), 102, 114. For Lincoln's correspondence on the matter, see Roy P. Basler, ed., *The Collected Works of Abraham Lincoln,* 9 vols. (New Brunswick, N.J.: Rutgers Univ. Press, 1953–55), 4:151–53, 155, 164, 170–71, 173.

13. [Samuel T. Williams] to Carroll, 26 Aug. 1861; Anna Ella Carroll, Memo on War Powers, 19 Aug. 1861, MDHS 3650-178, p. 7, Carroll Papers. Obviously Carroll was not impressed with Lincoln's inclusion of Missourian Edward Bates in his cabinet.

14. Carroll to Thurlow Weed, 17 Mar. 1861; Carroll to Weed, n.d., Weed Papers (this letter is undated but was obviously written after the 17 Mar. letter); John Minor Botts to Carroll, 31 Mar. 1861, Carroll Papers.

15. Carroll to Thurlow Weed, 15 Mar., 15 May 1861, Weed Papers. Carroll's friends badgered her. For example, John Fry wanted her to have a "little chat" with the president on his behalf. John B. Fry to Carroll, 9 Mar. 1861, Carroll Papers.

16. Abraham Lincoln in *Washington Star,* 22 Apr. 1861, cited in Earl Schenck Miers, ed., *Lincoln Day By Day, A Chronology 1809–1865,* 3 vols. (Washington, D.C.: Lincoln Sesquecentennial Commission, 1960), 3:37. See also Baker, *Politics of Continuity,* 53.

17. Carroll to Thomas H. Hicks, 21 Apr. 1861, Carroll Papers, CCJ.

18. Carroll to Salmon P. Chase, 24 Apr. 1861, Salmon Portland Chase Papers, Library of Congress; Carroll to Thurlow Weed, 26 Apr. 1861, Weed Papers; Carroll to Chase, 27 Apr. 1861, Chase Papers. Secretary of War Simon Cameron's ineptitude was pronounced enough that both Chase and Secretary of State Seward took part in activities normally beyond their purview. See J. W. Schuckers, *The Life and Public Services of Salmon Portland Chase, United States Senator and Governor of Ohio; Secretary of the Treasury, and Chief-Justice of the United States* (New York: D. Appleton, 1874), 419–20, 424. Carroll appealed to Chase for a safe escort to Annapolis. She may have met him through her friendship with Ohioan Thomas Corwin and may have chosen to approach him as well as Seward (through Weed), since

Seward and Weed were so unresponsive to her requests. Frederick J. Blue, *Salmon P. Chase: A Life in Politics* (Kent, Ohio: Kent State Univ. Press, 1987), found no evidence of as intimate a friendship as Carroll claimed in her later writings. As far as her letters to legislators, unfortunately, none of the delegates to the special session appear to have preserved their papers. Consequently, none of Carroll's letters have apparently survived. See also Evitts, *Allegiances,* 187–88; Baker, *Politics of Continuity,* 56; Clark, "Suppression and Control," 243; Henry Adams, *The Great Secession Winter of 1860–61 and Other Essays,* ed. George Rochfield (New York: Sagamore Press, 1958), 24; Carl M. Frasure, "Union Sentiment in Maryland, 1859–1861," *Maryland Historical Magazine* 24 (Sept. 1929), 210–11, 223–24.

19. Anna Ella Carroll, "Calhoun and His Nullification Doctrine," *Living Age* 70 (17 Aug. 1861): 444–46; Frank Moore, ed., *The Rebellion Record: A Diary of American Events, with Documents, Narratives, Illustrative Incidents, Poetry, Etc.,* 11 vols. (New York: G. P. Putnam and Charles T. Evans, 1861–63; D. Van Nostrand, 1864–68), 1 (1867): 5, 10, 14–15, 22–37, 41.

20. Carroll, "Calhoun," 444–45; John C. Calhoun, "A Discourse on the Constitution and Government of the United States," in *The Works of John C. Calhoun,* ed. Richard K. Cralle, 6 vols. (New York: Russell and Russell, 1968), 1:301. Calhoun's Fort Hill address was made 26 July 1831.

21. Anna Ella Carroll, *Reply to the Speech of Hon. J. C. Breckinridge, Delivered in the United States Senate, July 16, 1861, and, in Defence of the President's War Measures* (Washington, D.C.: Henry Polkinhorn, 1861), 3; [Breckinridge in] *Congressional Globe,* 37th Cong., 1st sess., 16 July 1861, 140; Lucille Stillwell, *John Cabell Breckinridge* (Caldwell, Idaho: Caxton Printers, 1936), 99–105.

22. Carroll, *Reply to Breckinridge,* 3, 9. Norma Cuthbert, *Lincoln and the Baltimore Plot* (San Marino, Calif.: Huntington Library, 1949), details the plot to assassinate Lincoln as he changed trains in Baltimore. See also Nevins, *Emergence of Lincoln,* 451; Miers, *Lincoln Day By Day* 3:19–21.

23. Carroll, *Reply to Breckinridge,* 10.

24. Carroll, *Reply to Breckinridge,* 10. See a similar interpretation from a contemporary in Horace Binney, "The Privilege of the Writ of Habeas Corpus Under the Constitution," in *Union Pamphlets of the Civil War 1861–1865,* ed. Frank Freidel, 2 vols. (Cambridge, Mass.: Belknap Press of Harvard Univ. Press, 1967), 1:202–5, 252. Lincoln defended his actions in his Message to Congress in Special Session, 4 July 1861; see Basler, *Works* 4:421–41.

25. Bates began to spell out this crucial distinction in his 5 July 1861 opinion on the suspension of the writ of habeas corpus. Edward Bates, 10 *Opinions of the Attorney General* 74 (1861); John P. Frank, "Edward Bates, Lincoln's Attorney General," *American Journal of Legal History* 10 (1966): 34–50; Harold H. Hyman and William M. Wiecek, *Equal Justice Under Law: Constitutional Development 1835–1875* (New York: Harper and Row, 1982), 263–64. The question of the Confederacy's status vis à vis belligerency is discussed in J. G. Randall, *Constitutional Problems Under Lincoln* (Gloucester, Mass.: Peter Smith, 1963), 51–69. Ludwell Johnson discusses the resolution of the matter in the courts in "The Confederacy: What Was It? The View from the Federal Courts," *Civil War History* 32 (Mar. 1986): 5–22. On the contemporary definition of belligerent rights see Henry Wheaton, *Elements of International Law: The Literal Reproduction of the Edition of 1866 by Richard Henry Dana, Jr.,* ed. George Grofton Wilson (Oxford: Clarendon Press, 1936), 29–32. Randall discusses the 5–4 Supreme Court decision in the Prize Cases that decided in favor of the president's actions in *Constitutional Problems,* 51–57. See also William Whiting, *The War Powers Under the Constitution of the United States* (1871; rpt. New York: DaCapo Press, 1972), 38–49, for his statement regarding belligerent rights; 82–83, for his interpretation of the general war powers of the president.

26. Basler, *Works* 4:430.
27. Carroll, *Reply to Breckinridge,* 7.
28. Hyman and Wiecek, *Equal Justice,* 232–42.
29. Carroll, *Reply to Breckinridge,* 11, 14; Basler, *Works* 4:429–31; Carroll, *Reply to Breckinridge,* 11; Binney, "Privilege," 252; Baker, *Politics of Continuity,* 59–60. Because the conditions permitting the suspension of the writ of habeas corpus were discussed in article I, section 9 of the Constitution, which article set out the duties of the legislative branch of the government, opponents of Lincoln's actions argued that he had no right to suspend the writ and that suspension was obviously a power reserved for Congress. Lincoln, Carroll, and pamphleteer Horace Binney all argued that if, in order to execute the laws and protect the Constitution against a rebellion, it was necessary to make arbitrary arrests and suspend the writ, that power was implicitly granted to the president in his capacity as commander-in-chief. See article II, section 1 (oath to protect the Constitution), section 2 (appointing the president commander-in-chief), section 3 (requiring the president to faithfully execute the laws).
30. Carroll, *Reply to Breckinridge,* 11, 14.
31. Samuel T. Williams to Carroll, 8 Aug. 1861; Caleb Smith to Carroll, 25 Sept. 1861; Edward Bates to Carroll, 21 Sept. 1861, Carroll Papers. Carroll, incidentally, has three copies of this Bates letter in her papers. Each copy, all in her hand, is slightly different. There is no doubt that Carroll and Bates knew each other fairly well; two other later letters from Bates make it clear they were on good terms. Apparently Carroll used this particular letter to advance her claim that the government ordered the printing of pamphlets she wrote. The first version states, "I have sent the President the copy you left"; the last, "The President requested me to thank you most cordially for the copy you sent. . . ." This incident of editing further reflects Carroll's tendency to twist reality into whatever would reflect her most favorably, making it most difficult for any historian to determine which of her claims was true or to what extent any were true.
32. Carroll to Abraham Lincoln, 21 June 1862, Carroll Papers; Thomas A. Scott to Carroll, 28 Jan. 1863, cited in Blackwell, *Military Genius,* 125–26; Lemuel D. Evans to Edwin M. Stanton, 8 Aug. 1862, Carroll Papers.
33. Anna Ella Carroll, "The Constitutional Power of the President to Make Arrests and Suspend the Writ of Habeas Corpus Examined" (Maryland, 1861), reprinted in Blackwell, *Life and Writings,* 92–98; Anna Ella Carroll, *The War Powers of the General Government* (Washington, D.C.: Henry Polkinhorn, 1861).
34. [Samuel T. Williams] to Carroll, 26 Aug. 1861; Carroll to Jefferson Davis, Feb. 1861, Carroll Papers. Davis's reply, in which he spoke of the finality of his "leave taking" from the Union, is a copy in Carroll's hand and is of questionable authenticity. Davis to Carroll, 1 Mar. 1861, Carroll Papers; Mary S. Dix, associate editor, The Papers of Jefferson Davis, to author, 29 Aug. 1985. Several letters from Davis to Carroll survive in Carroll's papers. He responded to patronage requests, sent her money, talked about his family, and promised to see her on his way home, "if my wife does not call for me before the adjournment." Davis to Carroll, 22 Dec. 1857, 20 Mar., 27 Feb. 1860, Carroll Papers.
35. Anna Ella Carroll, Memo on War Powers, 19 Aug. 1861, MDHS 3650-178, p. 17A, Carroll Papers.
36. Bruce Catton, *The Coming Fury* (New York: Doubleday, 1961), 397–401; Randall, *Constitutional Problems,* 294–302.
37. Carroll, Memo on War Powers, 22; Carroll, *War Powers,* 10.
38. Trumbull, *Congressional Globe,* 37th Cong., 2d sess., 2 Dec. 1861, 1; Carroll, *War Powers,* 12; Carroll to Thomas H. Hicks, 11 Jan. 1862, Carroll Papers. Carroll argued that "the idea of procuring the abolition of slavery by this war is the most chimerical one ever

conceived by the intelligent mind. . . ." See Carroll, Loose Papers on Slavery and the Civil War, Carroll Papers, CCJ, MDHS 3622-103, p. 42.

39. Carroll, *War Powers,* 10–11.

40. [Divenin] *Congressional Globe,* 37th Cong., 2d sess., 22 Jan. 1862, 438; Carroll to Abraham Lincoln, 21 June 1862, Carroll Papers; Blackwell, *Life and Writings,* 46–48. Carl Sandburg, *Abraham Lincoln: The War Years,* 4 vols. (New York: Harcourt Brace, 1939), 1:410–11, places the seal of the Department of State on her work, as does Blackwell's volume which reprints the pamphlet (*Life and Writings,* 48–91), but all claims filed by Carroll for payment were with the War Department. Sumner himself was impressed enough with Carroll's "Reply" to place a copy of it in Harvard University Library in 1862. See Armstrong, "The Story of Anna Ella Carroll," 199n. 2.

41. J. G. Randall and David Donald, *The Civil War and Reconstruction* (Lexington, Mass.: D. C. Heath, 1969), 371–76.

42. Carroll to Abraham Lincoln, 15 Apr. 1862, Carroll Papers.

43. Abraham Lincoln, Message to Congress, 16 Apr. 1862, in Basler, *Works* 5:192.

44. *Congressional Globe,* 37th Cong., 2d sess., 19 May 1862, 2188–96; Anna Ella Carroll, *The Relation of the National Government to the Revolted Citizens Defined* (Washington: Henry Polkinhorn, 1862).

45. *Congressional Globe,* 19 May 1862, 2189–90, 2193.

46. *Congressional Globe,* 19 May 1862, 2190, 2192, 2196.

47. Carroll to Abraham Lincoln, 19 May 1862, Carroll Papers. There was considerable disagreement among jurists in the 1860s regarding the right of confiscation in time of war. See Randall, *Constitutional Problems,* 294–302.

48. Randall, *Constitutional Problems,* 360–63; Hyman and Wiecek, *Equal Justice,* 251–52.

49. Carroll, *Relation,* 1–2.

50. *Congressional Globe,* 19 May 1862, 2190; Carroll, *Relation,* 3–6.

51. Carroll, *Relation,* 8, 12, 15.

52. Carroll to Abraham Lincoln, 4 July 1862, Carroll Papers. See Lincoln's response to Frémont's and Hunter's proclamations in Basler, *Works* 4:506 and 5:222. Black troops were first organized in April of 1862 and would be officially sanctioned by the War Department that August. See also Randall and Donald, *Civil War and Reconstruction,* 391–92.

53. Carroll to Abraham Lincoln, 14 July 1862, Robert Todd Lincoln Collection of Abraham Lincoln Papers (microfilm), Library of Congress.

54. Basler, *Works* 5:331; Randall, *Constitutional Problems,* 279–80.

55. Basler, *Works* 5:329–30. Randall, *Constitutional Problems,* 360–63, discusses the logistical problems in enforcing the provisions.

56. Anna Ella Carroll, Manuscript on Slavery, post-1864, MDHS 3652-430, Carroll Papers. For Lincoln's remarks on his emancipation program see his Annual Message to Congress, 1 Dec. 1862, in Basler, *Works* 5:518–37, especially 530–36; see also Richard N. Current, *The Lincoln Nobody Knows* (New York: McGraw-Hill, 1958), 221–22.

57. John B. Fry to Carroll, 5 Apr. 1861, Carroll Papers; James Grant to Aaron C. Burr, 31 Aug. 1860, Aaron Columbus Burr Papers, Yale University, New Haven, Conn.; Grant to Burr, 13 Sept. 1861, "Records of the Office of the Secretary of the Interior Relating to the Suppression of the African Slave Trade and Negro Colonization, 1854–72," U.S. Department of the Interior, Record Group 48, National Archives, Washington, D.C.; Carroll to Abraham Lincoln, 23 Apr. 1862, Department of the Interior, Record Group 48 (hereafter cited as DNA, RG 48).

58. Aaron C. Burr to Secretary [Caleb] Smith, 6 May 1862, DNA, RG 48.

59. James Grant to Aaron C. Burr, 9 Feb. 1861; Carroll to Burr, 3 Sept. 1861; James Grant to Burr, 3 Feb. [1862], Burr Papers; Carroll to Abraham Lincoln, 15 Apr. 1862, Carroll Papers. Carroll wrote to the newspapers as well. See Carroll to Editor, *New York Times,* 6 Mar. 1862.

60. Carroll to Abraham Lincoln, 23 Apr. 1862; Carroll to Secretary Smith, 27 Apr. 1862, DNA, RG 48. One reason Lincoln may have used when rejecting the idea was the pro-secession sentiment of many of the citizens of British Honduras, particularly traders. By early 1863 supporters were eager to accept free blacks for labor in British Honduras, but only those emancipated prior to the war, since they regarded freedmen as more "intelligent" than "Contrabands." See Wayne M. Clegern, *British Honduras: Colonial Dead End: 1859–1900* (Baton Rouge: Louisiana State Univ. Press, 1967), 22, 30, 38. Carroll also argued for a Central American site for free blacks in the *Washington National Republican,* 23 Apr. 1862.

61. Aaron C. Burr to Secretary Smith, 6 May 1862; Carroll to Secretary Smith, 13 May 1862, DNA, RG 48.

62. Anna Ella Carroll, Recollections of Lincoln, n.d., MDHS 3655-722, pp. 105–20, Carroll Papers.

63. Carroll to Abraham Lincoln, 19 May 1862, Lincoln Papers.

64. William Mitchell to Carroll, 13 May 1862, Carroll Papers; Carroll to Aaron C. Burr, 30 Aug. 1862, Burr Papers; Abraham Lincoln, "Address on Colonization to a Deputation of Negroes," in Basler, *Works* 5:370–75. Mitchell's letter, which describes the president's delighted reaction to the box sent and praises Carroll's abilities as a writer, is a copy in Carroll's hand, and may have been used at a later date in her claims against the government. It is one of three copies, none of which are exactly alike, and therefore must be viewed cautiously (see n. 31 above).

65. Carroll to Aaron C. Burr, 13 Sept. 1862, Burr Papers. Burr protested the decision to both Pomeroy and Lincoln and warned of dire consequences if colonization proceeded elsewhere, but to no avail. See Burr to Senator Pomeroy, 20 Sept., 5 Oct. 1862; Burr to Abraham Lincoln, 6 Oct. 1862, Burr Papers; Basler, *Works* 5:433–36; Carroll to Lincoln, 21 Oct. 1862, Lincoln Papers. A substantial work on the Ile A'Vache colony is by Jayme Ruth Spencer, "Abraham Lincoln and Negro Colonization: The Ile A'Vache, Hayti Experience, 1862–1864" (master's thesis, College of William and Mary in Virginia, Williamsburg, 1971).

66. Abraham Lincoln to Carroll, 19 Aug. 1862, in Basler, *Works* 5:381–82; Edward Bates to Carroll, 20 Aug. 1862, Garfield Papers. These two letters were enclosed in a letter from Carroll to Garfield in which she introduced herself and her claim against the government. Basler mistakenly has the Lincoln letter in Carroll's hand; both letters were copies, but not in Carroll's handwriting.

67. Basler, *Works* 5:423; Carroll to Abraham Lincoln, 15 Apr., 14 July 1862, Carroll Papers.

Chapter 5

1. Carroll to Abraham Lincoln, 21 June, 2 July 1862, Carroll Papers. These are drafts of the same letter with two different dates on it. There is no corroborative evidence that Carroll and Lincoln met, but since Carroll later quoted Lincoln's remark in a letter, no doubt the meeting took place. See n. 25 below.

2. "Lincoln's Lady Strategist," *Life* 25 (26 July 1948): 101–2; Greenbie, *My Dear Lady;* H. R. Shattuck, "Anna Ella Carroll: The Originator of the Tennessee Campaign," *Outing* 6

(July 1885): 403; Mark E. Neely, Jr., *The Lincoln Encyclopedia* (New York: McGraw-Hill, 1982), 48–49.

3. Lemuel D. Evans to William Henry Seward, 7 Sept. 1861, Carroll Papers.

4. Anna Ella Carroll, "Plan of the Tennessee Campaign," *North American Review* 42 (Apr. 1886): 344.

5. Carroll, "Plan," 343–44.

6. Carroll, "Plan," 344.

7. Shattuck, "Anna Ella Carroll," 407.

8. Marvin R. Cain, *Lincoln's Attorney General: Edward Bates of Missouri* (Columbia: Univ. of Missouri Press, 1965), 137–38.

9. Carroll, "Plan," 345.

10. Carroll to Thomas A. Scott, 10 Jan. 1862, Carroll Papers. Carroll was mistaken when she talked of a Memphis and Nashville Railroad at Hamburg. No such railroad existed. She was most likely referring to the Nashville and Decatur Railroad, further to the east. The original text of Carroll's plan was reprinted a number of times. Each version has minor changes in the text, but they are all virtually identical. There is one version, in what is presumably the hand of a professional amanuensis, in Carroll's papers. The version cited here is from Charles M. Scott, *The Origin of the Tennessee Campaign, by Capt. Charles M. Scott, As a Refutation of the Fradulent [sic] Claim of Miss Anna Ella Carroll* (Terre Haute, Ind.: Moore and Langen, 1889), 12–14.

11. Carroll, "Plan," 345.

12. Shattuck, "Anna Ella Carroll," 406, 407; Carroll, "Plan," 347.

13. [Lemuel D. Evans], *The Material Bearing of the Tennessee Campaign in 1862 upon the Destinies of Our Civil War* (Washington, D.C.: W. H. Moore [ca. 1872]), lists the effects of the plan's strategy most comprehensively. See also Shattuck, "Anna Ella Carroll," and Carroll, "Plan," as well as the entry for Carroll in the *National Cyclopedia of American Biography,* 62 vols. (New York: James T. White, 1893–1984), 5 (1894): 193.

14. Shattuck, "Anna Ella Carroll," 409. Lincoln's reaction is given in various words. This is the most dramatic version; it was taken from an interview conducted with Carroll late in her life. Since Carroll did not meet with Lincoln regarding the plan, and no direct evidence of Lincoln's reaction survives, all quotations of this kind can be regarded as poetical in nature.

15. *The War of the Rebellion: A Compilation of the Official Records of the Union and Confederate Armies,* 128 vols. (Washington, D.C.: GPO, 1880–1901), ser. 1, vol. 51, pt. 1: 369–70, 386–87 (hereafter cited as *OR*); Virgil Carrington James, *The Civil War at Sea,* 3 vols. (New York: Holt, Rinehart, Winston, 1960), 1:184, 216; Richard S. West, Jr., *Mr. Lincoln's Navy* (New York: Longmans, Green, 1957), 158–61.

16. *OR* 4:456–58, 408, 459–62; Ulysses S. Grant, *Personal Memoirs of U. S. Grant,* 2 vols. (New York: Charles L. Webster, 1885), 1:264–67.

17. Grant, *Memoirs* 1:345–46; Bern Anderson, *By Sea and By River: The Naval History of the Civil War* (1962; rpt. Westport, Conn.: Greenwood Press, 1977), 88. Whittlesey's letter to Halleck was dated 20 Nov. 1861. See *OR* 7:440.

18. West, *Mr. Lincoln's Navy,* 45; *Civil War Naval Chronology, 1861–1865,* comp. U.S. Naval Department, Naval History Division (Washington, D.C.: GPO, 1971), 14; Alfred T. Mahan, *The Gulf and Inland Waters* (New York: Charles Scribner's Sons, 1883), 12–13; *Official Records of the Union and Confederate Navies in the War of the Rebellion,* 30 vols. (Washington, D.C.: GPO, 1894–1922), ser. 1, 22:279 (hereafter cited as *ORN*). Missouri was added to the Department of the Ohio on 6 June 1861; the Western Department was constituted 3 July 1861, made up of Illinois and all states west of the Mississippi River to the Rocky Mountains. See Mark M. Boatner III, *Civil War Dictionary* (New York: David McKay, 1959), 606, 903.

19. *ORN* 22:284–85, 195, 277, 307–8, 355–56, 369, 375, 378; Grant, *Memoirs* 1:264; Mahan, *Gulf and Inland Waters,* 16. *ORN* 22:379–84 discusses the raid on Eddyville on the Cumberland River, 26–28 Oct. 1861. The raid on Belmont took place 7 Nov. 1861 on the Mississippi River. *ORN* 22:398–406.

20. *ORN* 22:388–89; Randall and Donald, *Civil War and Reconstruction,* 371–72.

21. Eads had had to threaten a work stoppage on the ironclads "for want of funds" in late October. See *ORN* 22:378. E. B. Long pointed out the difficulties in the Western Department in "Anna Ella Carroll: Exaggerated Heroine?" *Civil War Times Illustrated* 14 (July 1975): 33–35. For correspondence of Grant and Foote with Halleck and the reports on the capture of Fort Henry, see *OR* 7:119–416. See also Bruce Catton, *Terrible Swift Sword* (New York: Doubleday, 1963), 141–42, 146–47.

22. This denomination of Carroll is from a juvenile biography, Winifred E. Wise, *Lincoln's Secret Weapon* (New York: Chilton, 1961).

23. Carroll to Abraham Lincoln, 21 June 1862, Carroll Papers.

24. See Anna Ella Carroll, Claim against Government, Oct.-Nov. 1861, MDHS 3650-176, Carroll Papers; Howard K. Beale, ed., *Diary of Gideon Welles: Secretary of the Navy Under Lincoln and Johnson,* 3 vols. (New York: W. W. Norton, 1960), 1:127. While adequate as an employee in the War Department, Scott had also continued his position, unpaid, as vice-president of the Pennsylvania Railroad. The railroad obtained a number of lucrative contracts from the government during Scott's tenure. See Hendrick, *Lincoln's War Cabinet,* 220–21. Thomas A. Scott's statement dated 28 Jan. 1863 is cited in Blackwell, *Military Genius,* 125. See also Thomas A. Scott to Carroll [?], 2 and 28 Jan. 1863; Anna Ella Carroll, Claim against Government, 2 Jan. 1863, MDHS 3650-183, Carroll Papers. For an analysis of Lincoln's difficulties in working with women during the Civil War, see Roy P. Basler, "Lincoln, Blacks and Women," in *The Public and Private Lincoln: Contemporary Perspectives,* ed. Cullom Davis, Charles B. Strozier, Rebecca Monroe Leach, and Geoffrey C. Ward (Carbondale: Southern Illinois Univ. Press, 1979), 38–53.

25. Carroll to Abraham Lincoln, 21 June, 2 July 1862, Carroll Papers; Carroll to John Tucker, 26 Mar. 1862, Carroll Papers; Samuel Richey Kamm, *The Civil War Career of Thomas A. Scott* (Philadelphia: Univ. of Pennsylvania Press, 1940), 85–86; F. Lauriston Bullard, "Anna Ella Carroll and Her 'Modest' Claim," *Lincoln Herald* 50 (Oct. 1948): 5; Carroll to Lincoln, 14 Aug. 1862, Lincoln Papers. Carroll's 21 June letter is obviously a draft; the 2 July letter is an incomplete copy of the first, but does contain a notation by Carroll that it was read aloud to Lincoln, presumably about 2 July.

26. Carroll to Abraham Lincoln, 14 Aug. 1862, Lincoln Papers.

27. See, for example, Bullard, "Anna Ella Carroll"; Long, "Anna Ella Carroll," 28–35; Kenneth P. Williams, "The Tennessee River Campaign and Anna Ella Carroll," *Indiana Magazine of History* 46 (Sept. 1950): 221–48.

28. Scott, *Origin,* 6–7.

29. U. S. Grant to Captain Scott, 18 Mar. 1865, and U. S. Grant to Board of Inspectors, 15 Apr. 1862, both cited in Scott, *Origin,* 29. Neither of these letters appears in Grant's papers. See also Scott, *Origin,* 7.

30. Jones, *Revised History,* 297; Greenbie, *My Dear Lady,* 132; Lemuel D. Evans to William Henry Seward, 7 Sept. 1861, 3 Mar. 1862, Seward Papers (microfilm).

31. Scott, *Origin,* 8–9.

32. Scott, *Origin,* 8–9; Charles M. Scott to Anna Scott, 4 and 7 Feb. 1862; E. A. Scott to Carroll, 24 Mar. 1862, Carroll Papers.

33. E. A. Scott to Carroll, 25 May 1862; Charles M. Scott to Frank P. Blair, 31 May 1862; C. M. Scott to Carroll, 9 July 1862, Carroll Papers.

34. Charles M. Scott to Carroll, 2 May 1862, Carroll Papers; Williams, "Tennessee River

Campaign," 245; Charles M. Scott, Extracts, 23 Mar. 1862 through 7 June 1863, MDHS 3650-202, Carroll Papers; Carroll to Edwin Stanton, 14 May 1862, Carroll Papers and Carroll Papers, CCJ.

35. Carroll to John Tucker, 26 Mar. 1862; Carroll to Thomas A. Scott, 7 June 1862; Carroll to Tucker, 30 June 1862, Carroll Papers; Carroll to Edwin Stanton, 9 Sept. 1862, Carroll Papers, CCJ.

36. Thomas A. Scott to Carroll, 27 Oct. 1862, Carroll Papers; Anna Ella Carroll, "Captain Charles M. Scott: Plan of the Tennessee Campaign,"[Washington] *National Intelligencer,* 12 Apr. 1865.

37. The hearing before the House Committee on Military Affairs was held 11 July 1876. The proceedings were published the following August. U.S. Congress, House, Committee on Military Affairs, *Petition of Anna Ella Carroll for Compensation for services rendered to the War Department during the late war,* 44th Cong., 1st sess., 1876, H. Mis. Doc. 179 (hereafter cited as H.R. Doc. 179).

38. Scott, *Origin,* 10, 19. Ludwell H. Johnson, "Northern Profits and Profiteers: The Cotton Rings of 1864–1865," *Civil War History* 12 (June 1966), cites one instance in October 1864 where fifteen hundred bales of cotton was worth $1 million. If the price maintained itself at that level, Scott's cotton could have been worth about $650,000. Of course the price of cotton, as with all commodities, varied greatly year to year. Presumably that figure would be a gross rather than net worth, without accounting for the costs of transportation, taxes, and bribery of army and government officials for expediting its way through Union lines. See 101, 102, 106, 114.

39. Scott, *Origin,* 19–20. Scott claimed he left Carroll's and found General Grant, who took him to see Lincoln on "the very day" of his death. Lincoln took his papers and promised him a permit if they were in order. Scott had run out of money and had to leave Washington that evening, and heard of the president's death at Harrisburg the next day. His papers were never found. There is no corroborative evidence for Scott's statements. Lincoln did see Grant that day, but there is no mention of Scott then or at any time in the previous few weeks. Miers, *Lincoln Day By Day* 3:320–30.

40. H.R. Doc. 179, pp. 11–12. Carroll's claim that Scott paid to have the letter inserted was probably false. The letter was printed under the heading "Voluntary Communication." Such items were solicited and paid for by the *National Intelligencer.* See front page, *National Intelligencer,* 12 Apr. 1865 and any issue.

41. H.R. Doc. 179, pp. 11, 30, 31.

42. H.R. Doc. 179, pp. 115, 117, 122.

43. [Carroll] to Uncle [Charles Carroll?], n.d., 3622-27, Carroll Papers, CCJ.

44. [Evans], *Material Bearing;* letter to editor cited by Scott, H.R. Doc. 179, p. 122; letters from Samuel Hunt to Carroll throughout 1871 and 1872 in Carroll Papers, CCJ; L. S. McCoy to Carroll, 14 Mar. 1872, Carroll Papers, CCJ; Charles M. Scott to Carroll, 14 Mar. 1872, cited in H.R. Doc. 179, p. 116. Scott wished Carroll good luck on her claim and expressed his gratitude for her patronage search on his behalf in Scott to Carroll, 14 Jan. 1870, Carroll Papers.

45. H.R. Doc. 179, p. 121.

46. Scott, *Origin,* 3, 37; U. S. Grant to Board of Inspectors, 15 Apr. 1862, S. P. Lee to Captain Scott, 1 Mar. 1865, both cited in Scott, *Origin,* 29, 30, 31; H.R. Doc. 179, p. 122.

47. John Tucker to Carroll, 9 May 1865, Carroll Papers. Carroll had warned Scott not to breathe a word of his business in cotton, "for the reason that the Treasury Department gives all its instructions secretly and they do this to cut off all illicit trade." Carroll to Charles M. Scott, n.d., reprinted in H.R. Doc. 179, p. 30. See also Scott, *Origin,* 26.

48. U. S. Grant to Elihu B. Washburne, 22 Mar. 1862, *The Papers of Ulysses S. Grant,* ed.

John Y. Simon, 14 vols. (Carbondale: Southern Illinois Univ. Press, 1967–85), 4:409; see also Bruce Catton, *Grant Moves South* (Boston: Little, Brown, 1960), 123–26.

49. Two letters in the *New York Times* detail the same strategic importance of the rivers, including mention of their navigability and their closeness to the Memphis and Charleston Railroad. See correspondence signed "Tennessean," *New York Times,* 17 Nov. 1861 (the most complete of the two, with strategy remarkably similar in content to Carroll's plan) and 21 Dec. 1861. The author of the articles reported giving the information to a "loyal gentleman of some military experience in June 1861." For Lincoln's views on the importance of relieving Unionists in the border states, see Basler, *Works* 4:532. *OR* 52, pt. 1:191–92, contains Lincoln's overall plan regarding the western theater. It is not dated, but was written prior to 5 Oct. 1861. See chap. 7 herein for the conclusions of Civil War historians such as Kenneth Williams and E. B. Long regarding Carroll's claim.

Chapter 6

1. Carroll to War Department, 2 May 1862; Carroll to Edwin M. Stanton, 14 May 1862, U.S. War Department, Record and Pension Office, Anna Ella Carroll File, National Archives, Washington, D.C.

2. Carroll to Thurlow Weed, 17 Mar. 1861, Weed Papers; H.R. Doc. 179, p. 15; Carroll to Thomas King Carroll, 11 Jan. 1869; Carroll to Mary Carroll, 30 Jan. 1869; Truman Smith to Lemuel D. Evans, 22 Mar. 1874, Carroll Papers. Evans grew flustered when questioned about the trip in a congressional committee hearing on Carroll's claim, first saying that he had met Carroll in St. Louis, then Washington, then Baltimore, eventually admitting that they had traveled to St. Louis together.

3. Lemuel D. Evans to William H. Seward, 3 Mar. 1862, Seward Papers, (microfilm); Evans to Edwin Stanton, 8 Aug. 1862, Carroll Papers; Kamm, *Civil War Career,* 130–33; Carroll to War Department, 25 Aug. 1862; Carroll to Stanton, 9 Sept. 1862, War Department, Carroll File; Carroll, Claim, 2 Jan. 1863, MDHS 3650-183, Carroll Papers. No records survive in the State Department or War Department to confirm Evans's commission. Frémont's testimony before the Committee on the Conduct of the War indicated Evans was on his way to Texas by way of Tampico, Mexico to find out if the Confederates were receiving supplies from Mexico. See U.S. Congress, Senate, Committee on the Conduct of the War, *Report of the Joint Committee on the Conduct of the War,* 37th Cong., 3d sess., 1863, Rep. Com. 108, 4:120–21.

4. P. H. Watson to Carroll, 14 Sept. 1862, Carroll Papers; Carroll to War Department, 7 Oct. 1863, War Department, Carroll File. Receipt signed by Carroll is attached to the 14 Sept. letter. The money for this payment, like the payment made by Thomas Scott, may have been personal. No record of any payment to Carroll was found in the books of the War Department, the Provost Fund, the Secret Service Fund or by the Disbursing Clerk. The pamphlet Carroll mentions does not appear to have survived; a notation on the file indicates that it was received by the War Department. See also Carroll to Colonel Hardie, 7 Oct. 1863, Carroll Papers.

5. Carroll to P. H. Watson, 8 Jan. 1864, as noted on the War Department, Carroll File, and quoted in Carroll to Watson, 11 Jan. 1864, Carroll Papers; Watson to Carroll, 11 Jan. 1864, War Department, Carroll File, notation only; Carroll to Watson, 11 Jan. 1864; Watson to Carroll, 13 Jan. 1864, Carroll Papers. The 8 Jan. letter and the 11 Jan. Watson to Carroll letters are summarized on the file in the War Department but do not otherwise survive.

6. Carroll to Brigadier General Mayer[?], 9 Nov. 1862; Edward Bates to Carroll, 23 Sept.

1863; Carroll, "Essay on Military Government," MS draft, ca. 1869, MDHS 3652-425, Carroll Papers.

7. Carroll to [Sallie] Cradock, 12 May 1864; Carroll, "Recollections of Lincoln," undated MS, MDHS 3655-722, Carroll Papers; Carroll to Salmon P. Chase, 8 Dec. 1864, Chase Papers; James M. McPherson, *Ordeal By Fire: The Civil War and Reconstruction* (New York: Alfred A. Knopf, 1982), 440–42; Allan Nevins, *The War for the Union: The Organized War to Victory, 1864–1865* (New York: Charles Scribner's Sons, 1971), 98–103, 105–8; T. Harry Williams, *Lincoln and the Radicals* (Madison: Univ. of Wisconsin Press, 1969), 306–33.

8. Carroll to Salmon P. Chase, 5 Oct. 1863, Chase Papers; *National Intelligencer,* 18 Oct., 8 Nov. 1864. In her letter to Chase, Carroll may have been referring to the despotism of military rule rather than the despotism of racial slavery. If she was referring to the need for emancipation, it might have been solely for effect, since she was also attempting to pry funds loose from Chase's Treasury Department for her pamphlets at the same time.

9. Carroll to Thurlow Weed, 4 Nov. 1864, Weed Papers.

10. Edward Bates to Carroll, 5 Nov. 1864; Lemuel D. Evans to Carroll, 9 Nov. 1864, Carroll Papers. Carroll also wrote of Seaton's offer to her old friend and former minister, the Rev. Dr. Robert Breckinridge, 29 Nov. 1864, Breckinridge Family Papers. There is no mention of Carroll or her offer in Weed's biography or in his autobiography.

11. Josephine Seaton to Carroll, 1 Aug. 1866, 27 Jan. 1867, Carroll Papers; *National Intelligencer,* 31 Dec. 1864, 1 Jan. 1865; Carroll to Edwin Stanton, 15 Dec. 1864, War Department, Carroll File. Seaton finally wrote a short eulogistic biography of her father, published anonymously, *William Winston Seaton of the "National Intelligencer"* (Boston: James R. Osgood, 1871).

12. Carroll to William H. Seward, 4 Nov. 1865, Seward Papers; Carroll to Gideon Welles, 23 Feb. 1866, Gideon Welles Papers, Library of Congress; George Gibson, Recorder, Board of Claims, War Department, to Carroll, 14 July 1868; Carroll to Board of Claims, War Department, 22 July 1868; Thomas A. Scott to Gibson, 27 Nov. 1868; Brantz Mayer to Carroll, 7 Oct. 1867, Carroll Papers; Carroll to Aaron Columbus Burr, 11 Feb. 1869, Burr Papers. See also letters from Burr to Secretary of State Hamilton Fish, U.S. State Department, "Letters of Application and Recommendation During the Administration of U. S. Grant, 1869–1877," Record Group 59, National Archives, Washington, D.C. Carroll's history, *Annals of the Civil War,* was never finished or published, since it was stored in a trunk of papers lost when Carroll became ill, according to Blackwell, *Military Genius,* 151–52. J. S. Serrill to Carroll, 12 July 1869, Carroll Papers, refers to anti-Johnson pamphlets, but none have been found published under Carroll's name. Carroll was paid forty dollars for an article in *Harper's Magazine* on Maryland history, apparently never printed. See H. M. Alden to S. E. Carrell [*sic*], 9 Dec. 1870, Carroll Papers. *Harper's* printed "The First American Exploring Expedition," *Harper's New Monthly Magazine* 44 (Dec. 1871): 60–64, which Carroll rewrote from her essay by the same name in *The Star of the West. Harper's* continued to misspell her name in the table of contents as "S. E. Carrell."

13. Carroll to Mary H. Carroll, 16 Dec. 1868; Carroll to General Grant, 28 Dec. 1868, Carroll Papers.

14. Carroll to Thomas King Carroll, 3 Feb. 1869, Carroll Papers; Charles W. Ramsdell, *Reconstruction in Texas* (Austin: Univ. of Texas Press, 1970), 212–13, 248–50, 256–66; William C. Nunn, *Texas and the Carpetbaggers* (Austin: Univ. of Texas Press, 1962), 8–9; Lemuel D. Evans, *Speech of Hon. L. D. Evans on the Condition of Texas and the Formation of New States. Delivered in the Constitutional Convention of Texas on the 6th of January, 1869* (N.p., 1869); Carroll to Mary H. Carroll, 30 Jan. 1869; Carroll to brother, 8 Dec. 1868, Carroll Papers.

15. U.S. Congress, Senate, Committee on Military Affairs, *Petition of Anna Ella Carroll,*

Praying Compensation for suggesting certain plans of operation for the armies of the United States during the late war, 41st Cong., 2d sess., 1870, S. Mis. Doc. 100, pp. 1–2.

16. Benjamin P. Thomas and Harold Hyman, *Stanton: The Life and Times of Lincoln's Secretary of War* (New York: Alfred A. Knopf, 1962), 606–11, 637–38; Benjamin F. Wade to Carroll, 1 Mar. 1869, Carroll Papers. A copy of this letter, not in Carroll's hand, survives. It was reprinted first in U.S. Congress, Senate, Committee on Military Affairs, *Memorial of Anna Ella Carroll Asking compensation for service rendered the United States in the war of the rebellion,* 42nd Cong., 2d sess., 1872, S. Mis. Doc. 167, pp. 5–7; see also H. L. Trefousse, *Benjamin Franklin Wade: Radical Republican from Ohio* (New York: Twayne Publishers, 1963), 317.

17. *Memorial,* S. Doc. 167, p. 7; Trefousse, *Benjamin Franklin Wade,* 316–18.

18. U.S. Congress, House, Committee on Military Affairs, *Anna Ella Carroll: Report to accompany bill H.R. 7256,* 46th Cong., 3d sess., 1881, H. Rept. 386, pp. 1–3. Trefousse does not mention this letter.

19. *Report of the Joint Committee,* Rep. Com. 108, vol. 4.

20. See, for example, Caroline R. Wade to "My Dear Friend" [Anna Ella Carroll], 6 and 30 Apr., 20 Nov. 1869, 1 Mar. 1870, Carroll Papers. Wade supported woman suffrage, surely a factor in his support of Carroll. See Trefousse, *Benjamin Franklin Wade,* 284–85.

21. *Petition,* S. Doc. 100, pp. 1–2; Carroll to Robert G. Schenck, 9 Apr. 1870, Carroll Papers.

22. John Tucker to Carroll, 20 Apr. 1870, Carroll Papers.

23. Thomas A. Scott to Jacob M. Howard, 15 June 1870; Carroll to Senator [Howard?], 17 June 1870, Carroll Papers; T. A. Scott to Howard, 24 June 1870, reprinted in U.S. Congress, Senate, Committee on Military Affairs and the Militia, *Report to Accompany S. 1293,* 41st Cong., 3d sess., 1871, S. Rept. 339, p. 2.

24. Carroll to Thomas King Carroll, 11 Jan. 1871, Carroll Papers; *Report,* S. Rept. 339, p. 4.

25. *Congressional Globe,* 41st Cong., 3d sess., 1871, p. 895; George Vickers to Carroll, 2 and 30 Jan. 1871, Carroll Papers; Carroll to [Samuel Hunt], 3 Jan. 1871, Carroll Papers, CCJ; Carroll to sister, 2 Mar. 1871, Carroll Papers. Carroll fought against Republican party leader John Creswell in Maryland. See Baker, *Politics of Continuity,* 187.

26. Blackwell, *Life and Writings,* 133; Samuel Hunt to Carroll, 5 June 1871, Carroll Papers, CCJ; Carroll to Millard Fillmore, 7 Nov. 1871; Fillmore to Carroll, 10 Nov. 1871, Fillmore Papers; *Memorial,* S. Mis. Doc. 167, pp. 8–9, 4.

27. Samuel Hunt to Carroll, 31 May 1872, 22 Dec. 1871, Carroll Papers, CCJ.

28. [Evans], *Material Bearing,* 10. Evans admitted authorship of the pamphlet in H.R. Doc. 179, p. 29.

29. Carroll to John Tucker, [Oct. 1862], quoted in [Evans], *Material Bearing,* 15. Farragut had successfully come up the Mississippi in June of 1862 to join the Union river fleet coming down from Memphis to attack Vicksburg, but two-hundred-foot bluffs on the river side and swamps north and south of the city meant only an eastern assault would succeed. See McPherson, *Ordeal By Fire,* 233–34, 308–9, 311–12; Bruce Catton, *Never Call Retreat* (New York: Doubleday, 1965), 79–81. Carroll's suggestion (if in fact she made it, since the War Department file does not list receipt of the October 1862 letter in its Carroll file) neglected to take into account the vulnerability of Grant's supply lines that deep in enemy territory, or the fact that to move back to Memphis would be perceived by the public as a retreat, no matter how strategically sound. She also did not consider the near-impassable swamps of the Yazoo Delta east of the Mississippi as a potential problem in moving ground troops.

30. [Evans], *Material Bearing,* 15; Lemuel D. Evans to Carroll, 5 May 1872, Carroll Papers.

31. Samuel Hunt to Carroll, 13 Jan. 1874, Carroll Papers, CCJ Collection; Carroll to sister, 22 May 1872, Carroll Papers.

32. Carroll to Thomas King Carroll, 27 May 1872, Carroll Papers; *Memorial,* S. Doc. 167, p. 1; Carroll to sister, 2 June 1872, Carroll Papers.

33. Anna Ella Carroll, "Grant's Renomination," MS draft, ca. 1872, MDHS 3653-508, Carroll Papers; Carroll to Samuel Hunt, 4 and 6 Nov. 1872, Carroll Papers, CCJ; Carroll to Senator Wilson, 21 Nov. 1872, Carroll Papers.

34. [Anna Ella Carroll], *Miss Carroll's Claim Before Congress in Connection with the Tennessee Campaign* (Washington, D.C., 1873), 4, 18–19, 22–23, 36–37, 49.

35. Cassius M. Clay to Carroll, 24 Jan. 1873; George Vickers to Carroll, 31 Jan., 26 Aug. 1873; Carroll to Dr. Draper, 8 Mar. 1873; J. T. Headley to [Carroll], 14 Apr. 1873; Lemuel D. Evans to Carroll, 21 May 1873, Carroll Papers. Carroll's first claim was two pages; her 1871 memorial was nine; her 1873 publication ran to fifty-five pages.

36. Carroll to Millard Fillmore, 19 Nov. 1873, Fillmore Papers; Isaac D. Jones to Carroll, 15 Nov. 1873; C[harles] C. Carroll to Carroll, 12 Dec. 1873, Carroll Papers. Kingston Hall, purchased in 1837 by John Upsher Dennis at the sheriff's sale of the property for Thomas King Carroll's debts, still survives. A two-story brick house and kitchen connected by a brick colonnade are currently being restored.

37. [Anna Ella Carroll], *Miss Carroll's Claim Before Congress Asking Compensation for Military and Other Services in Connection with the Civil War* ([Washington, D.C.], 1874). This one was seventy pages long. A clipping of the *Daily Tribune* letter by Scott dated 24 Apr. 1874 was preserved in a letter, Charles M. Scott to Carroll, 20 Mar. 1865, Carroll Papers, CCJ. See also Carroll to Committee on War Claims, 6 June 1874, Carroll Papers, CCJ; [Anna Ella Carroll], *Miss Carroll's Literary Services to the Country During the Civil War Stated* ([Washington, D.C.], 1874), 1.

38. *New York Times,* 14 Apr. 1874; Carroll to Editor, *New York Times,* 4 May 1874; H.R. Doc. 179. For the full account of this confrontation see chap. 5 herein. The letter to the editor was a rough draft of Carroll's reply which, if sent, was apparently never published in the paper.

39. *Galveston* [Texas] *Daily News,* 6 July 1877; [L. D. Evans] to [Carroll], 8 Oct. 1867, Carroll Papers, CCJ; Evans to Carroll, 23 and 27 Feb. 1872, Carroll Papers. Evans had risen to chief justice of the Texas Supreme Court in 1870 and was its presiding judge until September 1873. He was United States marshal for the eastern district of Texas at the time of his death, but died in Washington, not Texas. Mentions of Evans in state and legal histories of the period are very brief. For a man whom John C. Frémont thought "so well known that it would scarcely be possible for him to reach Texas through Missouri country" because of his Unionist stance, Evans is surprisingly invisible in the history of the period. See J. H. Davenport, *The History of the Supreme Court of the State of Texas* (Austin, Tex.: Southern Law Book Publishers, 1917), 95–96; *The Handbook of Texas,* ed. Walter Prescott Webb, 2 vols. (Austin: Texas State Historical Association, 1952), 1:576; James D. Lynch, *The Bench and Bar of Texas* (St. Louis: Nixon-Jones Printing, 1885), 110–13; *A Comprehensive History of Texas, 1685–1897,* 2 vols., ed. Dudley G. Wooten (Dallas: William G. Scarff, 1898), 1:47; and Homer S. Thrall, *A Pictorial History of Texas* (St. Louis: N. D. Thomas, 1879), 532.

40. *Report of the Joint Committee,* Rep. Com. 108, 4:120–21; U.S. Congress, Senate, Committee on Military Affairs, *Memorial of Anna Ella Carroll of Maryland, Praying For compensation for services rendered to the United States during the late civil war,* 45th Cong., 1st sess., 1877, S. Mis. Doc. 5, p. 11; U.S. Congress, House, Committee on Military Affairs, *Memorial of Anna Ella Carroll, of Maryland, Praying For compensation for services rendered to the United States during the late civil war,* 45th Cong., 2d sess., 1878, H. Mis. Doc. 58, pp. 1, 2, 8.

41. U.S. Congress, Senate, Committee on Military Affairs, *Report,* 45th Cong., 3d sess., 1879, S. Rept. 775, pp. 6–7. This was in reply to *Memorial,* S. Mis. Doc. 5.

42. Carroll to Matilda Joslyn Gage, 17 Jan. 1873, reprinted in Matilda Joslyn Gage, *Who Planned the Tennessee Campaign of 1862? or Anna Ella Carroll vs. Ulysses S. Grant: A Few Generally Unknown Facts in Regard to Our Civil War,* National Citizen Tract No. 1 [Washington, D.C., 1880], preface.

43. Gage, *Who Planned the Tennessee Campaign,* 2–3, 16.

44. Nancy Woloch, *Women and the American Experience* (New York: Alfred A. Knopf, 1984), 309–24.

45. E. A. Rollins to Carroll, 5 Jan. 1881, Carroll Papers. Phoebe Couzins had interviewed Scott in 1880 at Carroll's request and found him in feeble enough health to fear he "might die at any moment." Phoebe Couzins, *The Military Genius of the War: Anna Ella Carroll, Author of the Tennessee Campaign,* pamphlet (St. Louis, 1882), 4.

46. Carroll to Mary H. Carroll, 30 Jan. 1881, Carroll Papers; U.S. Congress, House, Committee on Military Affairs, *Anna Ella Carroll,* H.R. 386, pp. 1–3; Carroll to Judge [Jeremiah S.] Black, 11 Feb. 1881, Frederick Dreer Collection, The Historical Society of Pennsylvania, Philadelphia.

47. Carroll to James A. Garfield, 15 July, 11 Sept., 6 Aug., 3 Nov. 1880, 16 Mar. 1881, Garfield Papers.

48. James A. Garfield to Carroll, 20 Aug. 1880, Garfield Papers; *New York Times,* 15 Sept. 1881. The story was, literally, front-page news, presumably because of Carroll's spring victory in the congressional committee. The pension was apparently set at fifty dollars a month, but never passed. See Couzins, *Military Genius,* 5.

49. Elizabeth Cady Stanton, Susan B. Anthony, and Matilda Joslyn Gage, eds., *History of Woman Suffrage,* 6 vols. (Rochester, N.Y.: Susan B. Anthony, Charles Mann, 1881–1922), 2 (1881): 1–2; Couzins, *Military Genius,* 5, 8; *Biographical Directory of Congress,* 760; William Warden to Mary H. Carroll, 23 Feb. 1884, Carroll Papers; Edward S. Bragg to Carroll, 26 Apr. 1881, reprinted in Blackwell, *Life and Writings,* 133–34.

50. William Warden to Mary H. Carroll, 23 Feb. 1884, Carroll Papers.

51. Hon. John D. White, *Speech of Hon. John D. White, of Kentucky, in the House of Representatives, Thursday, February 7, 1884* (Washington, D.C., 1884), 6, 10.

52. William W. Warden to Miss Carroll, 29 Jan. 1885, Carroll Papers. It is unclear whether Carroll, who was recovering from her stroke by 1885, instigated the lawsuit or if her sister Mary did. All of Warden's letters but this one are to Mary who, living in Washington, may have simply been acting as her sister's agent. Anne did not join Mary in Washington until after Mary had a job. See n. 59 below.

53. William W. Warden to Chief Justice Richardson, 13 Feb. 1885; Warden to Mary H. Carroll, 27 Oct. 1884, 20 and 26 Apr., 1 June 1885, Carroll Papers. Aid in the form of subscriptions came from pleas in the press. See n. 58 below.

54. *Anna Ella Carroll v. United States,* 20 Court of Claims 426 (Court of Claims 1885), 429–31; H.R. Bill 4835, 51st Cong., 1st sess., 13 Jan. 1890, copy of printed bill preserved in Carroll Papers.

55. Shattuck, "Anna Ella Carroll," 405–6.

56. Shattuck, "Anna Ella Carroll," 407–9.

57. C. C. Hussey, *Miss Anna Ella Carroll, as Author of the Tennessee Campaign, in the Late Civil War,* pamphlet (East Orange, N.J.: Gazette Steam Book and Job Print, 1885); Carroll, "Plan of the Tennessee Campaign," 342–47; Mary A. Livermore, *My Story of the War: A Woman's Narrative of Four Years Personal Experience as Nurse in the Union Army, and in Relief Work at Home, in Hospitals, Camps, and at the Front, During the War of the Rebellion* (Hartford, Conn.: A. D. Worthington, 1889), 175; Blackwell, *Military Genius.* Liv-

ermore's book sold sixty thousand copies; see "Mary A. Livermore," *Notable American Women 1607–1950,* ed. Edward T. James, 3 vols. (Cambridge, Mass.: Harvard Univ. Press, 1971), 2:410–13. Blackwell's small volume was available at the offices of the Woman Suffrage Society in Washington and at the offices of the *Woman's Journal* in Boston, a suffragist magazine edited by Blackwell's sister-in-law, Lucy Stone.

58. Sarah Ellen Blackwell to Carroll, 24 July 1885, Carroll Papers; Blackwell to Alice Stone Blackwell, 3 Jan. 1891, Blackwell Family Papers, Library of Congress; Susan B. Anthony to Mary H. Carroll, 19 Dec. 1889, Carroll Papers. *Woman's Journal* has monthly reports throughout 1885 on Carroll and the Carroll Fund; see also S. Ellen Blackwell, "The Anna Ella Carroll Fund," *Woman's Column* 6 (18 Jan. 1888); clipping preserved in Anna Ella Carroll File, National American Woman Suffrage Association Papers, Library of Congress (hereafter NAWSA Papers); S. E. Blackwell, "The Case of Miss Carroll," *Century Magazine* 40 (Aug. 1890): 638–39; C. C. Hussey to Editor, *Woman's Journal* 16 (7 Nov. 1885): 356; Abbie M. Gannett to [Mary H. Carroll], 30 Nov. 1885, Carroll Papers, CCJ; Lucy Stone, "Editorial," *Woman's Journal* 16 (19 Dec. 1885): 404.

59. Representative Charles F. Manderson to Carroll, 9 July 1890, Carroll Papers; Mary H. Carroll to Grover Cleveland, 26 July 1885, 27 Aug. 1888, 6 Sept. 1893; Mary H. Carroll to Rose Cleveland, 18 Nov. 1885, Grover Cleveland Papers, Library of Congress (microfilm); appointment given 15 June 1886, U.S. Department of the Treasury, Personnel Applications, National Archives, Washington D.C.; Sarah Ellen Blackwell to Alice Stone Blackwell, 9 Feb. 1891, Blackwell Papers; Isabel Howland to Editor, *Inter-Ocean,* 30 May 1891, reprinted in Blackwell, *Life and Writings,* 136–39; Mary H. Carroll to Mrs. Frances Cleveland, 1 Dec. 1893, Cleveland Papers. A note attached to this letter indicates that President Cleveland interested himself enough in Mary's case to examine her record. Her pay was eventually reinstated. See Carroll File, Treasury Department Personnel Applications.

60. Death Certificate, Vital Records Division, Department of Human Resources, District of Columbia; Dr. William J. Perry to author, 24 Apr. 1986; Blackwell, *Life and Writings,* 140–42, Anna Ella Carroll, gravestone, Old Trinity Churchyard, Church Creek, Md.

Chapter 7

1. *National Cyclopedia of American Biography* 5 (1894): 193; Albert Gallatin Riddle, *Recollections of War Times: Reminiscences of Men and Events in Washington, 1860–1865* (New York: G. P. Putnam's Sons, 1895), 190, 193.

2. Blackwell, *Life and Writings;* Advertisement, *Woman's Journal* 26 (19 Jan. 1895): 21; Lucinda B. Chandler, "Anna Ella Carroll: The Great Unrecognized Genius of the War of the Rebellion," *Godey's Magazine* 133 (Sept. 1896): 255, 257. Blackwell, *Military Genius,* 150–63, gives some idea of the numbers of women that wrote on behalf of Carroll's cause. A *Woman's Journal* advertisement of 19 Jan. read, "The pamphlets form a valuable contribution . . . and an able dissertation on the principles of the constitution. As such we recommend it for study by equal suffrage clubs and clubs for political study." See also articles, letters, and even poetry in issues of *Woman's Journal* from 1885 through 1896. Carroll's story was also published in *American Women,* ed. Frances E. Willard and Mary A. Livermore, 2 vols. (1897; rpt. Detroit: Gale Research, 1973), 1:153–54.

3. Ida M. Tarbell, "The American Woman: How She Met the Experience of War," *American Magazine* 69 (Apr. 1910): 811.

4. Tarbell, "American Woman," 801–2, 814.

5. Tarbell, "American Woman," 814; Aileen S. Kraditor, *The Ideas of the Woman Suf-*

frage Movement, 1890–1920 (New York: Anchor Books, 1971), 16–17, 21–22; Woloch, *Women,* 337–43; "Ida M. Tarbell," *Notable American Women* 3:430.

6. Jones, *Revised History,* 298; May Irene Copinger, "Maryland Woman Influenced U.S. Destiny," *Baltimore Sun,* 11 Oct. 1925; Dr. Milton H. Shutes, "Meet an Unheralded Heroine," *National Republic Magazine* 22 (Nov. 1934): 3–4, 34. The *Sun* article misdated Carroll's death as 21 Feb. and also credits her, probably mistakenly, with a biography of General Joseph Warren.

7. [Marjorie Greenbie], "My Dear Lady," *Woman's Home Companion* 67 (Feb. 1940): 13–14, (Mar. 1940): 26. *Woman's Home Companion,* edited by Gertrude B. Lane, was the number-one women's magazine in the United States in 1937. See "Gertrude B. Lane," *Notable American Women* 2:363–65.

8. Greenbie, *My Dear Lady;* Sydney and Marjorie Barstow Greenbie, *Anna Ella Carroll and Abraham Lincoln: A Biography* (Manchester, Maine: Univ. of Tampa Press in cooperation with Falmouth Publishing House, 1952), viii (hereafter cited as *Carroll and Lincoln*).

9. Greenbie, *My Dear Lady,* vi–vii. See reviews of the Greenbies' work in *American Historical Review* 32 (Oct. 1926): 172–73, and particularly 45 (July 1940): 972, wherein the reviewer of *Furs to Furrows* remained "completely baffled as to why the book was ever written."

10. Livermore, *My Story of the War,* 174; Greenbie, *My Dear Lady,* especially 260–61; Carroll to Abraham Lincoln, 30 July 1862, Lincoln Papers; Greenbie, *My Dear Lady,* 111.

11. Greenbie, *My Dear Lady,* xii, 39.

12. F. Lauriston Bullard, "Anna Ella Carroll Career Persuasively, Eloquently Told," *Boston Herald,* 19 Oct. 1940; Lyman Beecher Stowe, "In Lincoln's Kitchen Cabinet," *New York Times Book Review,* 8 Dec. 1940; Ralph Thompson, "Books of the Times," *New York Times,* 8 Dec. 1940; all clippings preserved in Carroll File, NAWSA Papers.

13. Greenbie, *Suit with Red Lining,* 47, 3, 49, 56; "Anna Ella Carroll," writ. Robert Tallman, *Cavalcade of America,* NBC Radio, 2 June 1941.

14. Hollister Noble, *Woman with a Sword* (New York: Doubleday, 1948), 3–5, 408. Doubleday issued a separate pamphlet which reprinted Noble's bibliography and sources, apparently for distribution to book stores; Hollister Noble, "The Facts about Anne Carroll and the Story behind *Woman with a Sword,*" pamphlet (New York: Doubleday, 1948).

15. Alice Dixon Bond, "Biography Discloses Woman Whose Strategy Saved Union," *Boston Sunday Herald,* 24 Oct. 1948, clipping in Carroll File, NAWSA Papers; "Lincoln's Lady Strategist"; "Woman with a Sword," writ. Hollister Noble, *Playhouse 25,* Armed Forces Radio and Television Services, n.d. (rebroadcast 1974); "Woman with a Sword," writ. Hollister Noble, *Cavalcade of America,* adapt. Virginia Radcliffe, NBC Radio, 23 May 1949; Herbert Allen, "New Light on Lincoln's 'Secret' War Tactician," *Boston Herald,* 2 Feb. 1949, clipping in Carroll File, NAWSA Papers; H. E. Neal, "Secret Heroine of the Civil War," *Coronet* 26 (May 1949): 148–52.

16. Bullard, "Anna Ella Carroll"; Woloch, *Women,* 462.

17. Armstrong, "Story of Anna Ella Carroll," 199.

18. Williams, "Tennessee River Campaign," 223; Greenbie, *Suit with Red Lining,* 60.

19. Williams, "Tennessee River Campaign," 230–34, 235–37, 247.

20. Carroll to Thomas A. Scott, 10 Jan. 1862, Carroll Papers. This document contains the 30 Nov. plan and an appended letter reiterating her advice, dated 10 Jan. 1862, a letter Carroll persistently misdated in her petitions and memorials as 5 Jan. 1862.

21. Sydney Greenbie to Monroe F. Cockrell, n.d., reply written on letter, Monroe F. Cockrell to University of Tampa Press, 9 Jan. 1952, Monroe F. Cockrell Papers, William R. Perkins Library, Duke University, Durham, N.C. Cockrell, a friend of Williams, was a businessman whose avocation was Civil War history.

22. Avery Craven, "Review," *New York Herald Tribune Book Review,* 26 Oct. 1952; Greenbie and Greenbie, *Carroll and Lincoln,* 505.

23. Greenbie and Greenbie, *Carroll and Lincoln,* 193, 366–75, 400–404, 140, 91, 233. Richard Bardolph reviewed *Carroll and Lincoln* in the *Journal of Southern History* 18 (Nov. 1952): 511–13.

24. Greenbie and Greenbie, *Carroll and Lincoln,* 505.

25. Sydney Greenbie to Editor and Richard Bardolph to Editor, *Journal of Southern History* 19 (Nov. 1953): 549–51; M[arjorie] B. G[reenbie], "The Making of a Best Seller," epigraph to Sydney Greenbie, *Suit with Red Lining;* Greenbie, *Suit with Red Lining,* 124–25.

26. J. G. Randall, *Lincoln the President,* 4 vols. (New York: Dodd, Mead, 1945–55), 2 (1945): 66–67; Allan Nevins, *The War for the Union: War Becomes Revolution, 1862–1863* (New York: Charles Scribner's Sons, 1960), 15–16; Abraham Lincoln to Carroll, 19 Aug. 1862, in Basler, *Works* 5:381–82; Kenneth P. Williams, *Lincoln Finds a General,* 5 vols. (New York: Macmillan, 1949–59), 3 (1952): 456, and 4 (1956): 455–57. The letter in Lincoln's papers was written a few days after Carroll's angry reply to Lincoln's refusal of her propaganda proposition, and was cited by the Greenbies to prove that his refusal was caused by ill temper and that Lincoln and Carroll quickly returned to their close companionship. The letter is not an original, but a copy which Carroll enclosed in a letter introducing herself to James Garfield, 6 Aug. 1880, Garfield Papers. The copy is not in her hand, which makes its authenticity less suspect, but it is really just a polite note to a citizen who had done work on behalf of the Union. Lincoln, Basler suggested, was simply trying to soothe Carroll's anger at being refused after what she perceived as his earlier support for her activities, a perception based upon the administration's distribution of her pamphlets. In reality, Lincoln's action was simple courtesy, no more. Carl Sandburg also mentioned Carroll's pamphlets briefly in *Abraham Lincoln* 1:410–11.

27. "Woman with a Sword," writ. Hollister Noble, *Hallmark Hall of Fame,* NBC Television, 10 Feb. 1952; Greenbie, *Suit with Red Lining,* 121, 138; *Marjorie Barstow Greenbie v. Noble, et al.,* United States District Court, Southern District of New York, Civil 94-300, National Archives, New York Branch, Bayonne, N.J. A copy of the *Hallmark Hall of Fame* performance, which featured Jayne Meadows as Anna Ella Carroll, survives on kinescope at the Radio and Television Archives, University of California at Los Angeles.

28. *Greenbie v. Noble, et al.,* The Honorable Richard Levet, "Opinion," 4, 45–48, 54; Greenbie, *Suit with Red Lining,* 138.

29. Greenbie, *Suit with Red Lining,* 219, 220–21.

30. Greenbie, *Suit with Red Lining,* 224–25; Noble, *Woman with a Sword,* 291, 332, 333–34; Greenbie, *Suit with Red Lining,* 187.

31. Agatha Young, *The Women and the Crisis: Women of the North in the Civil War* (New York: McDowell, Oblensky, 1959), 143–47, 369. Wise, *Lincoln's Secret Weapon;* see also Anna Ella Carroll, "The Relation of the National Government to Revolted Citizens Defined," in *Union Pamphlets* 1:357–80; "Anna Ella Carroll," in *Notable American Women* 1:289–92. Wise's work drops a number of years from Carroll's age, as Noble had, and tries valiantly to distinguish between the American party and the more pejoratively denominated Know-Nothings as two entirely separate organizations. An earlier juvenile article was Kenneth M. Gould, "Lincoln's Unknown Soldier," *Senior Scholastic* 68 (9 Feb. 1956): 16. Carroll's tale was also told in Otto Eisenschiml, *The Hidden Face of the Civil War* (New York: Bobbs-Merrill, 1961), 74–82. Eisenschiml's conspiratorial approach to the history of the Civil War would no doubt have appealed to the Greenbies.

32. Snyder, "Anna Ella Carroll," 36–63; Baker, *Politics of Continuity,* 187; Baker, *Ambivalent Americans,* 35–36, 156–57; E. B. Long, "Anna Ella Carroll," 29, 33, 35. Long was no

doubt referring to the Greenbie lawsuit, in which he was called in as an expert on Lincoln. Greenbie had unkindly characterized him as a "Bonga Thrower for the lords of the Lincoln industry." A bonga thrower, wrote Greenbie, was a poet laureate of African chiefs whose task was to whisper praise in the chief's ear three times a day, and to find a way to praise all his actions, even those that had failed. Greenbie, *Suit with Red Lining,* 199.

33. Basler, "Lincoln, Blacks, and Women," 45–48.

34. Anne Firor Scott, *The Southern Lady: From Pedestal to Politics, 1830–1930* (Chicago: Univ. of Chicago Press, 1970), was the first to delineate the image of the Southern lady, the restrictions placed upon her by Southern society, and the ways in which women were politically active while still working within that restrictive framework. See also Anne Goodwyn Jones, "Southern Literary Women as Chroniclers of Southern Life," in *Sex, Race, and the Role of Women in the South,* ed. Joanne V. Hawks and Sheila L. Skemp (Jackson: Univ. Press of Mississippi, 1983), 84–85, 81, 92. Jones uses Mary Boykin Chesnut as one example in her study of the restrictions, both social and psychological, under which Southern literary women worked.

35. Jones, "Southern Literary Women," 92; Carroll, *Review,* iii–iv.

36. Linda Kerber, *Women of the Republic: Intellect and Ideology in Revolutionary America* (Chapel Hill: The Institute for Early American History and Culture by the Univ. of North Carolina Press, 1980), 269–88, examines women's political methodology prior to enfranchisement. See also Mary Beth Norton, *Liberty's Daughters: The Revolutionary Experience of American Women, 1750–1800* (Boston: Little, Brown, 1980), 155–94.

37. Scott, *Southern Lady;* Gerda Lerner, *The Grimké Sisters from South Carolina: Pioneers for Woman's Rights and Abolition* (New York: Schocken Books, 1967); Ellen Carol Dubois, *Feminism and Suffrage: The Emergence of an Independent Woman's Movement in America, 1848–1869* (Ithaca, N.Y.: Cornell Univ. Press, 1978); Anne Firor Scott, *Making the Invisible Woman Visible* (Urbana: Univ. of Illinois Press, 1984); Eleanor Flexner, *Century of Struggle: The Woman's Rights Movement in the United States* (New York: Atheneum, 1973); Paula Baker, "The Domestication of Politics: Women and American Political Society, 1780–1920," *American Historical Review* 89 (June 1984): 620–47. Catherine Clinton, *The Plantation Mistress: Woman's World in the Old South* (New York: Pantheon Books, 1982), and Mary P. Ryan, *Cradle of the Middle Class: The Family in Oneida County, New York, 1790–1865* (Cambridge: Cambridge Univ. Press, 1981), both discuss the symbolic status generated by a leisured wife who could create a sanctuary at home for her working husband. See also Barbara Welter, "The Cult of True Womanhood," *American Quarterly* (1966): 151–74, for a delineation of the cult's prescriptive characteristics. Thomas Dublin discusses the working patterns of unmarried women in *Women at Work: The Transformation of Work and Community in Lowell, Massachusetts, 1826–1860* (New York: Columbia Univ. Press, 1979). One reason Carroll did not join a voluntary association may have been lack of opportunity. Religious reform societies, such as the American Home Missionary Society that would have appealed to Carroll, were nearly nonexistent in Maryland. See Van Ness, "Economic Development," 188.

38. Howe, "Victorian Culture," 21–23, 14.

39. Blackwell, *Life and Writings,* 22.

40. Jean Gould Hales, " 'Co-laborers in the Cause': Women in the Ante-bellum Nativist Movement," *Civil War History* 25 (June 1979): 119–38; Carroll, *GAB,* 28.

Selected Bibliography

Note on Sources: Sources listed in the bibliography are primarily those cited in the text. Additional sources which were used but not cited directly are also included. Carroll's works and works on her life are listed separately.

Primary Sources

Unpublished Personal Papers

Anthony Autograph Collection. New York Public Library, New York, New York.
Biographical Folders Collection. University of Pennsylvania Archives, Philadelphia, Pennsylvania.
Blackwell Family. Library of Congress, Washington, D.C.
Breckinridge Family. Library of Congress, Washington, D.C.
Burr, Aaron Columbus. Manuscripts and Archives, Yale University Library, New Haven, Connecticut.
Carroll, Anna Ella. Manuscripts Division, Maryland Historical Society Library, Baltimore, Maryland.
———. Carroll, Cradock, Jensen Papers, Manuscripts Division, Maryland Historical Society Library, Baltimore, Maryland.
Carroll Family. Library of Congress, Washington, D.C.
Chase, Salmon Portland. Library of Congress, Washington, D.C.
Clayton, John M. Library of Congress, Washington, D.C.
Cleveland, Grover. Library of Congress, Washington, D.C.
Cockrell, Monroe F. William R. Perkins Library, Duke University, Durham, North Carolina.

Corwin, Thomas. Library of Congress. Washington, D.C.

Davis, Jefferson. Rice University, Houston, Texas.

Dreer, Frederick. The Historical Society of Pennsylvania, Philadelphia, Pennsylvania.

Fillmore, Millard. Buffalo and Erie County Historical Society, Oswego, New York.
———. Penfield Library, State University College at Oswego, Oswego, New York.

Fish, Hamilton. Library of Congress, Washington, D.C.

Garfield, James Abram. Library of Congress, Washington, D.C.

Hicks, Thomas H. Manuscripts Division, Maryland Historical Society Library, Baltimore, Maryland.

Lincoln, Abraham. Robert Todd Lincoln Collection, Library of Congress, Washington, D.C.

Marcy, William Learned. Library of Congress, Washington, D.C.

Mason Family. Virginia Historical Society, Richmond, Virginia.

National American Woman Suffrage Association Papers. Library of Congress, Washington, D.C.

Seward, William Henry. Rus Rhees Library, University of Rochester, Rochester, New York.

Smith, Gerrit. The George Arents Research Library, Syracuse University, Syracuse, New York.

Ullmann, Daniel. New-York Historical Society, New York, New York.

Weed, Thurlow. Library of Congress, Washington, D.C.
———. Rus Rhees Library, University of Rochester, Rochester, New York.

Welles, Gideon. Library of Congress, Washington, D.C.

Whittlesey, Elisha. Western Reserve Historical Society, Cleveland, Ohio.

Government Documents

Annapolis, Maryland. Maryland State Archives, Hall of Records.
  Baltimore City Superior Court Records
  Dorchester County Probate Records
  Dorchester County Tax Assessment Ledgers
  Governor's Letterbook
  Proceedings of the Governor
  Somerset County Chancery Court Records
  Somerset County Deed Books
  Somerset County Tax Assessment Ledgers

Baltimore, Maryland. Baltimore City Archives.
  Chattel Records of Baltimore City
  Manumission Records

Congressional Globe, 1861–1873

Congressional Record, 1874–1897

U.S. Congress. House. Committee on Military Affairs. *Anna Ella Carroll: Report to accompany bill H.R. 7256.* 46th Cong., 3d sess., 1881. H. Rept. 386.

_____. *Memorial of Anna Ella Carroll, of Maryland, Praying For compensation for services rendered to the United States during the late civil war.* 45th Cong., 2d sess., 1878. H. Mis. Doc. 58.

_____. *Petition of Anna Ella Carroll For Compensation for services rendered to the War Department during the late war.* 44th Cong., 1st sess., 1876. H. Mis. Doc. 179.

_____. Senate. Committee on Military Affairs. *Memorial of Anna Ella Carroll, Asking compensation for service rendered the United States in the war of the rebellion.* 42d Cong., 2d sess., 1872. Sen. Mis. Doc. 167.

_____. *Memorial of Anna Ella Carroll of Maryland, Praying For compensation for services rendered to the United States during the late civil war.* 45th Cong., 1st sess., 1877. S. Mis. Doc. 5.

_____. *Petition of Anna Ella Carroll, Praying Compensation for suggesting certain plans of operation for the armies of the United States during the late war.* 41st Cong., 2d sess., 1870. S. Mis. Doc. 100.

_____. *Report.* 45th Cong., 3d sess., 1879. S. Rept. 775.

_____. Committee on Military Affairs and the Militia. *Report to accompany bill S. No. 1293.* 41st Cong., 3d sess., 1871. S. Rept. 339.

_____. Committee on the Conduct of the War. *Report of the Joint Committee on the Conduct of the War.* 37th Cong., 3d sess., 1863. Rep. Com. 108.

U.S. Department of the Interior. "Records of the Office of the Secretary of the Interior Relating to the Suppression of the African Slave Trade and Negro Colonization, 1854–1872." Record Group 48. National Archives, Washington, D.C.

U.S. Department of State. "Despatches From United States Minister to Honduras, 1861–1873." Record Group 59. National Archives, Washington, D.C.

_____. "Letters of Application and Recommendation During the Administration of U. S. Grant, 1869–1877." Record Group 59. National Archives, Washington, D.C.

U.S. Department of the Treasury. Personnel Applications. National Archives, Washington, D.C.

U.S. War Department. Anna Ella Carroll File, Record and Pension Office. National Archives, Washington, D.C.

Newspapers and Periodicals

Louisville [Kentucky] *Journal*
New York Daily News
New York Express
New York Morning Express
New York Times
Washington Daily National Intelligencer
Washington National Republican
Woman's Journal

Reference Works

American Directories through 1860. New Haven, Conn.: Research Publishers, 1969. Microfiche.

American Women. Ed. Frances E. Willard and Mary A. Livermore. 2 vols. 1897. Reprint. Detroit: Gale Research, 1973.

Appleton's Cyclopedia of American Biography. Ed. James Grant Wilson and John Fiske. 6 vols. New York: D. Appleton, 1886–91.

A Biographical Dictionary of the Maryland Legislature, 1635–1789. Ed. Edward C. Papenfuse, Alan F. Day, David W. Jordan, and Gregory A. Stiverson. 2 vols. Baltimore: Johns Hopkins Univ. Press, 1979–85.

Biographical Directory of the American Congress, 1774–1971. Washington, D.C.: GPO, 1971.

Biographical Directory of the Governors of the United States, 1798–1978. Ed. Robert Sobel and John Raimo. 4 vols. Westport, Conn.: Meckler Books, 1978.

Civil War Dictionary. Ed. Mark M. Boatner III. New York: David McKay, 1959.

Congressional Quarterly. *Guide to U.S. Elections.* Washington, D.C.: Congressional Quarterly, 1975.

Dictionary of American Biography. Ed. Allen Johnson. 12 vols. New York: Charles Scribner's Sons, 1964–73.

1800 Census Index. Ed. Ronald V. Jackson et al. Bountiful, Utah: Accelerated Indexing Systems, 1976.

The Handbook of Texas. Ed. Walter Prescott Webb. 2 vols. Austin: Texas State Historical Association, 1952.

Martis, Kenneth C. *The Historical Atlas of United States Congressional Districts, 1789–1983.* New York: Free Press, 1982.

National Cyclopedia of American Biography. 62 vols. New York: James T. White, 1893–1984.

National Register of Historic Places. Washington, D.C.: U.S. Department of Interior, 1976.

Notable American Women, 1607–1950. Ed. Edward T. James. 3 vols. Cambridge, Mass.: Harvard Univ. Press, 1971.

Portrait and Biographical Record of the Eastern Shore of Maryland. New York: Chapman Publishing, 1898.

Works by Carroll

American Nominations Fillmore and Donelson, Being an Extract from a Work Entitled The Great American Battle; or, The Contest Between Christianity and Political Romanism. New York: Miller, Orton and Mulligan, 1856.

"Calhoun and His Nullification Doctrine." *Living Age* 70 (17 Aug. 1861): 444–46.

"The Constitutional Power of the President to Make Arrests and Suspend the Writ of Habeas Corpus Examined." Baltimore, 1861. In Sarah Ellen Blackwell, *Life and Writings of Anna Ella Carroll,* 92–98. Washington, D.C.: Judd and Detweiler, 1895.

"The First American Exploring Expedition." *Harper's New Monthly Magazine* 44 (Dec. 1871): 60–64.

The Great American Battle; or, the Contest Between Christianity and Political Romanism. New York: Miller, Orton and Mulligan, 1856.

Miss Carroll's Claim Before Congress Asking Compensation for Military and Other Services in Connection with the Civil War. [Washington, D.C., 1874.]

Miss Carroll's Claim Before Congress in Connection with the Tennessee Campaign. Washington, D.C., 1873.

Miss Carroll's Literary Services to the Country During the Civil War Stated. [Washington, D.C., ca. 1874.]

"Plan of the Tennessee Campaign." *North American Review* 42 (Apr. 1886): 342–47.

Pope or President? Startling Disclosures of Romanism As Revealed By Its Own Writers. Facts for Americans. New York: R. L. Delisser, 1859.

The Relation of the National Government to the Revolted Citizens Defined. Washington, D.C.: Henry Polkinhorn, [1862].

Reply to the Speech of Hon. J. C. Breckinridge, Delivered in the United States Senate, July 16, 1861, and, In Defence of the President's War Measures. Washington, D.C.: Henry Polkinhorn, 1861.

Review of Pierce's Administration; Showing Its Only Popular Measures to Have Originated with the Executive of Millard Fillmore. Boston: James French, 1856.

The Star of the West; or, National Men and National Measures. 3d ed. Boston: James French, 1857.

The Union of the States. Boston: James French, 1856.

The War Powers of the General Government. Washington, D.C.: Henry Polkinhorn, 1861.

Which? Fillmore or Buchanan! Boston: James French, 1856.

Who Shall Be President? An Appeal to the People. Boston: James French, 1856.

Works on Carroll

A. Articles

Armstrong, Walter P. "The Story of Anna Ella Carroll: Politician, Lawyer and Secret Agent." *American Bar Association Journal* 35 (Mar. 1949): 198–200, 275.

Basler, Roy P. "Lincoln, Blacks, and Women." In *The Public and Private Lincoln: Contemporary Perspectives,* ed. Cullom Davis, Charles B. Strozier, Rebecca Monroe Leach, and Geoffrey C. Ward, 38–53. Carbondale: Southern Illinois Univ. Press, 1979.

Blackwell, S. E. "The Case of Miss Carroll." *Century Magazine* 40 (Aug. 1890): 638–39.

Blackwell, S. Ellen. "The Anna Ella Carroll Fund." *Woman's Column* 6 (18 Jan. 1888).

Bradley, Sylvia. "Anna Ella Carroll, 1815–1894: Military Strategist—Political

Propagandist." In *Notable Maryland Women,* ed. Winifred G. Helms, 62–70. Cambridge, Md.: Tidewater Publishers, 1977.

Bullard, F. Lauriston. "Anna Ella Carroll and Her 'Modest' Claim." *Lincoln Herald* 50 (Oct. 1948): 2–10, 47.

Chandler, Lucinda B. "Anna Ella Carroll: The Great Unrecognized Genius of the War of the Rebellion." *Godey's Magazine* 133 (Sept. 1896): 250–67.

Copinger, May Irene. "Maryland Woman Influenced U.S. Destiny." *Baltimore Sun,* 11 Oct. 1925.

Gould, Kenneth M. "Lincoln's Unknown Soldier." *Senior Scholastic* 68 (9 Feb. 1956): 16.

[Greenbie, Marjorie B.] "My Dear Lady." *Woman's Home Companion* 67 (Feb. 1940): 13–14, 93, 96; 67 (Mar. 1940): 26, 86, 88–91.

"Lincoln's Lady Strategist." *Life* 25 (26 July 1948): 101–2, 105.

Long, E. B. "Anna Ella Carroll: Exaggerated Heroine?" *Civil War Times Illustrated* 14 (July 1975): 28–35.

Neal, H. E. "Secret Heroine of the Civil War." *Coronet* 26 (May 1949): 148–52.

Shattuck, H. R. "Anna Ella Carroll: The Originator of the Tennessee Campaign." *Outing* 6 (July 1885): 403–9.

Shutes, Dr. Milton H. "Meet an Unheralded Heroine." *National Republic Magazine* 22 (Nov. 1934): 3–4, 34.

Snyder, Charles McCool. "Anna Ella Carroll, Political Strategist and Gadfly to President Fillmore." *Maryland Historical Magazine* 68 (Spring 1973): 36–63.

Tarbell, Ida M. "The American Woman: How She Met the Experience of War." *American Magazine* 69 (Apr. 1910): 801–14.

Williams, Kenneth P. "The Tennessee River Campaign and Anna Ella Carroll." *Indiana Magazine of History* 46 (Sept. 1950): 221–48.

B. Books

Blackwell, Sarah Ellen. *Life and Writings of Anna Ella Carroll.* Washington, D.C.: Judd and Detweiler, 1895.

———. *Life of a Military Genius: Anna Ella Carroll of Maryland.* Washington, D.C.: Judd and Detweiler, 1891.

Greenbie, Marjorie. *My Dear Lady: The Story of Anna Ella Carroll, the "Great Unrecognized Member of Lincoln's Cabinet."* New York: McGraw-Hill, 1940.

Greenbie, Sydney. *Suit with Red Lining.* Penobscot, Maine: Traversity Press, 1958.

Greenbie, Sydney, and Marjorie Barstow Greenbie. *Anna Ella Carroll and Abraham Lincoln: A Biography.* Manchester, Maine: Univ. of Tampa Press in cooperation with Falmouth Publishing House, 1952.

Noble, Hollister. *Woman with a Sword.* New York: Doubleday, 1948.

Wise, Winifred E. *Lincoln's Secret Weapon.* New York: Chilton, 1961.

C. Pamphlets

Couzins, Phoebe W. *The Military Genius of the War: Anna Ella Carroll, Author of the Tennessee Campaign.* St. Louis, 1882.

[Evans, Lemuel D.] *The Material Bearing of the Tennessee Campaign in 1862 upon the Destinies of Our Civil War.* Washington, D.C.: W. H. Moore, [ca. 1871].

Gage, Matilda Joslyn. *Who Planned the Tennessee Campaign of 1862? Or Anna Ella Carroll vs. Ulysses S. Grant: A Few Generally Unknown Facts in Regard to Our Civil War.* National Citizen Tract No. 1 [Washington, D.C., 1880].

Hussey, C. C. *Miss Anna Ella Carroll, as Author of the Tennessee Campaign, in the Late Civil War.* East Orange, N.J.: Gazette Steam Book and Job Print, 1885.

Noble, Hollister. "The Facts about Anne Carroll and the Story behind *Woman with a Sword.*" New York: Doubleday, 1948.

Scott, Capt. Charles M. *The Origin of the Tennessee Campaign by Capt. Charles M. Scott, As a Refutation of the Fradulent Claim of Miss Anna Ella Carroll* [sic]. Terre Haute, Ind.: Moore and Langen, 1889.

White, Hon. John D. *Speech of Hon. John D. White, of Kentucky, in the House of Representatives, Thursday, February 7, 1884.* Washington, D.C., 1884.

D. Lawsuits

Anna Ella Carroll v. United States. 20 Court of Claims 426. Court of Claims, 1885.

Marjorie Barstow Greenbie v. Hollister Noble, Doubleday and Company, Inc., Sears, Roebuck and Company, National Broadcasting Company, Inc., Batten, Barton, Durstine & Osborne, Inc., E. I. Dupont Nemours & Co., (Inc.), Foote, Cone & Belding, Inc., and Hallmark Cards. United States District Court, Southern District of New York, Civil 94-300. Bayonne, N.J.: National Archives, New York Branch.

E. Book Reviews

Allen, Herbert. "New Light on Lincoln's 'Secret' War Tactician." Rev. of *Woman with a Sword* by Hollister Noble. *Boston Herald,* 2 Feb. 1949.

Bardolph, Richard. "Anna Ella Carroll and Abraham Lincoln." Rev. of *Anna Ella Carroll and Abraham Lincoln: A Biography* by Sydney and Marjorie Barstow Greenbie. *Journal of Southern History* 18 (Nov. 1952): 511–13.

Bond, Alice Dixon. "Biography Discloses Woman Whose Strategy Saved Union." Rev. of *Woman with a Sword* by Hollister Noble. *Boston Sunday Herald,* 24 Oct. 1948.

Bullard, F. Lauriston. "Anna Ella Carroll Career Persuasively, Eloquently Told." Rev. of *My Dear Lady* by Marjorie Barstow Greenbie. *Boston Herald,* 9 Oct. 1940.

Craven, Avery. "Review." Rev. of *Anna Ella Carroll and Abraham Lincoln* by Sydney and Marjorie Barstow Greenbie. *New York Herald Tribune Book Review,* 26 Oct. 1952.

Greenbie, Sydney. "Reply to Kenneth Williams." Rev. of *"Anna Ella Carroll and Abraham Lincoln"* review of Kenneth Williams. *Lincoln Herald* 55 (Spring 1953): 37–41.

Stowe, Lyman Beecher. "In Lincoln's Kitchen Cabinet." Rev. of *My Dear Lady* by Marjorie Barstow Greenbie. *New York Times Book Review,* 8 Dec. 1940.

Thompson, Ralph. "Books of the Times." Rev. of *My Dear Lady* by Marjorie Barstow Greenbie. *New York Times,* 8 Dec. 1940.

Williams, Kenneth P., and Ruth A. Trantina. "Anna Ella Carroll and Abraham Lincoln." Rev. of *Anna Ella Carroll and Abraham Lincoln: A Biography* by Sydney and Marjorie Barstow Greenbie. *Lincoln Herald* 54 (Summer 1952): 54–57.

F. Media Productions

"Anna Ella Carroll." Writ. Robert Tallman. *Cavalcade of America.* NBC Radio, 2 June 1941.

Greenbie, Sydney, and Marjorie Barstow Greenbie. *The General Was a Lady.* T. S. Theatre Collections. New York Public Library, New York, N.Y.

Strange Glory. Dir. Jacques Tourneur. Metro-Goldwyn-Mayer, 1938.

"Woman with a Sword." Writ. Hollister Noble. *Cavalcade of America.* Adapt. Virginia Radcliffe. NBC Radio, 23 May 1949.

"Woman with a Sword." Writ. Hollister Noble. *Hallmark Hall of Fame.* Dir. William Corrigan. NBC Television, 10 Feb. 1952.

"Woman with a Sword." Writ. Hollister Noble. *Playhouse 25.* Armed Forces Radio & TV Services, n.d.; rebroadcast, 42d week, 1974.

Contemporary Works

Adams, Henry. *The Great Secession Winter of 1860–61 and Other Essays.* Ed. George Rochfield. New York: Sagamore Press, 1958.

[Anspach, Friedrich]. *The Sons of the Sires.* Philadelphia: Lippincott, Grambo, 1885.

Anti-Catholicism in America, 1841–1851: Three Sermons. Reprint. New York: Arno Press, 1977.

Barre, W. L. *The Life and Public Services of Millard Fillmore.* 1856. Reprint. New York: Lenox Hill, 1971.

Basler, Roy P., ed. *The Collected Works of Abraham Lincoln.* 9 vols. New Brunswick, N.J.: Rutgers Univ. Press, 1953–55.

Bates, Edward. 10 *Opinions of the Attorney General* 74 (1861).

Beale, Howard K., ed. *Diary of Gideon Welles: Secretary of the Navy Under Lincoln and Johnson.* New York: W. W. Norton, 1960.

Binney, Horace. "The Privilege of the Writ of Habeas Corpus Under the Constitution." In *Union Pamphlets of the Civil War, 1861–1865,* ed. Frank Freidel. 2 vols. Cambridge, Mass.: Belknap Press, Harvard Univ. Press, 1967.

Botts, John Minor. *The Great Rebellion: Its Secret History, Rise, Progress, and Disastrous Failure.* New York: Harper and Brothers, 1866.

[Chamberlain, Ivory]. *Biography of Fillmore.* Buffalo, 1856.

Chittenden, L. E. *A Report of the Debates and Proceedings in the Secret Sessions of the Conference Convention for Proposing Amendments to the Constitution of the United States. Held at Washington, D.C., in February, A.D. 1861.* New York: D. Appleton, 1864.

Cralle, Richard K., ed. *The Works of John C. Calhoun.* 6 vols. New York: Russell and Russell, 1968.

Evans, Lemuel D. *Speech of the Hon. L. D. Evans on the Condition of Texas and the Formation of New States. Delivered in the Constitutional Convention of Texas on the 6th of January, 1869.* N.p., 1869.

Grant, Ulysses S. *The Papers of Ulysses S. Grant.* Ed. John Y. Simon. 14 vols. Carbondale: Southern Illinois Univ. Press, 1967–85.

――――. *Personal Memoirs of U. S. Grant.* 2 vols. New York: Charles L. Webster, 1885.

Greeley, Horace, and John F. Cleveland. *A Political Textbook for 1860: Comprising a Brief View of Presidential Nominations and Elections: Including all the National Platforms Ever Yet Adopted: Also A History of the Struggle respecting Slavery in the Territories, and of the Action of Congress As to the Freedom of the Public Lands, with the Most Notable Speeches and Letters of Messrs. Lincoln, Douglas, Bell, Cass, Seward, Everett, Breckinridge, H. V. Johnson, etc., etc., Touching the Questions of the Day; and Returns of all Presidential Elections Since 1836.* New York: The Tribune Association, 1860.

Halstead, Murat. *Caucuses of 1860.* Columbus, Ohio: Follet, Foster, 1860.

Hesseltine, William B., and Rex G. Fisher, eds. *Trimmers, Trucklers and Temporizers: Notes of Murat Halstead from the Political Conventions of 1856.* Madison: The State Historical Society of Wisconsin, 1961.

Hibernicus. *What Brings So Many Irish to America!* 1845. Reprint. San Francisco: R & E Research Associates, 1972.

Livermore, Mary A. *My Story of the War: A Woman's Narrative of Four Years Personal Experience as Nurse in the Union Army, and in Relief Work at Home, in Hospitals, Camps, and at the Front, During the War of the Rebellion.* Hartford, Conn.: A. D. Worthington, 1889.

Marsh, Ephraim. *North American Documents. Letters from George Law, Ephraim Marsh, and Chauncey Shaffer.* Reprint. Louisville, Ky.: Lost Cause Press, 1962. Microcard.

Moore, Frank, ed. *The Rebellion Record: A Diary of American Events, with Documents, Narratives, Illustrative Incidents, Poetry, Etc.* 11 vols. New York: G. P. Putnam and Charles T. Evans, 1861–63; D. Van Nostrand, 1864–68.

Morse, Samuel F. B. *Imminent Dangers to the Free Institutions of the United States through Foreign Immigration.* 1835. Reprint. New York: Arno Press and the *New York Times,* 1969.

Official Records of the Union and Confederate Navies in the War of the Rebellion. 30 vols. Washington, D.C.: GPO, 1894–1922.

Population Schedules of the Eighth Census of the United States, 1860. Washington, D.C.: National Archives and Records Service, 1959. Microfilm.

Population Schedules of the Fifth Census of the United States, 1830. Washington, D.C.: National Archives and Records Service, 1959. Microfilm.

Population Schedules of the Fourth Census of the United States, 1820. Washington, D.C.: National Archives and Records Service, 1959. Microfilm.

Population Schedules of the Seventh Census of the United States, 1850. Washington, D.C.: National Archives and Records Service, 1959. Microfilm.

Population Schedules of the Sixth Census of the United States, 1840. Washington, D.C.: National Archives and Records Service, 1959. Microfilm.

Population Schedules of the Third Census of the United States, 1810. Washington, D.C.: National Archives and Records Service, 1959. Microfilm.

Proceedings of the First Three Republican National Conventions. Minneapolis: Charles W. Johnson, 1893.

Richardson, James D., ed. *A Compilation of the Messages and Papers of the Presidents, 1798–1902.* 10 vols. Washington, D.C.: Bureau of National Literature and Art, 1905.

Saunders, Frederick. *A Voice to America.* New York: Edward Walker, 1855.

[Seaton, Josephine.] *William Winston Seaton of the "National Intelligencer."* Boston: James R. Osgood, 1871.

Severance, Frank H., ed. *Millard Fillmore Papers.* 2 vols. Buffalo: Buffalo Historical Society, 1907.

Walker, General William. *The War in Nicaragua.* 1860. Reprint. Detroit: Blaine Ethridge-Books, 1971.

The War of the Rebellion: A Compilation of the Official Records of the Union and Confederate Armies. 128 vols. Washington, D.C.: GPO, 1880–1901.

Weed, Harriet A., ed. *Life of Thurlow Weed.* 1883. Reprint. New York: Da Capo Press, 1970.

Whitney, Thomas R. *A Defense of the American Policy.* 1856. Reprint. N.p.: Jerome S. Ozer, 1971.

Secondary Sources

Articles

Baker, Paula. "The Domestication of Politics: Women and the American Political Society, 1780–1920." *American Historical Review* 89 (June 1984): 620–47.

Brewer, James H. Fitzgerald. "The Democratization of Maryland, 1800–1837." In *The Old Line State: A History of Maryland,* ed. Morris L. Radoff, 49–66. Annapolis: Hall of Records Commission, 1971.

Brewer, W. W. "Lincoln and the Border States." *Journal of Negro History* 34 (Jan. 1949): 46–72.

Brown, Richard D. "Modernization: A Victorian Climax." In *Victorian America,* ed. Daniel Walker Howe, 29–44. Philadelphia: Univ. of Pennsylvania Press, 1976.

Carman, Harry J., and Richard H. Luthin. "Some Aspects of the Know-Nothing Movement Reconsidered." *South Atlantic Quarterly* 39 (1940): 213–34.

Clark, Charles B. "Suppression and Control of Maryland, 1861–1865: A Study of Federal-State Relations During Civil Conflict." *Maryland Historical Magazine* 54 (Sept. 1959): 241–71.

Crenshaw, Ollinger. "The Speakership Contest of 1859–1860." *Mississippi Valley Historical Review* 29 (Dec. 1942): 323–38.

Crofts, Daniel W. "A Reluctant Unionist: John A. Gilmer and Lincoln's Cabinet." *Civil War History* 24 (Sept. 1978): 225–49.

Davis, David Brion. "Some Ideological Functions of Prejudice in Ante-Bellum America." *American Quarterly* 60 (Summer 1963): 115–25.

_____. "Some Themes of Counter-Subversion: An Analysis of Anti-Masonic, Anti-Catholic, and Anti-Mormon Literature." *Mississippi Valley Historical Review* 47 (Sept. 1960): 205–24.

Duncan, Richard R. "The Era of the Civil War." In *Maryland: A History, 1632 to 1974,* ed. Richard Walsh and William Lloyd Fox, 309–95. Baltimore: Maryland Historical Society, 1974.

Fehrenbacher, Don E. "The Origins and Purpose of Lincoln's 'House-Divided' Speech." *Mississippi Valley Historical Review* 46 (Mar. 1960): 615–43.

Frank, John P. "Edward Bates, Lincoln's Attorney General." *American Journal of Legal History* 10 (1966): 34–50.

Frasure, Carl M. "Union Sentiment in Maryland, 1859–1861." *Maryland Historical Magazine* 24 (Sept. 1929): 210–24.

Garnett, James Mercer. "John Francis Mercer, Governor of Maryland, 1801–1803." *Maryland Historical Magazine* 2 (Sept. 1907): 191–213.

Gienapp, William E. "Nativism and the Creation of a Republican Majority in the North Before the Civil War." *Journal of American History* 72 (Dec. 1985): 529–59.

Hales, Jean Gould. " 'Co-laborers in the Cause': Women in the Ante-bellum Nativist Movement." *Civil War History* 25 (June 1979): 119–38.

Haller, Mark H. "The Rise of the Jacksonian Party in Maryland, 1820–1829." *Journal of Southern History* 28 (Aug. 1962): 307–26.

Hicks, John D. "The Third Party Tradition in American Politics." *Mississippi Valley Historical Review* 20 (June 1933): 3–28.

Holt, Michael F. "The Antimasonic and Know Nothing Parties." In *History of U.S. Political Parties,* ed. Arthur M. Schlesinger, Jr., 1:575–740. 4 vols. New York: Chelsea House Publishers, in association with R. R. Bowker, 1973.

_____. "The Politics of Impatience: The Origins of Know Nothingism." *Journal of American History* 60 (Sept. 1973): 309–31.

Howe, Daniel Walker. "Victorian Culture in America." In *Victorian America,* ed. Daniel Walker Howe, 3–28. Philadelphia: Univ. of Pennsylvania Press, 1976.

Jackson, Donald Dale. "Around the World with Wilkes and His 'Scientifics.' " *Smithsonian* 16 (Nov. 1985): 48–63.

Janes, Henry L. "The *Black Warrior* Affair." *American Historical Review* 12 (Jan. 1907): 280–98.

Johnson, Ludwell H. "The Confederacy: What Was It? A View from the Federal Courts." *Civil War History* 32 (Mar. 1986): 5–22.

_____. "Contraband Trade During the Last Year of the Civil War." *Mississippi Valley Historical Review* 49 (Mar. 1963): 635–52.

_____. "Northern Profits and Profiteers: The Cotton Rings of 1864–1865." *Civil War History* 12 (June 1966): 101–15.

Jones, Anne Goodwyn. "Southern Literary Women As Chroniclers of Southern

Life." In *Sex, Race, and the Role of Women in the South,* ed. Joanne V. Hawks and Sheila L. Skemp, 75–93. Jackson: Univ. of Mississippi Press, 1983.

Kelly, J. Reaney. "Cedar Park, Its People and Its History." *Maryland Historical Magazine* 58 (Mar. 1963): 30–53.

Maizlish, Stephen E. "The Meaning of Nativism and the Crisis of the Union: The Know-Nothing Movement in the Antebellum North." In *Essays on American Antebellum Politics, 1840–1860,* ed. Stephen E. Maizlish and John J. Kushma, 166–98. College Station: Univ. of Texas at Arlington by Texas A&M Univ. Press, 1982.

Smith, Donnal V. "The Influence of the Foreign-Born of the Northwest in the Election of 1860." *Mississippi Valley Historical Review* 19 (Sept. 1932): 192–204.

Smith, W. Wayne. "Politics and Democracy in Maryland, 1800–1854." In *Maryland: A History, 1632–1974,* ed. Richard Walsh and William Lloyd Fox, 239–308. Baltimore: Maryland Historical Society, 1974.

Smith, Willard H. "Schyler Colfax and the Political Upheaval of 1854–1855." *Mississippi Valley Historical Review* 28 (Dec. 1941): 383–98.

Smith-Rosenberg, Carroll, and Charles Rosenberg. "The Female Animal: Medical and Biological Views of Woman and Her Role in Nineteenth-Century America." *Journal of American History* 60 (Sept. 1973): 332–56.

Stephenson, George M. "Nativism in the Forties and Fifties, with Special Reference to the Mississippi Valley." *Mississippi Valley Historical Review* 9 (Dec. 1922): 185–202.

Tuska, Benjamin. "Know-Nothingism in Baltimore, 1854–1860." *Catholic Historical Review* 5 (July 1925): 217–51.

Van Ness, James S. "Economic Development, Social and Cultural Changes: 1800–1850." In *Maryland: A History, 1632–1974,* ed. Richard Walsh and William Lloyd Fox, 156–238. Baltimore: Maryland Historical Society, 1974.

Vevier, Charles. "American Continentalism: An Idea of Expansion, 1845–1910." *American Historical Review* 65 (Jan. 1960): 323–35.

Webster, Clyde C. "John Minor Botts, Anti-Secessionist." *Richmond College Historical Papers* 1 (June 1915): 9–37.

Welter, Barbara. "The Cult of True Womanhood." *American Quarterly* 18 (1966): 151–74.

Wilson, Charles R. "The Original Chase Organization Meeting and the Next Presidential Election." *Mississippi Valley Historical Review* 23 (June 1936): 61–79.

Books

Anderson, Bern. *By Sea and By River: The Naval History of the Civil War.* 1962. Reprint. Westport, Conn.: Greenwood Press, 1977.

Baker, Jean H. *Ambivalent Americans: The Know-Nothing Party in Maryland.* Baltimore: Johns Hopkins Univ. Press. 1977.

———. *The Politics of Continuity: Maryland Political Parties from 1858 to 1870.* Baltimore: Johns Hopkins Univ. Press, 1973.

Beals, Carleton. *Brass-Knuckle Crusade: The Great Know-Nothing Conspiracy, 1820–1860.* New York: Hastings House Publishers, 1960.

Benson, Lee. *The Concept of Jacksonian Democracy: New York as a Test Case.* Princeton, N.J.: Princeton Univ. Press, 1961.

Billington, Ray Allen. *The Origins of Nativism in the United States, 1800–1844.* New York: Arno Press, 1974.

_____. *The Protestant Crusade, 1800–1860.* 1938. New York: Rinehart, 1952.

Blue, Frederick J. *The Free-Soilers: Third-Party Politics, 1848–1854.* Urbana: Univ. of Illinois Press. 1973.

_____. *Salmon P. Chase: A Life in Politics.* Kent, Ohio: Kent State Univ. Press, 1987.

Burnham, W. Dean. *Presidential Ballots, 1836–1892.* Baltimore: Johns Hopkins Univ. Press, 1955.

Cain, Marvin R. *Lincoln's Attorney General: Edward Bates of Missouri.* Columbia: Univ. of Missouri Press, 1965.

Campbell, Penelope. *Maryland in Africa: The Maryland State Colonization Society, 1831–1857.* Urbana: Univ. of Illinois Press, 1971.

Catton, Bruce. *The Coming Fury.* New York: Doubleday, 1961.

_____. *Grant Moves South.* Boston: Little, Brown, 1960.

_____. *Never Call Retreat.* New York: Doubleday, 1965.

_____. *Terrible Swift Sword.* New York: Doubleday, 1963.

Civil War Naval Chronology, 1861–1865. Comp. U.S. Naval Department, Naval History Division. Washington, D.C.: GPO, 1971.

Clegern, Wayne M. *British Honduras: Colonial Dead End, 1859–1900.* Baton Rouge: Louisiana State Univ. Press, 1967.

Clinton, Catherine. *The Plantation Mistress: Woman's World in the Old South.* New York: Pantheon Books, 1982.

A Comprehensive History of Texas, 1685–1897. Ed. Dudley G. Wooten. 2 vols. Dallas: William G. Scarff, 1898.

Cox, La Wanda. *Lincoln and Black Freedom: A Study in Presidential Leadership.* Columbia: Univ. of South Carolina Press, 1981.

Current, Richard N. *The Lincoln Nobody Knows.* New York: McGraw-Hill, 1958.

Cuthbert, Norma. *Lincoln and the Baltimore Plot.* San Marino, Calif.: Huntington Library, 1949.

Davenport, J. H. *The History of the Supreme Court of the State of Texas.* Austin, Tex.: Southern Law Book Publishers, 1917.

Davis, David Brion, ed. *The Fear of Conspiracy: Images of Un-American Subversion from the Revolution to the Present.* Ithaca, N.Y.: Cornell Univ. Press, 1971.

Degler, Carl. *The Other South: Southern Dissenters in the Nineteenth Century.* Boston: Northeastern Univ. Press, 1982.

Dublin, Thomas. *Women at Work: The Transformation of Work and Community in Lowell, Massachusetts, 1826–1860.* New York: Columbia Univ. Press, 1979.

Dubois, Ellen Carol. *Feminism and Suffrage: The Emergence of an Independent Women's Movement in America, 1848–1869.* Ithaca, N.Y. Cornell Univ. Press, 1978.

Eisenschiml, Otto. *The Hidden Face of the Civil War*. New York: Bobbs-Merrill, 1961.

Ettinger, Amos Aschbach. *The Mission to Spain of Pierre Soulé, 1853–1855*. New Haven, Conn.: Yale Univ. Press, 1932.

Evitts, William J. *A Matter of Allegiances: Maryland from 1850 to 1861*. Baltimore: Johns Hopkins Univ. Press, 1974.

Fell, Sister Marie Leonore. *The Foundations of Nativism in American Textbooks, 1783–1860*. Washington, D.C.: The Catholic Univ. of America Press, 1941.

Fite, Emerson David. *The Presidential Campaign of 1860*. New York: Macmillan, 1911.

Flexner, Eleanor. *Century of Struggle: The Women's Rights Movement in the United States*. New York: Atheneum, 1973.

Foner, Eric. *Free Soil, Free Labor, Free Men: The Ideology of the Republican Party Before the Civil War*. New York: Oxford Univ. Press, 1970.

Franklin, John Hope. *From Slavery to Freedom: A History of Negro Americans*. 3d ed. New York: Vintage Books, 1969.

Freidel, Frank, ed. *Union Pamphlets of the Civil War, 1861–1865*. 2 vols. Cambridge, Mass.: Belknap Press, Harvard Univ. Press, 1967.

Gilligan, Carol. *In a Different Voice: Psychological Theory and Women's Development*. Cambridge, Mass.: Harvard Univ. Press, 1982.

Gosnell, H. Allen. *Guns on Western Waters*. Baton Rouge: Louisiana State Univ. Press, 1949.

Griffis, William Elliot. *Millard Fillmore*. Ithaca, N.Y.: Andrus and Church, 1915.

Harris, Caspar, M.D. *Memoir of Miss Margaret Mercer*. 2d ed. Philadelphia: Lindsay and Blakiston, 1848.

Hendrick, Burton J. *Lincoln's War Cabinet*. Boston: Little, Brown, 1946.

Hofstadter, Richard. *The Paranoid Style in American Politics and Other Essays*. New York: Alfred A. Knopf, 1966.

Holt, Michael F. *Forging a Majority: The Formation of the Republican Party in Pittsburgh, 1848–1860*. New Haven, Conn.: Yale Univ. Press, 1969.

————. *The Political Crisis of the 1850s*. New York: John Wiley and Sons, 1978.

Howe, Daniel Walker. *The Political Culture of the American Whigs*. Chicago: Univ. of Chicago Press, 1979.

Hyman, Harold, and William M. Wiecek. *Equal Justice Under Law: Constitutional Development 1835–1875*. New York: Harper and Row, 1982.

Jennings, Thelma. *The Nashville Convention: Southern Movement for Unity, 1848–1851*. Memphis, Tenn.: Memphis State Univ. Press, 1980.

Jensen, Gary Dennis. *Joseph Sabin and His "Dictionary of Books Relating to America."* Ann Arbor Mich.: University Microfilms, 1983.

Johnson, Ludwell H. *Division and Reunion: America 1848–1877*. New York: John Wiley and Sons, 1978.

Jones, Elias, *Revised History of Dorchester County, Maryland*. Baltimore: Read-Taylor Press, 1925.

Jones, Virgil Carrington. *The Civil War at Sea*. 3 vols. New York: Holt, Rinehart, Winston, 1960.

Kamm, Samuel Richey. *The Civil War Career of Thomas A. Scott.* Philadelphia: Univ. of Pennsylvania Press, 1940.

Karnes, Thomas L. *The Failure of Union: Central America, 1824–1975.* Tempe: Arizona State Univ. Press, 1976.

Kerber, Linda K. *Women of the Republic: Intellect and Ideology in Revolutionary America.* Chapel Hill: Institute for Early American History and Culture by Univ. of North Carolina Press, 1980.

Kraditor, Aileen S. *The Ideas of the Woman Suffrage Movement, 1890–1920.* New York: Anchor Books, 1981.

Lerner, Gerda. *The Grimké Sisters from South Carolina: Pioneers for Woman's Rights and Abolition.* New York: Schocken Books, 1967.

Luthin, Reinhard H. *The First Lincoln Campaign.* 1964. Reprint. Cambridge, Mass.: Harvard Univ. Press, 1964.

Lynch, James D. *The Bench and Bar of Texas.* St. Louis: Nixon-Jones Printing, 1885.

McKee, Thomas Hudson. *The National Conventions and Platforms of All Political Parties, 1789–1905.* Baltimore: The Friedenwald Company, 1906.

McPherson, James M. *Ordeal By Fire: The Civil War and Reconstruction.* New York: Alfred A. Knopf, 1982.

Mahan, Alfred T. *The Gulf and Inland Waters.* New York: Charles Scribner's Sons, 1883.

Manakee, Harold R. *Maryland in the Civil War.* Baltimore: Maryland Historical Society, 1961.

May, Robert E. *The Southern Dream of a Caribbean Empire, 1854–1861.* Baton Rouge: Louisiana State Univ. Press, 1973.

Miers, Earl Schenck, ed. *Lincoln Day By Day, A Chronology, 1809–1865.* 3 vols. Washington, D.C.: Lincoln Sesquecentennial Commission, 1960.

Neely, Mark E., Jr. *The Lincoln Encyclopedia.* New York: McGraw-Hill, 1982.

Nevins, Allan. *The Emergence of Lincoln: Prologue to Civil War, 1859–1861.* New York: Charles Scribner's Sons, 1950.

————. *Ordeal of the Union: A House Dividing, 1852–1857.* New York: Charles Scribner's Sons, 1947.

————. *The War for the Union: The Organized War to Victory, 1864–1865.* New York: Charles Scribner's Sons, 1971.

————. *The War for the Union: War Becomes Revolution, 1862–1863.* New York: Charles Scribner's Sons, 1960.

Nichols, Roy Franklin. *Franklin Pierce: Young Hickory of the Granite Hills.* Philadelphia: Univ. of Pennsylvania Press, 1969.

Norton, Mary Beth. *Liberty's Daughters: The Revolutionary Experience of American Women, 1750–1800.* Boston: Little, Brown, 1980.

Nunn, William C. *Texas and the Carpetbaggers.* Austin: Univ. of Texas Press, 1962.

Overdyke, W. Darrell. *The Know-Nothing Party in the South.* Baton Rouge: Louisiana State Univ. Press, 1950.

Paullin, Charles Oscar. *Paullin's History of Naval Administration, 1755–1911.* Annapolis: U.S. Naval Institute, 1968.

Pleasants, Samuel A. *Fernando Wood of New York.* New York: AMS Press, 1966.

Potter, David M. *The Impending Crisis.* Ed. Don E. Fehrenbacher. New York: Harper and Row, 1976.

―――. *Lincoln and His Party in the Secession Crisis.* New Haven, Conn.: Yale Univ. Press, 1942.

Radcliffe, G. L. P. *Governor Hicks of Maryland and the Civil War.* Johns Hopkins University Studies in Historical and Political Science, ed. Herbert B. Adams, series vol. 19. Baltimore: Johns Hopkins Univ. Press, 1901.

Ramsdell, Charles W. *Reconstruction in Texas.* Austin: Univ. of Texas Press, 1970.

Randall, J. G. *Constitutional Problems Under Lincoln.* Gloucester, Mass.: Peter Smith, 1963.

―――. *Lincoln the President.* 4 vols. New York: Dodd, Mead, 1945–55.

Randall, J. G., and David Donald. *The Civil War and Reconstruction.* 2d ed. Lexington, Mass.: D. C. Heath, 1969.

Rayback, Robert J. *Millard Fillmore: Biography of a President.* Buffalo: Buffalo Historical Society, 1959.

Richardson, Hester Dorsey. *Sidelights on Maryland History with Sketches of Early Maryland Families.* Baltimore: Williams and Wilkins, 1913.

Riddle, Albert Gallatin. *Recollections of War Times: Reminiscences of Men and Events in Washington, 1860–1865.* New York: G. P. Putnam's Sons, 1895.

Ryan, Mary P. *Cradle of the Middle Class: The Family in Oneida County, New York, 1790–1865.* Cambridge: Cambridge Univ. Press, 1981.

Safire, William. *Freedom.* Garden City, N.Y.: Doubleday, 1987.

Sandburg, Carl. *Abraham Lincoln: The War Years.* 4 vols. New York: Harcourt Brace, 1939.

Scarry, Robert J. *Millard Fillmore: 13th President of the United States.* Moravia, N.Y.: Robert J. Scarry, 1982.

Schmeckebier, Laurence F. *History of the Know-Nothing Party in Maryland.* Johns Hopkins University Studies in Historical and Political Science, ed. Herbert B. Adams, series vol. 17. Baltimore: Johns Hopkins Univ. Press, 1899.

Schuckers, J. W. *The Life and Public Services of Salmon Portland Chase, United States Senator and Governor of Ohio; Secretary of the Treasury, and Chief-Justice of the United States.* New York: D. Appleton, 1874.

Scott, Anne Firor. *Making the Invisible Woman Visible.* Urbana: Univ. of Illinois Press, 1984.

―――. *The Southern Lady: From Pedestal to Politics, 1830–1930.* Chicago: Univ. of Chicago Press, 1970.

Scroggs, William O. *Filibusters and Financiers: The Story of William Walker and His Associates.* New York: Macmillan, 1916.

Setzekorn, William David. *Formerly British Honduras: A Profile of the New Nation of Belize.* Athens: Ohio Univ. Press, 1981.

Shalhope, Robert E. *Sterling Price: Portrait of a Southerner.* Columbia: Univ. of Missouri Press, 1971.

Silbey, Joel H. *The Partisan Imperative: The Dynamics of American Politics Before the Civil War.* New York: Oxford Univ. Press, 1985.

────. *The Transformation of American Politics, 1840–1860.* Englewood Cliffs, N.J.: Prentice-Hall, 1967.

Sklar, Kathryn Kish. *Catherine Beecher: A Study in American Domesticity.* New Haven, Conn.: Yale Univ. Press, 1973.

Smith, Elbert B. *The Presidencies of Zachary Taylor and Millard Fillmore.* Lawrence: Univ. Press of Kansas, 1988.

Stanton, Elizabeth C., Susan B. Anthony, and Matilda Joslyn Gage, eds. *History of Woman Suffrage.* 6 vols. Rochester, N.Y.: Susan B. Anthony, Charles Mann, 1881–1922.

Staudenraus, P. J. *The African Colonization Movement, 1816–1865.* New York: Columbia Univ. Press, 1961.

Steiner, Bernard C. *Life of Reverdy Johnson.* Baltimore: Norman, Remington, 1914.

Stern, Madeline B., ed. *Publishers for Mass Entertainment in Nineteenth Century America.* Boston: G. K. Hall, 1980.

Stillwell, Lucille. *John Cabell Breckinridge.* Caldwell, Idaho: The Caxton Printers, 1936.

Tercentenary History of Maryland. Comp. Henry Fletcher Powell. 4 vols. Baltimore: S. J. Clarke, 1925.

Thomas, Benjamin P. *Abraham Lincoln.* New York: Alfred A. Knopf, 1952.

Thomas, Benjamin P., and Harold Hyman. *Stanton: The Life and Times of Lincoln's Secretary of War.* New York: Alfred A. Knopf, 1962.

Thrall, Homer S. *A Pictorial History of Texas.* St. Louis: N. D. Thomas, 1879.

Trefousse, H. L. *Benjamin Franklin Wade: Radical Republican from Ohio.* New York: Twayne Publishers, 1963.

Van Deusen, Glyndon G. *Thurlow Weed: Wizard of the Lobby.* Boston: Little, Brown, 1947.

────. *William Henry Seward.* New York: Oxford Univ. Press, 1967.

Walker, Thomas Holmes. *One Hundred Years of History, 1802–1902: A History of the Second Presbyterian Church.* Baltimore, 1902.

West, Richard S., Jr. *Mr. Lincoln's Navy.* New York: Longmans, Green, 1957.

Wheaton, Henry. *Elements of International Law: The Literal Reproduction of the Edition of 1866 by Richard Henry Dana, Jr.* Ed. George Grafton Wilson. Oxford: Clarendon Press, 1936.

White, Frank F. *The Governors of Maryland, 1777–1970.* Annapolis, Md.: The Hall of Records Commission, 1970.

Whiting, William. *The War Powers Under the Constitution of the United States.* 1871. Reprint. New York: Da Capo Press, 1972.

Williams, Kenneth P. *Lincoln Finds a General.* 5 vols. New York: Macmillan, 1949–59.

Williams, T. Harry. *Lincoln and the Radicals.* Madison: Univ. of Wisconsin Press, 1969.

Woloch, Nancy. *Women and the American Experience.* New York: Alfred A. Knopf, 1984.

Woodward, Ralph Lee, Jr. *Central America: A Nation Divided.* New York: Oxford Univ. Press, 1976.

Wright, William Cook. *The Secession Movement in the Middle Atlantic States.* Cranbury, N.J.: Associated Univ. Presses, 1973.

Young, Agatha. *The Women and the Crisis: Women of the North in the Civil War.* New York: McDowell, Oblensky, 1959.

Dissertations and Theses

Harmon, Judd Scott. "Suppress and Protect: The United States Navy, The African Slave Trade, and Maritime Commerce, 1794–1862." Ph.D. diss., College of William and Mary in Virginia, 1977.

Smith, Wilbur Wayne. "The Whig Party in Maryland, 1826–1856." Ph.D. diss., University of Maryland, 1967.

Spencer, Jayme Ruth, "Abraham Lincoln and Negro Colonization: The Ile A'Vache, Hayti Experience, 1862–1864." Master's thesis, College of William and Mary in Virginia, 1971.

Index